Between Couch

Between Couch and Piano links well-established psychoanalytic ideas with historical and neurological theory to help us begin to understand some of the reasons behind music's ubiquity and power.

Drawing on new psychoanalytic understanding as well as advances in neuroscience, this book sheds light on the role of the arts as stimulus, and as a key to creative awareness. Subjects covered include:

- Music in relation to the trauma of loss.
- Music in connection with wholeness and the sense of identity.
- The ability of music to jump-start normal feelings, motion and identity where these have been seemingly destroyed by neurological disease.
- The theory of therapeutic efficacy of music and art.

Between Couch and Piano is a comprehensive overview that will be of interest to all those intrigued by the interrelation of psychoanalysis and the creative arts.

Gilbert J. Rose is in private practice of psychiatry and psychoanalysis and is a member of the Muriel Gardiner Program in Psychoanalysis and Humanities at Yale.

Between Couch and Piano

Psychoanalysis, music, art and neuroscience

Gilbert J. Rose

Brunner-Routledge
Taylor & Francis Group

HOVE AND NEW YORK

First published 2004
by Brunner-Routledge
27 Church Road, Hove, East Sussex BN3 2FA

Simultaneously published in the USA and Canada
by Brunner-Routledge
29 West 35th Street, New York NY 10001

Brunner-Routledge is an imprint of the Taylor & Francis Group

Copyright © 2004 Gilbert J. Rose

Typeset in Times by Mayhew Typesetting, Rhayader, Powys
Printed and bound in Great Britain by MPG Books, Bodmin, Cornwall
Paperback cover design by Lisa Dynan

This publication has been produced with paper manufactured to strict
environmental standards and with pulp derived from sustainable forests.

British Library Cataloguing in Publication Data
A catalogue record for this book is available from the British Library

Library of Congress Cataloging-in-Publication Data
Rose, Gilbert J., 1923–
    Between couch and piano : psychoanalysis, music, art and
neuroscience
/Gilbert J. Rose.
        p. cm.
Includes bibliographical references (p.   ) and index.
    ISBN 1-58391-972-4 (alk. paper) – ISBN 1-58391-973-2 (pbk.: alk.
paper)
1. Psychoanalysis and music. 2. Music–Psychological aspects. 3.
Psychoanalysis and literature. I. Title.
    ML3830 R74 2004
    781'.11–dc21
                                                          2003022367

ISBN 1-58391-972-4 (hbk)
ISBN 1-58391-973-2 (pbk)

To Graciela

I learned that words are no good; that words don't ever fit even what they are trying to say at . . . sin and love and fear are just sounds that people who never sinned nor loved nor feared have for what they never had and cannot have until they forget the words . . . .

(William Faulkner, *As I Lay Dying*)

The cosmos works by harmony of tensions, like the lyre and bow.

(Heraclitus)

Contents

Foreword: a musician listens to a psychoanalyst listening to music

Gilbert Rose's book is full of fascinating and sophisticated insights about the musical experience. As a music theorist, composer, and listener, I have learned a lot from what he has written. Since my knowledge of psychoanalysis is rudimentary, I no doubt have a partially skewed view of his work. But this is inevitable: as Rose explains, each reader creates in his/her mind a unique version of a verbal text (more on that later). And so I write as a musician, reading this book and taking from it (and constructing out of its words and ideas) something of value to me.

Some parts of the book naturally speak to me more directly than others, and it is those about which I am writing. I am pleased to find many of Rose's ideas on communication, for example, paralleling my own. Furthermore, his centralizing of time in the musical experience certainly wins the warm approval of the author of a book called *The Time of Music*! I also find his explanations of the therapeutic powers of music to be fascinating.

Communication

In Chapter 3, Rose bravely tackles a challenging and problematic question: does music communicate? Are a composer's ideas actually in the music, and if so do they emerge through a performance in order to reach a listener? Does the listener hear what the composer has "said"?

In attempting to answer these difficult questions, we need to be aware (as Rose clearly is) of the distinctions between music as conceived by a composer, as represented in the product of the composer's activity (what music theorist Jean-Jacques Nattiez calls the "trace"), and as understood by a listener (Nattiez, 1990: 10–

32). The composer's creative processes depend on his/her inspiration, personality, intentions, influences, moods, techniques, etc. The performer subsequently exercises his/her own creative (as well as re-creative) processes to make a performance, using not only the score but also his/her own inspiration, personality, intentions, etc. In other words, the performer receives, perceives, and reconceives the score by means of a personal receptive process, which is then turned around into a creative process.

Since he does not fully distinguish different traces of the musical work – score, performance, and recording (or broadcast) – Nattiez's ideas need further refinement. If the performance is recorded and/or broadcast (as many performances are), then an additional receptive–creative link is added to the chain. The recording engineer receives, perceives, and reconceives the performance, which is then turned into a creative product dependent not only on the performance but also on the engineer's inspiration, influences, techniques, equipment, etc. When this recording is heard, the listener's receptive processes make sense of it and personalize the music. This process is also creative, as the listener constructs a mental image of the music which depends not only on the recorded sounds as heard but also on the listener's predilections, preferences, prior listening experiences, musical abilities, etc.

If it actually existed, the complete communication chain (with every link present) would be long and complex: from the composer's initial thoughts and intentions through his/her creative act to the score, which is altered somewhat by an editor and/or publisher, and then through the performer to the performance, and then through the recording engineer to the recording, and then through the listener to an internalized representation of the music. While a particularly strong idea may actually be communicated through this chain all the way from composer to listener,[1] such message-sending is relatively rare, I believe. Each person in the chain interprets, reads, misreads, and adds his/her own ideas, which may well alter or replace those of the composer. In cases where the chain is shorter – a jazz improviser playing unamplified to a live audience, for example – the communication may be more direct. But when all links are present, the communication model for musical transmission is quite suspect. Expressiveness, yes: music is a means and a context for composers, performers, engineers, and listeners to express themselves. Emotion, yes: the expression can be quite moving. But communication? Rarely, I believe.

Even language is not fixed. As Rose says, "Words are flexible, meanings change, language is a living organism." And people who speak and people who listen are in flux. Rose writes of "the improbability of conveying anything more than very partial truth by language. Facts, yes [I would have said 'maybe']; the feelings about facts, no." Objective communication – verbal as well as musical – is difficult. As Rose writes, language "leaves out more than it includes, yet it includes so much that any number of connections can be made among the elements that are encompassed."

We express ourselves all the time, in all sorts of ways. And we listen to one another. But we do not simply, passively receive a communication. We construct the message (and even the sender!) for ourselves, using a mix of what we have heard, what we think we have heard, what we want to have heard, what we hope we did not hear, who we are, who we think the message sender is, what our values and expectations are, what our moods and contexts are, our memories of previous interactions, etc. So, misunderstanding between two people is inevitable, no matter how much they try to communicate, no matter who they are, no matter what their relationship. This situation is inevitable, and it should be accepted rather than fought.

The same is true of reading as it is of conversation: as Rose writes, each "reader uses the given narrative as material from which to form his own fantasy." And so it is with music: each listener uses the sounds presented to his/her ear, sounds which the composer may have conceived in terms of some narrative structure, to create his/her own personal narrative-fantasy.

In a previous article I related an incident that showed me just how tenuous the communication model can be for music:

I asked a graduate analysis seminar to study [Ives's] *Putnam's Camp*. Several of the seminar participants were from countries other than the United States and hence had little knowledge of American folk music and patriotic songs. Even some of the American participants did not recognize most of the quotations in Ives's score. One student recognized only "The Star-Spangled Banner" in the penultimate measure – a possibly obscure quotation, since it contains only the first four notes, which constitute a generic major triad. I suggested that those who did not recognize the distinction between quoted and original material, and those who did not know anything about the historical and cultural contexts of the quoted music, had a skewed understanding of the music. Several students objected vehemently, claiming that they recognized American vernacular idioms as such and that was sufficient. I am not so concerned with how valid or complete the understanding of such students was, as I am intrigued by how utterly different the piece must have been for them compared to how it was for me. Despite a lot of analysis about shared perceptions (of such structural aspects as rhythmic irregularities, harmony, set constructs, interplay of tonality and atonality, etc.), everyone in the seminar had different (as well as common) experiences with the music. In a certain sense, there were as many pieces as there were seminar members!

(Kramer, 1997: 34–45)

Putnam's Camp may be an extreme case, given the large number of quotations and references to other music it contains, but I believe that all music elicits individual associations, responses, and meanings in listeners. As Rose states about a study of reading, "each reader interacted with the story in terms of his own personality and intrapsychic life and in the light of this constructed something new which was most consonant with himself . . . . In short, he takes from the work what is most consonant with himself, rewrites it in his own mind and becomes its co-author . . . . Art does not 'communicate' meanings; it *generates* them in the receptive mind." Similarly, if each listener to a piece of music constructs "something new," something which reflects the self more than it reflects the music heard, then how can anyone maintain that there is direct communication from composer to listener?

I do not deny that it is tempting, and comforting, to believe that composers speak to listeners. Rose offers many insights into why the communication model of art is appealing. But it is, if not outright false, then at best less than half the story.

What I am suggesting may sound heretical: a listener who is deeply moved by a performance is not primarily responding to a message sent out by a composer. The composer has not, to any appreciable degree, communicated with this listener. I am not denying the validity or the depth of the listener's response, but rather its source. The listener himself/herself has a lot to do with his/her emotional experience – otherwise, how could we explain different people having different experiences while hearing the same performance? The performer also influences the listener's reaction, although probably less than the listener himself/herself. And the audio technician (if there is one in the chain) has an impact on the listener. But the composer's expression must traverse a long, circuitous route, during which what may have been intended as communication is inevitably distorted and altered.

Rose's thinking parallels these ideas. He courageously goes against accepted psychoanalytic ideas about "the emotional appeal of art." In writing about "the 'communication' by the artist through the work to the recipient," he states quite rightly that "the possibility of such communication retains little credit in the field of aesthetics." Many in the music community, however, continue to accept the communication metaphor as literal truth. Often listeners do believe they have received a communication from the composer. Consider this not uncommon example, which appeared in a newspaper account of how Mozart's G Minor Symphony was believed to have helped a man recover from a serious operation.

> I blissfully sink back as the opening chords of his glorious 40th Symphony start easing every sore spot in my body . . . . The first movement, *Molto Allegro*, is . . . a cloud that picks me up, lifts me up from the pains and fear of my hospital stay . . . . Today, where there was pain, the life-assuring hand of Mozart once again leads me back to joy . . . . [In the second movement] Mozart will not just rescue me from despair. He will tell me of the glorious paths I have yet in front of me . . . . [In the third movement] Mozart sprays me with a dozen more clear inspirations. I hear him saying, "All those delights are there for you. I know you can do them. I know your will" . . . . The music [of the last movement] is Mozart at his highest appreciation of life.
>
> (Atlas, 1995: 5E)

These feelings originated in this particular listener, not in the man Mozart (who most likely did not intend to offer solace to ailing patients), and not even really in the G Minor Symphony. I do not mean to belittle the profundity of this man's experience with the symphony. I believe his account, if I take the more direct invocations of communication as metaphorical. Nor do I mean to suggest that his experience came only from within, that the actual music had nothing to do with it. This man would surely not have had a comparable experience listening, for example, to rap music. Mozart's symphony certainly has something to do with the man's cathartic experience, even if the experience depended even more on the listener: on his needs ("I know Mozart will have something I need to hear and to hear now," (Atlas, 1995: 5E)), his desires, his veneration of Mozart's work, his prior experiences with the symphony, and possibly the opinions others have expressed of K. 550.

Indeed, this particular work – like the second movement of Beethoven's Seventh Symphony, as Rose reports – seems to have elicited a wide variety of responses throughout its 200-year existence:

> Otto Jahn, for example, called it "a symphony of pain and lamentation" (1856), while C. Palmer called it "nothing but joy and animation" (1865). Alexandre Dimitrivitch Oulibicheff (1843) wrote of the finale, "I doubt whether music contains anything more profoundly incisive, more cruelly sorrowful, more violently abandoned, or more completely impassioned," while A.F. Dickinson (1927) felt that "the verve of this movement is tremendous. It is . . . the best possible tonic for the low in spirits." Georges de Saint-Foix wrote in 1932 of "feverish precipitousness, intense poignancy, and concentrated energy," while Donald Francis Tovey wrote at about the same time of "the rhythms and idioms of comedy." Robert Dearling called it "a uniquely moving expression of grief," while H. Hirschbach thought it "an ordinary, mild piece of music." While Alfred Einstein found the symphony "fatalistic" and Pitts Sanborn thought it touched with "ineffable sadness," composers seem to have had happier opinions. Berlioz noted its "grace, delicacy, melodic charm, and fineness of workman-ship"; Schumann found in it "Grecian lightness and grace"; Wagner thought it "exuberant with rapture."
>
> (Kramer, 1988b: 480)

A traditional music analyst might discourage *all* such responses to the G Minor Symphony, saying that the composer never intended to convey such images (or, even if he had, that his intentions are irrelevant: only the music counts, not how or why it came to be).[2] Confronted with a student writing a comparable interpretation, such a music analyst might try to get him/her to listen more abstractly, more in terms of patterns of tension and release, rhythmic development, motivic derivation, metric structure, and harmonic drive. But we should accept that the student's hearing is perfectly appropriate – *for that particular student.*

Musical amateurs (such as the man who believed that Mozart helped him recover after surgery) are hardly the only ones to anthropomorphize works of music into their composers, to identify the force behind the perceived music with the actual person who wrote it. This tendency is common among performers, who readily speak of, for example, "how Serkin plays Beethoven." This phrase is a telling abbreviation of "how Serkin plays the music composed by Beethoven." Such an identification of the music with its composer may be taken as a tacit equation of the music and the person who created it. To the extent that such a locution is a personification of the music, I find little trouble with it: there *is* something about music that is not badly served by the concept of a personality. But is it Beethoven's personality? Or is it a personality (or persona) created (only in part, since both Serkin and his listeners have a role in the construction of musical personae) by Beethoven, much as Shakespeare (and actors, directors, and theatergoers) created Hamlet? Because Hamlet has his own name, we do not usually conflate him with Shakespeare. We know that Hamlet's ideas came (in part) from the man Shakespeare, but we also know that a playwright is capable of creating diverse personae, none of whom need be the author's *alter ego.* The characters in a piano sonata of Beethoven do not have individual names, and indeed it is not obvious just how they inhabit the music. But the sense of personality in the music is palpable. Lacking anyone else to identify with the personalities, musicians (and listeners) happily call the personalities by the name of the composer (or, sometimes, by that of the performer: commentators have written about the personality – whether or not they use that exact word – of a Glenn Gould performance, for example). This is especially evident when performers refer, in rehearsals and other contexts, to "playing the Mozart." Less often do we hear them say they are playing the C Major Quartet, or K. 465, or the "Dissonant" Quartet.

As I have tried to indicate, the pseudo-communication chain is problematic. Nowadays music scholars are beginning to shift their focus from one end of the chain (the composer) to the other (the listener). Thus Rose's ideas are particularly valuable, as he writes of the ways music becomes meaningful, and even therapeutic, for individual listeners. If the listener is understood to be active in the creation of musical meaning, then he/she – more than the composer – is the source (not simply the destination) of what is loosely taken to be communication. Yet many listeners – such as the essayists writing on K. 550 quoted above – still think they have received communications from composers. The composers who allegedly communicate with them are not the real flesh-and-blood people who created the scores that the performers interpreted, but rather a mental construct. Music theorist Nicholas Cook writes of denying "that the author is a free agent, the source from which meaning flows; instead the author is seen as a construction of ideological forces, and meaning is seen as being negotiated between those forces and the reader" (Cook, 1995: 426).

In their minds, each of the people who wrote interpretations of the G Minor Symphony created their own Mozart, who is only tangentially related to the Mozart who actually lived. These virtual Mozarts are believed to communicate to these listener–interpreters, but since all these Mozarts are different their "communications" are different.

Time and therapy

Rose is quite right when he states in Chapter 5 that music "is meaningful primarily through time." I find fascinating Rose's explanations of how music's temporality gives it its power to help neurologically damaged individuals, such as those suffering from the sundown syndrome. Up to a point, it would seem to be the cyclic and repetitive nature of music (e.g. the constant beat to which listeners may entrain their bodily motions, and the four-measure phrases succeeding one another throughout much of a piece) that makes it calming. But if this were the whole story, it would be the repetitive, unchanging nature of music, more than its march through time, to which disturbed patients react. And then we might expect the most repetitive music to be the most soothing. But I wonder if that would be the case. I do not know if anyone has tried to soothe patients by playing pieces like Steve Reich's *Piano Phase*, Philip Glass's *Music in Fifths*, Maurice Ravel's *Boléro*, Erik Satie's *Vexations*, or certain piano sonatas of Clementi, but I would doubt that such music would be as tranquilizing as the examples Rose cites, extending from country music to that of Bach and Handel. This is because excessive repetition, excessive sameness, begins to produce not an inner calm but rather an inner tension: there is only so much repetition or predictability that a listener can take before beginning to feel trapped by the music, before experiencing the tension of a small sound-world seeming to close in on the self. This is where temporal orderliness can turn against itself: musical calm, I suspect, comes not from a maximum of order but from a balanced admixture of (mostly) order and (some) disorder, of regularity and irregularity, of predictability and surprise. Excessive order (as in the works just mentioned) and excessive disorder (as in the second movement of Ives's Fourth Symphony, for example, or in certain compositions of Iannis Xenakis) can produce a profoundly unsettling experience of musical time.

And so, let us not lose sight of music's ability to produce the opposite effect from calming: music can upset otherwise calm people! I am not sure it is the same music which does both, but music with irregularities, discontinuities, etc. – music that goes against the expected regularity which (as Rose demonstrates) is what makes it a powerful tranquilizer – can be disturbing. The harrowing effects of, for example, Beethoven's *Grosse Fugue* or the first movement of Mahler's Seventh Symphony, or the barbaric asymmetries of Stravinsky's *Rite of Spring*, depend in part on the denial of regularity and of expectation. This music unsettles as much as regular music that Rose mentions soothes. Hence this music requires some getting used to, as does any new learning.

I do not wish to discount the extraordinary calming power of certain music, but I do believe that music which deeply disquiets us has an equally wondrous power. This is the ability to induce strangely new, at once unfamiliar and shockingly familiar, emotional states in listeners who are able to give themselves over to the vulnerability of such musical experiences.

The question of the orderly versus the disorderly is ultimately temporal: soothing music tends to be predominantly (but not exclusively) temporally regular. Unsettling music tends to compromise its temporal regularity with striking irregularities. And so I can, on one level, scarcely object to Rose's idea that "one normal function of music is to support the illusion that time 'flows' in an ultimately orderly way." But on another level this statement hardly tells the whole story (nor does Rose believe that it does). Music whose time flow is mostly ordered may soothe disturbed patients, but it can bore other listeners. It may provide a comforting context for dancing, or for entering into the rituals of a rock concert, or for humming away in the background as we go about other tasks. But music which is listened to with deep involvement and complete concentration, without accompanying other activities, often appeals not because of its even temporal flow but precisely because of its deviations from the expected regularity to which listeners have become entrained.

Rose calls musical time flow an illusion, and I agree. Perhaps it is not time that flows in music but rather music that flows through time. Perhaps time is not a river flowing by us, but rather it is we who move, along with the music we hear, through a temporal landscape. Whether or not time flows is a major philosophical question, not likely to be resolved here. But it is useful to keep clear these two alternative ways to regard musical temporality – the flow of time through music versus the flow of music through time. Thus, I think Rose is being too loose when, in discussing nonrational intuition, he equates "the flow of time" with "human advance through time." One of these two concepts says that time moves (and we observe it do so), the other that we move through (a presumably static or eternal) time.

Rose is aware of this distinction, and of its insolubility. Thus he is able to end one section of Chapter 5 by stating that "it is not time that passes but we," yet near the beginning of the next section he invokes music's power to destroy the sense of time's passage.[3] We can have such seemingly contradictory views of time because time is not like any other life experience, nor like any other entity or concept we know. Trying to pin it down as either in motion or static serves only to obscure its profound pervasiveness in all we do and all we are. As Rose states elsewhere, music offers the opportunity for reordering beyond the conventional categories of temporal succession.

If time neither solely flows nor solely stands still, what can we say about music? That it too neither flows nor stands still? I prefer to think of music as both moving through time and standing still. Music accomplishes the apparent impossibility of moving and not moving *simultaneously*. This is because virtually all music is at once progressive and cyclic, linear and nonlinear, diachronic and synchronic, irregular and regular, becoming and being. Music in which cyclic, nonlinear, synchronic, and regular qualities predominate may be the music that is most soothing, the music that works best as "temporal prosthesis" for the neurologically impaired. Music in which the progressive, linear, diachronic, and irregular qualities prevail is the music which can shake some listeners to the depths of their souls.

Interestingly, Rose discusses Javanese gamelan music, which is unusually cyclic. The temporal regularity of this music would seem to make it a good candidate for temporal prosthesis. I would indeed be curious to know what their responses would be if gamelan music were played for disturbed Western patients (I would also be interested in its effect on troubled Javanese). Would its unfamiliar sound world preclude it from calming them, or would its ordered cyclicity soothe the patients?[4]

Actually, traditional Western music also contains temporal cycles embedded within larger cycles, somewhat like those in Javanese music. I am referring to musical meter and its hierarchic properties (for example, a prototypical four-measure phrase acts like a large, slow 4/4 measure). What is the distinction between Javanese musical cycles and those of the West? A major temporal difference is that the higher levels of the hierarchy in most Western music contain frequent irregularities (when, for example, a phrase expected to last four measures is extended by one or two "extra" measures). These irregularities are subtle: we do not realize we are experiencing, for example, a five-measure phrase until it fails to end in its fourth measure. These so-called "hypermetric" irregularities might make Western classical music not the best candidate for "temporal prosthesis," and indeed the soft rock and country music Rose mentions generally have regular hypermetrical structures.

Since Rose is particularly interested in music's temporal regularity, it is hardly surprising that he is attracted to Epstein's theory of proportional tempo. Epstein has shown a predilection in much music for proportional tempos. Proportional tempo is indeed a seductive force in music, particularly since the relative tempos of the levels of the hypermetric hierarchy are usually 2:1 and sometimes 3:1 but only occasionally some other ratio. Neither composers nor performers (nor, let us hope, listeners), however, are slaves to proportional tempo. Not every performance or every composition follows Epstein's theories. Non-proportional tempos can be startling or even upsetting to a listener, but it is sometimes in the very process of being confused – as in any new learning – that listeners ultimately gain their greatest meanings from music.

Epstein does not discuss exceptions very much, since he is trying to explicate the widespread occurrence of proportionality. However, as a composer and a listener, I know that I often relish, and am taken by, and moved by unpredictable tempo relationships – precisely those that do not follow simple proportions. Unusual tempo ratios can jolt me out of my complacency, and cause me to pay close attention to the temporality of the music I am hearing. Such music can be exhilarating precisely because of its unpredictability. In our praise of music's orderliness, let us not lose sight of the irrational nature of certain music (here I specifically go beyond Rose's "non-rational" qualities of music), which can be among the most profound music we have. Proportional tempo may well be the norm, it may be expected, it may (as Epstein claims) have a biological basis, and it may possibly even contribute to temporarily resetting a dementing process in those who listen to it, but it is not inevitable.

I would caution Rose not to accept all of Epstein's ideas uncritically. Epstein certainly offers a strong case for proportional tempo (and for the cubic curve underlying rubato), but these ideas remain controversial and have been challenged on a number of grounds by various scholars.

I am impressed by the numerous instances Rose discusses wherein music integrates and cures (to use Sacks's terms, as quoted in Chapter 5). I find that the therapeutic uses of music speak volumes about its fundamental importance. And I imagine that well people react to music in some of the same ways. But I think it is important to remember that not all music has therapeutic potential, and that well listeners may react to aspects of the music other than its temporal regularity. Disturbed patients, and patients with Parkinson's disease, may respond to music's soothing regularity because it fulfills a need they have for stability. But those of us who live in the outside world, which in some ways is already too full of order and predictability, may well crave – or at least respond deeply to – musical instances of instability, irregularity, discontinuity, unexpectedness, or irrationality. This may be because we need some amount of those qualities, precisely because they unsettle us. As Morse Peckham (1965) has suggested, in dealing with the most challenging art – in trying to impose some sort of order on, or discover some sort of order within, its apparent disorder – we grow, as individuals and ultimately as a culture. This kind of intellectual and emotional growth, occasioned by challenging and seemingly irrational music, is as necessary for the well among us as the stability provided by temporally regular music is for the disturbed and sick among us.

Rose explains in Chapter 3 that music tends to lose some of its irregularities in memory: "a system left to itself [I would have said 'to a perceiver'] tends to lose asymmetries and become more regular. Memory reinforces this tendency; less good shapes tend to be forgotten." Indeed, this fact has been substantiated through experiments in music perception. Irregular music is often recalled in a version more regular than what was originally heard. This process of regularization is similar to what happens with muzak, when it uses some music of the classical or romantic eras. Muzak's arrangers often recompose the music they borrow so as to remove striking harmonies or irregular meters or rhythms – things which they believe may be too startling, too noticeable. As a result, the music is supposed to soothe people in grocery stores or wherever, and even encourage them to buy. It tends to annoy rather than soothe those who are deeply involved in the music that is being watered down, however. But background use of simplified music is akin to the use of temporally regular music to calm the disturbed. I am not against such uses of music, of course, but I think it is important to remember the power of music, when carefully listened to, to do just the opposite. "Music heard so deeply that it is not heard at all, but you are the music while the music lasts," as T.S. Eliot (1943) wrote.

Music's therapeutic power may go beyond temporal regularity and muzak's simplifications. As Rose remarks (in Chapter 5), music "may have to do with self-recognition, union, reinforcement." This is, according to Rose, because of not only music's periodicity and motion but also its patterns of tension and release. Music may indeed mirror the mind in these ways. But, again, let us also remember the darker side of music. Challenging music, unusual music, may force us beyond our selves. It may help us to forge new selves. It may provoke us with disunion rather than welcome us with union. It may not mirror our minds as they are but rather suggest ways to expand our minds, ways to have new temporal experiences, ways to find new meanings, new personae.

Rose ends up saying that we create music "in our own image." But some of the most profound composers (of all eras) have gone beyond that, creating a music in the image not of what we are but of what they glimpse we might become. Theirs is the music of the greatest profundity, but it may also be the least useful as temporal prosthesis. This is music in which there may, in fact, be an *imbalance* of tension and release (Rose suggests in Chapter 3 that a dynamic balance of tension and release is central to all art), and in which the frame is not always "secure and sensitive." When I think about the music that has moved me, and changed me, the most – Beethoven's A Minor String Quartet (Opus 132), Mahler's Ninth Symphony, Schubert's C Major String Quintet, Sibelius's *Tapiola*, Bach's B Minor Mass, Brahms's Clarinet Quintet, Mozart's G Minor Quintet, Ives's Trio, Bartók's *Music for Strings, Percussion, and Celeste*, Stravinsky's *Symphonies of Wind Instruments*, Messiaen's *Chronocromie*, Xenakis's *Eonta* – I find music of considerable tension (with releases, to be sure, but not necessarily with a balance between the two). This is music in which "returning to the central tonality of the 'home' key" (Chapter 3) may not "always bring a relief of tension." This is music which does not consistently offer "a dynamically-balanced holding environment of virtual tension and release." I have difficulty imagining such pieces as soothing mentally or physically impaired patients, because soothing is precisely what they do not try to be.

Music and words

In Chapter 7, Rose recounts fascinating stories about people turning to music at times of severe stress. These stories are compelling and moving. They make me want to know more: *how* does music serve to comfort the frightened? I suspect the answer is something more than music's temporal regularity, something more than what seems to calm disturbed mental patients. Echoing Zuckerkandl, Rose suggests that singing together melts away people's separateness. This is no doubt true, but why is music-making such an efficient communal activity for bringing people together? How does music succeed so well in uniting people under stress?

Since the music produced by people bonding together in the face of adversity is usually texted, I wonder particularly why singing has its unique power, compared to simply reciting verses or humming music without words. Rose is on the right track when he states in Chapter 7 that "the content of the song was always secondary to the music." By "content" he must mean verbal content. But does not the real content of song lie in the amalgamation of the words and the tones? In the most effective songs – including of course songs that bring a sense of strength to threatened people – the total experience of singing and/or listening is more than the sum of the experiences of hearing the words and listening to the music.

Rose suggests a reason why people under emotional stress turn to song, why words alone are not sufficient to provide comfort and solidarity. As he notes, tunes are experienced as entities, not note by note.[5] The unitary wholeness of a musical melody is not an objective fact. Composers and performers do not communicate wholeness in the melodies they produce. As Rose explains in Chapter 3, a musical line is not literally an organic whole, but if it has certain requisite characteristics, listeners will sense in it a sufficient similarity to their own inner notion of wholeness that they will mentally constitute it as unitary.

The same is true of words, I believe, but less so. When I listen to speech, I of course take in the meaning (as I construe it in my mind) of a verbal phrase as a whole, but I am also aware of the individual words and morphemes[6] that help to convey that meaning. But I am less aware of the individual phonemes,[7] just as I am less aware of individual tones in a melody.[8]

I would like to suggest, on a hunch and without any scientific justification, that people are less aware of individual notes in a heard melody than of morphemes (or syllables or words) in heard speech. Why would this be? Perhaps because we are all experts at listening to and parsing speech, whereas most of us are amateurs at singing and at analytic listening to music. Amateur musicians hear complete gestalts more than individual components; experts hear both. When words are sung to music, the integrated listening that is second nature to music listeners casts its unifying influence over the words, so that we hear musical gestalts binding together verbal morphemes.

The reason that melodies may be experienced as more nearly unitary than speech may be this: there are far fewer possible tones that can continue a melody begun than there are words that may come next in a speech pattern. The repertory of tones available in most musical languages is far smaller than the repertory of words or syllables available in most natural languages. Hence strings of morphemes may go many places, but strings of notes are more constrained, and hence are understood more as a unit.

It is true that natural languages have relatively small repertories of phonemes, however, but I do not believe that we construct meanings from the phonemes as we hear them so much as we react to the morphemes, which have far greater variety. The phonemes have a basic importance, of course – it is they that we literally hear. But it seems to me that the morphemes, more than phonemes, correspond to individual notes of a melody, and musical notes create greater continuity and greater unity than do spoken morphemes.

Music can provide a comfort of wholeness that is stronger than that of speech. By singing we bind the words together into unitary experiences, and being unitary is precisely what is needed in the face of the fragmented experiences of fear and loss. Words alone can support the fragmentation of a damaged personality, whether hurt through loss of a loved one, fear, or illness. But words sung to music resist that breaking apart and offer to the person who sings, and to the people who listen, the integration that has been taken from their lives.

As a professional musician, and in particular as a professional analyst of music, I have a more difficult time achieving that wholeness than does someone who listens to melodies only as entities, someone who does not have the habit of pulling melodies apart to look for relationships between individual tones. It is often noted that professional musicians and music scholars may lose some of their emotional responses to music, the very responses that attracted them to music earlier in their lives. This paradoxical change is sometimes explained by an alleged shift of musical responses from the right to the left brain hemisphere (relevant research is cited in Kramer, 1988b: 404, notes 31–32). But another explanation is what I have just suggested, inspired by Rose's ideas: that amateur listeners and singers sense mainly the wholeness of melodies, which have the power to concatenate possibly disparate words. Music for them is an integrating and an integrated experience, an ordered experience, an experience of continuity and wholeness. Once musicians begin to pull melodies apart into individual motives or single notes – whether in rehearsal or under music analysis – then it becomes less automatic, and possibly more difficult, to sense only their wholeness. And so music performers (particularly those who play or sing from notated scores) and music theorists may have a richer understanding of music than amateurs do, but they also may find it rare to be profoundly moved by continuous, integrated melodies.

For most people, music is comforting and integrative, and it has the ability to console and to cure. It is therefore hardly surprising that music plays an important part in almost everyone's life. There are no cultures on earth without music. Music pervades our daily lives, our rituals, our religions, our leisure activities, our times of stress and loss. Few people have asked how or why music is so potent and pervasive. Now, thanks to Rose's groundbreaking work, we can begin to understand from a psychoanalytic perspective some of the reasons behind music's ubiquity and power – the power to stretch as well as to soothe.[9]

Jonathan D. Kramer
Professor of Music
Columbia University

Notes

1   An example: Justin London suggested (in a private conversation) that communication must be present for the jokes in Haydn's music to work. Even today, two centuries after the composer placed his rather specific messages into his scores, listeners "get" the jokes. The communication chain is complete, and listeners understand what Haydn wanted them to understand. So, communication is possible. But jokes are more specific than most musical expression, and I maintain that, on average, most Western art music fails to communicate specific ideas from composer to listener.

2   Perhaps the most influential statement of this attitude is Wimsatt and Beardsley's (1954) "Intentional Fallacy."

3   I suggest that these apparent contradictions arise from trying to think of time in the same way we conceive other life experiences and other entities. The best way out of this conundrum, I believe, is that offered by Arlow (as quoted in Chapter 5): "time does not flow or stand still." Seeger's idea (also quoted in Chapter 5) is equally relevant: "the experience of time flow . . . is . . . a socially constructed form of order imposed on experience."

4   Indeed, Rose does not tell us enough about therapeutic music, although he does mention, in Chapter 7, that not all music works therapeutically, and some pieces may even be epileptogenic. Some of the things I still want to know are: Does the same music always calm the same patients? Different patients? Does some music soothe some patients but not others? What aspects, if any, do the most soothing musics have in common?

5   This is certainly true of short melodies, but those whose duration exceeds that of the perceptual present may be conceived, but are not perceived, as entities. However, listeners do chunk longer tunes into segments of manageable length, which are felt as unitary entities.

6   A morpheme is the smallest unit of language that carries meaning, such as a syllable. A morpheme cannot be subdivided without losing its meaning. Thus a morpheme is analogous to a molecule (but not to an atom, which does not possess the same characteristics as does the substance of which it is a part). The musical analog of a morpheme is a

motive – a small figure with a recognizable rhythmic and/or melodic shape.

7 A phoneme is the smallest unit of language that has a distinct sound, such as what is represented in written language by a letter. In spoken language, a phoneme consists of a single sound. Morphemes usually consist of more than one phonemes. A phoneme is thus analogous to an atom. The musical analog of a phoneme is an individual note or tone.

8 Unless I force myself to listen analytically, something I do reasonably often because I am a music theorist but which I did far less often in my younger years, before I had learned how to pull apart and analyze melodies.

9 I would like to acknowledge the help of Norma Kramer and Deborah Bradley, who carefully and critically read preliminary versions of this foreword.

References

Atlas, E.E. (1995), "The Magic of Mozart's Music Soothes a Hurting Heart", *Sarasota Herald-Tribune*, 22 January.

Cook, N.J. (1995), "Music Theory and the Postmodern Muse: An Afterword", in E.W. Marvin and R. Hermann (eds), *Concert Music, Rock, and Jazz Since 1945: Essays and Analytical Studies*, Rochester, NY: University of Rochester Press.

Eliot, T.S. (1943), "The Dry Salvages", *Four Quartets*, New York: Harcourt, 1968.

Kramer, J.D. (1988a), *Listen to the Music*, New York: Schirmer Books.

—— (1988b), *The Time of Music*, New York: Schirmer Books.

—— (1997), "Postmodern Concepts of Musical Time", *Indiana Theory Review* 17/2.

Nattiez, J.-J. (1990), *Music as Discourse*, trans. C. Abbate, Princeton, NJ: Princeton University Press.

Peckham, M. (1965), *Man's Rage for Chaos*, Philadelphia: Chilton.

Wimsatt, W. and Beardsley, M.C. (1954), "The Intentional Fallacy", *The Verbal Icon*, Lexington, KY: University of Kentucky Press.

Preface

Why do music and abstract art pack universal emotional appeal? And, sometimes, "therapeutic" efficacy?

The main thesis of this book is that they tap into a biological need to grow and develop by newly reintegrating thought and feeling.

This is key to a creative expansion of awareness. Thus, the inquiry itself sheds light on the creative process.

My focus on this theme stems from long-standing interest in the arts and from clinical experience as a psychoanalyst. In the latter capacity, I continue to be struck by the shortcomings of words alone to touch emotions in order to effect change and growth. In contrast, abstract art, especially music, can have a direct emotional appeal. Without having to be representational, and irrespective of words or eventual verbalization, they both generate feelings and help to process them.

Closely related to this is their mysterious "therapeutic" efficacy. Like truly satisfying work or the magical mutuality of love, music and art appear to rank among the "natural" means for expanding the apprehension of the riches of reality.

My psychoanalytic understanding suggests that this draws upon the earliest wordless – largely vocal and kinesthetic – emotional rapport between infants and their parents. The infant's survival actually depends on the quality of this nonverbal relationship. So, too, do emotional growth and development. Later on, one's attachment to art encourages ongoing elaboration and refinement of emotions, thus deepening the quality of life.

This volume is based on my trilogy on nonverbal aesthetic form and psychoanalysis (G.J. Rose, 1980, 1987, 1996). It incorporates an overview of that work but also advances the project of building a theory of psychoanalytic aesthetics with new material, as well as by concentrating primarily on music as the ultimate abstract art.

While fundamentally beholden to Winnicott's (1953) theory of an intermediate transitional area between self and objects, and the spirit of Marion Milner, it is essentially an original body of work. Most of the chapters have never been previously published, apart from "On the Shores of Self: Samuel Beckett's *Molloy*" (1973); "The Music Of Time in Faulkner's *Light in August*" (1979); "In Pursuit of Slow Time: Modern Music and a Clinical Vignette" (1984).

The nature of the project is such that it seems fitting to share some of its personal background.

As a youngster I kept being reminded by my parents that these were the best years of my life. I had every reason to be happy, they rightly said; and they, every reason to expect that I be grateful in return. I could only agree. But felt more woeful than ever.

Fortunately, along the way I learned that nothing could beat Beethoven's piano sonatas for expressing emotion – safely. And the best place to listen to my sister play Beethoven's sonatas (far better than I could ever hope to) was lying under the piano. From rage to yearning, I could connect with a whole range of emotion without being accused of being ungratefully unhappy.

There I could listen to myself, too: feel feelings, think thoughts, think feelings, feel thoughts. And be whole again.

The same baby grand piano and a couch have long shared space in my office. There, my entire adult professional life has been spent listening – behind the couch or often face to face – to other people's thoughtful feelings, feelingful thoughts – and my own responsive resonances. The organizing principle has been the importance of exercising minds of our own in such a way that feeling and thought are equal partners.

In my office I listen for the "music" – i.e., the feeling – behind others' speech and behavior as I try to help them with their task of mastery and integration. As music led me under the piano to find a wholeness of thoughts and feelings, the "music" of feeling guides me through seemingly endless variations toward the inner coherence of underlying identity themes.

* * *

It is astonishing that, until recently, feelings – the very origin of psychoanalysis – have been down-played in psychoanalysis. Likewise, art. It has been almost a mantra in organized psychoanalysis that it is a science and hence worthy of respect. Art is not only not science, it is based on its very opposite: illusion. Art is also worthy of respect, of course. There is no denying that great writers anticipated psychoanalytic truths.

Whatever the reasons, whether the security of a century of accumulated experience and expansion, or the threat from rivalrous contenders – its own intellectual offspring – the centrality of feelings is being restored into the field of psychoanalysis. Art stands ready to be mined as a treasured resource for their study. Just as psychoanalysis can shed light on why one needs art, art can help teach psychoanalysis more about emotions.

Since art can play a significant role in helping to modulate emotions, as indeed I so maintain, then we need to rethink the primacy accorded to psychoanalytic insight via verbalization on the couch as *the* royal route to access and integrate feelings with thought. Nonverbal affect embodied in abstract art like music may need to be assigned a status alongside the established importance of narrative fantasy, free association, interpretation and insight. Contrary to what I was taught to believe in years of school-room Latin, it appears that first-class thinking may not be substantially limited to if not synonymous with language.

It may be suspected that raising such possibilities reflects early, unresolved rebelliousness now aimed at analytic orthodoxy. And so it may. But, if so, it also arises from a richly savored personal and cultural life and, most importantly, the privilege of a fulsome career in clinical psychoanalysis, itself. So I believe.

* * *

It remains to say a few words about the use of the terms "feeling," "emotion" and "affect," which I have been using fairly loosely. "Feeling" and "emotion" are almost synonymous except that while we are aware of feelings we may not always be aware of emotions. Emotions are accompanied by physical manifestations such as shortness of breath, or rapid heart beat; these may then call one's attention to the existence of underlying feelings. As for the term "affect," because of the metapsychological thicket that surrounds the concept, I try to limit its use to technical matters such as affect regulation or nonverbal affect.

A recent explication (Matthis, 2000) brings needed clarification to the concept. Affect arises from an affective matrix whose ultimate location is embodied within the nervous system. Affect comprises feelings, emotions, and "affect equivalents" in the form of psycho-somatic symptoms or somatic illnesses. Because of its basic origin in the body, affect reflects an ongoing bodily potential to react in two different directions: *psychically* with conscious, subjective feelings or emotions, as well as to respond *physically* with the objective physical signs of "affect equivalents." Thus, most importantly, the term "affect" emphasizes the fact of *embodiment* for feelings, emotions and affect equivalents.

The same bodily aspect holds for words. To Lacan's dictum that the unconscious is structured like a language we may rejoin that the ego is first and foremost a bodily ego. As Freud pointed out in one of his earliest works (*On Aphasia*, 1891), words are also physical events arising from sensory sources in parental language and intonation. Early analysts found bodily sources of language in the infant's gestures (Ferenczi, 1913), sphincter activity (Sharpe, 1940), and nursing patterns (Spitz, 1957). The philosopher, Cassirer (1923), demonstrated the first conceptual differentiations of language in the body.

The physicality of words is exploited most eloquently in poetry where a context of pulse and silences convey sense through sound (Rose, 1980). Thus relating poetry to music.

Words, music, feelings – and embodiment.

As music led me originally to what I consider the heart of psycho-analysis, namely, feeling, it seems a natural development that the perspectives of psychoanalysis now lead me more deeply into the nature of music and abstract visual art.

As I sought words to express feelings, I learned to value music the more: it frames the silences untouched by words. And the mystery. Contemplating which seems not an unfitting task for the later days of one's years.

Among the most puzzling mysteries is the almost magical way in which music can sometimes almost instantly, if temporarily, "jump-start" normal feelings, motion and identity where these have been seemingly destroyed by inexorable neurological disease. Specula-tions are offered in terms of (1) the power of "implicit motion" in music reinforcing faulty neurobiological rhythms, and (2) all art stimulating affect-regulating internalizations – both old, preverbal ones and perhaps providing external transferential models for building new, nonverbal ones.

This book is not primarily a clinical investigation. Therefore, although it makes use of case examples, it does not rely mainly on psychoanalytic observational data as evidence emerging from the couch. Rather, the methodology makes use of basic psychoanalytic concepts – the interplay of primary and secondary processes, the implicit motion embedded in their patterns of tension and release – plus trauma theory and data from early development and neuroscience; it applies these tools to such questions as how nonverbal abstract art integrates thought and feeling.

The effort succeeds, I believe, in contributing new heuristic perspectives to perplexing problems. Perhaps more importantly, it stimulates new questions such as how ongoing emotional differentiation and psychic integration take place other than by verbal insight and analytic working through.

For the benefit of lay readers who are put off by technical jargon, I try as far as possible to favor ordinary usage. For example, primary and secondary processes are often rendered into imagination and knowledge or cognition. However, these terms, whether technical or popular, are never divorced from their underlying economic attributes of tension (the long-circuiting of secondary process) or release (the short-circuiting of primary process). These are retained as fundamental to the argument.

Freud's own writing style might well serve as a model. It illustrates a "marriage" of primary process imaginative freedom with secondary process logical control such that the "music" of his prose "enacts" the ideational content (Mahoney, 1987). I would like to think that a combination of some degree of poetical style and terse, nontechnical clarity helps bring my work to the appreciative attention of receptive readers.

* * *

The book as a whole owes its being to my life companion. Deprived of self and memory in the long dying of vascular dementia, a radiant smile at times still bore witness that a soul yet lived. None other than hers who was our Anne, it inspirits this effort.

Acknowledgments

I gratefully acknowledge the use of personal material by Etienne Abelin; the generous guidance to pertinent references by Eugene Goldberg; the council of Morton Reiser and Robert Scharf not to exceed a prudent depth in neuroscience; a shared intellectual affinity with the late David Epstein across the boundaries of our respective fields of psychoanalysis and music; the tactful correction by Jonathan Kramer of errors in the use of musical terminology; the drawings of Giacometti's figures contributed by an anonymous artist; the reliable backing of friend and agent, Sidney Kramer; the enthusiastic interest of grandson, Alexander Rose; the unfailing moral support of John Gedo; the late José Barchilon; and others.

Thanks are extended to the publishers for permission to reprint (as Chapters 2, 4 and 6) the following previously published article and chapters by the author: Rose, G.J. (1973), "On the Shores of Self: Samuel Beckett's *Molloy*", *Psychoanalytic Review* 60: 587–604, © 1973 The Guilford Press, New York; Rose, G.J. (1980), "The Orchestration of Time in William Faulkner's *Light in August*", in G.J. Rose *The Power of Form: A Psychoanalytical Approach to Aesthetic Form* by permission of International Universities Press, Inc., © 1980 International Universities Press, Inc.; Rose, G.J. (1987), "In Pursuit of Slow Time", in G.J. Rose *Trauma and Mastery in Life and Art* (expanded with an original docudrama, 1996) by permission of International Universities Press, Inc., © 1987 International Universities Press, Inc.

Chapter 1

Between words and music

Where does aesthetic responsiveness arise? A prototype may well lie in the nonverbal emotional rapport and empathy of the earliest infant–parent interplay. Within this matrix are found, too, the rhythmic sing-song and syllables that universally comprise the rudiments of music and words. Reaching further back, there is the interactional synchrony that neonates manifest within twenty minutes of birth: they react to voices with synchronized movements (cited by Benzon, 2001). And still further, since auditory systems become active three to four months before birth, perhaps the fetus becomes entrained to speech patterns *in utero*. Little is known about any of this.

We know perhaps even less about the continuum between knowing and feeling. Or words and music. We do know that words and music are both rooted in the body. As Freud (1891) made clear in a number of his writings beginning with *On Aphasia*, every word has been bathed in sensory sources coming from parental speech and intonation. There is no such thing as a disembodied word.

Emboldened by recent neuroscience, it would seem more apparent than ever that cognition and feeling are basically inseparable and not only in infancy. In the course of development and the attrition of daily life they become more differentiated from each other.

It is a common problem of clinical practice to attempt to rejoin them and thereby help restore a sense of inner and outer wholeness without the danger of flooding. The early discovery of transference, then counter-transference, and now an increased sensitivity to intersubjectivity are among the tools in this direction.

As for words and music, words tend to cluster towards the knowing end of the intellect–feeling spectrum; music towards the opposite pole.

Let us begin with clinical technique and then turn to other matters which arguably can be located somewhere in the mid-range between words and music: the difference in how verbal and nonverbal information is registered; the contribution of musical sensitivity to therapeutic communication including predicting suicidality; some bodily correlates of poetry and music; and recent thinking about the neurobiological basis of the sensory qualities of our subjective world. We will return specifically to words and music via one musician's brave attempt to translate eight bars of music into words – only to demonstrate once again its ineffability within what has been termed the "mysterious leap" between body and mind.

* * *

It is a truism of psychoanalysis that insight without emotional involvement is of little therapeutic value. How can treatment unite thinking and feeling?

The long-established principle is that of "working through." For however long it takes, one hopes that a new cognitive insight will eventually percolate down toward the depths of one's affective core; at the same time, the defenses that keep deeper feelings sequestered from mature thought may gradually yield to the emotional constancy of the treatment alliance and tactful, timely interpretations of its transferential distortions.

Alas, life is short and psychoanalysis – perhaps necessarily – long.

In actual practice, experienced therapists find their own guiding principles the better to bridge between abstract theory and the pressing needs of reality.

Here are some of mine.

The arts sensitized me, and clinical experience confirmed, that psychic boundaries are permeable rather than being firm structures. Accomplishing what language does not readily do, the arts subjectify the outer world and objectify the inner; they show that the boundaries of subjectivity and objectivity are more permeable than traditional psychoanalytic theory used to teach. (Think of Munch's painting of the experience of a kiss as a graphic representation of a meltdown of boundaries. Or the conflation of inner and outer surfaces in a Möbius strip.) They pioneered the insight that there is no immaculate perception without subjective interpretation, no reality without imagination, no thought without feeling. Contemporary neuroscience is adding heft to these principles.

It is useful to think that the constant interplay of imagination and knowledge helps each evolve to higher levels of development and complexity. One does not simply outgrow and abandon earlier forms of imagination and graduate to mature secondary process knowledge of reality. A less simplistic (and less dour) view: the past is an ever-present accompaniment and an only partially accessible resource, supplying the potential for both harmony and dissonance.

A child may outgrow an actual comfort blanket or other transitional *object*; but much of adult feelingful thinking continues to take place in Winnicott's (1953) intermediate area. Here a transitional *process* of continuous interplay of inner and outer (Rose, 1978) in an open system (von Bertalanffy, 1968) reflects the dynamic between a breathing self and a changing reality – each shaping the other to create a unique synchronous totality. It is a minor, everyday version of the creative process bringing novelty to the tired, old familiar and building a bridge to the new and heretofore strange.

Ego boundaries expand and constrict as a person's need for privacy alternates with the wish to share, be silent as well as communicate, savor distance as well as closeness, regress perhaps to consolidate further before venturing again to progress and explore.

All these dynamic shifts arise out of a field of dynamic forces which may be understood in time. Or not. In the meantime, professional name-calling such as "Resistance!" connotes an adversarial static state and recalls an outdated early era in the history of psychoanalysis.

The therapeutic process may usefully be thought of in terms of music. Music is not about playing notes; music consists of silences that breathe and shape the sound, engendering depths of feeling to be experienced without the necessity for immediate understanding.

As in music, a holding environment based on attunement and stability provides a reliable structure conducive to affect. Unrelieved structure, however, like a blank screen, may degenerate into a shared torpor rather than encouraging the freedom to discover and learn to express affect.

In addition to interpretation, other active measures consistent with objective neutrality and abstinence may well be required to promote affective interaction and keep the process from languishing. Flexible spontaneity and a readiness to improvise are called for, such as introducing discrete doses of controlled dissonance like changes of tempo and rhythm.

All this depends, of course, on the therapist's own subjectivity: constraints and possibilities inherent in one's character and humanity, assurance arising from the thoroughness of one's personal training analysis, an ingrained habit of self-appraisal, and the confidence that accrues from successful clinical experience and learning from one's mistakes. For the practitioner, the immense good fortune of a full personal life may be nothing less than a mental hygiene necessity.

Flexibility and spontaneity, however much hedged with cautions about respecting traditional parameters of neutrality and abstinence, the constancy of a reliable holding environment, and the necessity for self-appraisal should not be dismissed as mere boilerplate. On the other hand, since nothing short of a handbook of clinical illustrations would be sufficient, I will limit myself to sketching some of the ways I try to connect with a patient's unverbalized affect – without scrupling too much about whether this is "real analysis" or "just therapy."

Simply put, I try to discern and speak in the person's natural language. This includes noting, accommodating and perhaps matching – not aping – phonological features of speech such as tempo, rhythm and volume. Also pertinent are the frequency and quality of silences, accompanying body language, congruity or discrepancy between style and content. I pay particular attention to trying to discover the latently operating metaphors that so often connect content with underlying feeling. All this may happen quickly or take many sessions.

The phonology and metaphors seem closely related to and embodied in much that is nonverbal. As I become comfortable with the style, like attending to a new language and adopting some of it, I frequently notice a mutual unbending taking place. Even the breathing seems easier. These considerations must be closely related to empathy, for it has been noted that adult partners who match their patterns of vocalization and pauses tend to feel more empathically related (Jaffe and Feldstein, 1970: 95–96).

A personal example far removed from professional life comes to mind and may convey what is difficult to express. As a pre-adolescent I spent some summers on a farm and hung out with the adult son of the owner, who seemed to enjoyed teaching me how to do some of the chores like milking. As a young adult years later I traveled to that part of the country and looked for the farm. It was boarded up and seemingly abandoned. Walking over the fields I saw a man. As we approached each other I called out, "Fred?" He, squinting, replied: "You look kinda natural!"

I often wondered later what went into the homey acknowledgement. Had I unconsciously reverted to an earlier gait, and/or perhaps mirrored his? Was it this whole gestalt, as well as my voice and "tonality" – certainly not my features for I was now grown in total appearance – that had allowed him to recognize me *through himself* as "kinda natural"?

As in relating this anecdote, as time has gone on I am not shy about using personal examples to illustrate something or make a point *if it is apposite*. It sets an example of my feeling comfortable and inviting the other to join me. I may also free associate aloud to something the person has said, or has not said, or expressed posturally or in some other nonverbal way. It sets an example of daring to be free even if it risks looking foolish or making a mistake, which I am also ready to admit. An instructor long ago defined doing therapy as: "two people sitting in a room, one is probably anxious, and it better not be you!"

In the ambience that I am describing, humor comes naturally to me. At its best, its use does not detract from always remaining serious if seldom solemn. In the course of time I have refined its use in therapy and have previously discussed it (Rose, 1969). It is an important aspect of my style along with striving to find the right metaphors, being guided largely by nonverbal cues, and using myself as a human instrument to invite a freer affective interchange.

As an example of using myself as an instrument, there are times when ironic self-directed humor emerges spontaneously. This can serve as an inoculation against unhealthy self-importance. It also sets a further example that there be no immunity – myself included – from detached objectivity. When directed towards the other person, it licenses me to be direct without being cruel, as it also counteracts any tendency to infantilize by being overly compassionate and over-identified. When it occasionally misfires, it offers an opportunity for clarification and a yet closer working alliance in which it is clear that I am not above – indeed, I invite – mutual criticism and candor.

* * *

Progress in cognitive psychology has brought a clarifying restatement of the problem of connecting underlying feeling with conscious thinking, if not how to solve it. Instead of feeling versus thinking, it offers a different duality: verbal versus nonverbal information processing. They are encoded and organized in different formats and are stored in separate systems specialized for each type. We turn now to summarizing some of the work of Wilma Bucci (1985, 1997).

Mental representations appear to be stored in dual codes: verbal and nonverbal. Verbal information is encoded and stored in linguistic form and may involve abstract phonological or semantic codes. The verbal system is activated by words, whether in the form of inner speech or verbal thought.

Nonverbal input is encoded and stored in perceptual forms which includes kinesthetic and visceral as well as other sensory representations. The nonverbal system is directly activated by pictures, sounds, tastes, smells and *feelings*.

Experimental studies show how important imagery is in forming mental representations; and that both imagery and emotion are associated with the nonverbal system. Since thought depends on mental representations, which require imagery, which is stored in the nonverbal system, it follows that the nonverbal system is closely implicated in thought. More cogently, language can no longer be considered the major vehicle of thought; the nonverbal, imagistic component of thought – closely related to affect – may be an equal if silent partner in cognition.

Repression is more likely to involve the nonverbal system. This is where much painful material may be stored, de-linked from words and never represented in verbal form.

The problem for psychoanalytic treatment is that the verbal and nonverbal systems are linked but often insufficiently. A person's affective core is linked to nonverbal perceptual schemata. Treatment must go beyond dealing with verbalizable mental contents and reach down to the nonverbal levels where so much of the emotion is encoded. Free association and dreams aid in this. So, too, do the various devices beyond verbal interpretation that we have been discussing, like humor, and the analyst using his/her own personal style as an instrument for attunement and change.

Verbal interpretations often leave untouched emotional material that either has never been linked to words, as in alexithymia or somatization, or has been wrongly named. Language is necessary to disentangle faulty verbal connections that reflect emotional confusions.

Common examples in my own experience: disagreeing and being disagreeable; liking and being alike; objective aloneness and subjective loneliness; having wishes or needs and being wishful or needy; being objectively broke as against feeling poor, deprived, or helpless; authoritative and authoritarian; making judgments and being judgmental; moral and moralistic.

In addition to such linguistic disentanglement, Bucci appears to support the traditional view that conveying insight through language is the goal of psychoanalysis. Is linkage to language necessary to influence emotions encoded in the nonverbal system and thus effect structural change? One may question this partly on the basis of her own work, which shows that there is more to thought than language.

By now, many therapists agree that there is more to treatment than words. Much change in analytic therapy comes by way of an internalization of the emotional ambience of the therapeutic relationship, which in turn effects a more benevolently critical relation with oneself. Though this may never become fully conscious or verbalizable, it may yet prove enduring.

* * *

A recent book (Knoblauch, 2000) is a treasury of clinical illustrations of the phonological as contrasted to the semantic significance of verbalization. As a former jazz musician as well as therapist, the author is able to spell out how music can serve as a descriptive analog for tuning in to affect. This has the merit of helping to make manifest what has undoubtedly been implicit and intuitive in the hands of many therapists.

The following summarizes relevant aspects.

Jazz provides a way of thinking about some nonverbal dimensions of psychoanalytic dialogue like tone, rhythm, tempo, volume, and gesture. In therapy these are intuitive and silent considerations; but among members of a musical ensemble group playing and improvising together they are explicitly musical. Improvising and accompaniment in jazz can be used as a metaphor for a clinical technique for interacting with certain patients.

In a therapeutic dialogue musical considerations can serve to sensitize a therapist to nonverbal cues and thereby do more skillfully what he/she may be doing intuitively – such as bring out a nonverbalized affect, introduce a new facet of personality, or prevent a premature closure.

Rhythm, especially, is the connecting link between music and the body's respiration and pulse. Respiration and pulse may become entrained – namely, synchronized – with musical rhythms to provide either soothing regularity or jolting tempo shifts and breaks.

Some of the elements that provide order in ensemble playing are rhythm, tone, and each performer taking turns for soloing. In therapy, such nonverbal elements assume equal importance with the semantic content of the verbal interchange. A therapist may employ a rhythmic dimension to slow or accelerate the pace, increase the arousal, or, by using an upward turn of tone, to avoid sounding officious.

These microdimensions of nonverbal communication were first recognized in infant–caregiver observations. There it was repeatedly observed that each of the pair influences the other's actions and feelings long before verbal communication is available to them. Out of such interactions with each other, temporal shapes of feeling emerge continuously. As music structures the experience of time, so do these interactions.

Attending to the nonverbal, musical dimensions of the dialogue can provide a point of departure for dealing with otherwise inaccessible, dissociated affects. As in the original work with infants, one may, for example, match a patient's vocal rhythm, tone, and volume and then slowly reduce and soften them in a gradual process of nonverbal affect regulation.

Knoblauch makes clear that the type of patient he is describing is often so inarticulate and sensitive to intrusiveness that little more than the most tactfully timed, nonverbal accompaniment – informed by musical considerations – is tolerable until considerable progress is accomplished. This is a slow process of symbolic elaboration and silent dialogue. At a much later stage this may be supplemented by verbal interpretation to facilitate gradual verbal articulation of feelings and eventually self-regulation and integration.

A cautionary note may still be added, however. If the interplay between patient and therapist be thought of as a musical collaboration, we must respect that each intrinsically represents a different perspective. Also, the balance between them is constantly shifting in focus and weight. A "democratic" principle of intersubjective equality can be misleading if applied uncritically.

On the one hand, it is the patient who has composed the material and is the primary performing artist; the therapist is the sensitively attentive, supportive, non-intrusive accompanist and as such is essential but secondary.

However, while the therapist surely acts as accompanist, there is more to his/her function to be applied when it becomes possible: for example, experienced listener, critic and professional tutor. The patient does not come (and pay!) in order to enjoy solo privileges only, but for a basically asymmetrical working partnership.

Patient and therapist each has priority in the area where he/she has most to contribute. From this, meaning may emerge or be discovered, and perhaps surprise either one or both and eventually turn out to be the work primarily of either, both, or, indeed, essentially indivisible.

* * *

In contrast to the foregoing account of what makes for "musically" good sessions, the following communication from a young musician friend just beginning treatment offers a lucid account of what getting off to a bad "musical" start feels like. I quote with his permission.

> In the first session I felt rather free but there were things that I felt uncomfortable with: his interest and way of listening and talking seemed a bit acted. I had a hard time feeling where he is as a person. As it was the first session I didn't let it bother me too much.
>
> I walked out of my second session really down and out and after today's (third) session I'm really not sure if I want to continue working with him.
>
> I can't locate him as a person and feel like it's a space of theatre (the theatre of therapist and patient) which wouldn't be all that bad if I didn't feel that there's not much space for emotions. In the way he talks and moves, somehow affected, nervous. I imagined him on stage as a musician. I believe I would be really put off. I can imagine having a creative session with him every now and then but I don't see a basis for a relationship of several years.
>
> It all reminds me of the feeling I get (and other musicians, too) when I play chamber music with a new person: he/she may

be a great musician, but if the chemistry isn't right and the energy and soundcolors don't match, it just doesn't work.

I think what bothered me most was a lack of smooth transition between this guy's silences and his talking. The language – the sound – did not meet the silence. So I wasn't able to perceive an organic rhythm of breath etc. – and the silence (and the talking) didn't mean much. The silences seemed empty and the sounds forced, that is, not enough tension or too much.

Wonder what you think . . .

* * *

Generally speaking, musicians like the one just cited are probably more sensitive to attributes of pitch, prosody and voice quality. A work in progress by two authors (Silverman and Silverman, 2002), one a jazz musician, has to do with the sound of the voice of individuals judged to be at immediate risk of suicide. As such it offers another contrast to the foregoing accounts of good and bad "ensemble playing" by a patient and therapist.

It is a familiar finding that suicidal speech seems often to trigger in the listener a wish to deny communications of end-stage despair. However, for one who is attuned to the musical qualities of speech, the sound of a person's voice, irrespective of the content, can often alert one to a significant suicidal risk.

Silverman and Silverman studied audiotapes, both private and loaned by nationwide suicide organizations, of individuals who either had completed suicide or had attempted it with lethal means. Diagnostically they covered a broad range: bipolar illness, depression and both histrionic and psychotic character disorders, including a number with histories of prior suicide attempts and familial suicides.

Not surprisingly, some of the vocal patterns included features commonly noted in depression: loss of energy and power, and monotonous, repetitious, uninflected speech. The most compelling finding, however, was that the voice sounded hollow and toneless, as though lacking a center, and, irrespective of volume and tempo, already "dead and gone." In contrast to the hollowness of depression, the lifelessness of near-term suicidal persons' voices may reflect a decrease in harmonic overtones and resonance, reflecting an internal state different from depression. (Further acoustic studies are in process, e.g. the distribution of overtones in spectral patterns.)

These persons report an experience of "falling into a hole" – suggesting radical disturbances in representation and imagery. In contrast to the voice of the depressed person, which strikes the listener as that of one suffering an illness, the high-risk near-term suicidal person sounds as though already dying. Also in contrast to depression, and probably unique for suicidality, is an absence of vocal patterns associated with anxiety, such as tremulousness.

Another compelling feature is that of unexpected accent. This can take the form of an abrupt affective burst of sudden effort, out of keeping with the ongoing rhythm, followed by an abrupt depletion. (The authors speculate that this dysrhythmia may reflect a sympathetic/parasympathetic autonomic imbalance.)

They conclude that, overall, the vocal patterns of near-term suicidal patients are sufficiently distinct from the depressive profile as to warrant designating the former to be a unique pathological configuration.

* * *

We turn now from the already nearly dead atonal sound of suicidality to the living pulse of the body softly beating in the voices of poetry and music. First we shall consider a paper elucidating the relationship between poetic meter and the body (Turner and Poppel, 1988).

The fundamental unit of metered poetry, the line, nearly always takes from two to four seconds to recite (peak distribution 2.5 to 3.5 seconds). The three-second poetic line is the salient feature of metered poetry. Its prevalence in human poetry appears to be universal, being found in cultures as diverse as classical Greece and Japan.

The sense of hearing essentially makes temporal distinctions; it hears time. That is to say, it detects differences between temporal periods and organizes them in a hierarchy.

Less than three thousandths of a second (0.003 s) apart, sounds are perceived as simultaneous. Between three thousandths of a second (0.003 s) and three hundredths of a second (0.03 s) one can hear that they are separate sounds but not which came first. When two sounds are about three hundredths of a second (0.03 s) apart one can passively experience their sequence but not yet organize a response before the second sound arrives. Three tenths of a second (0.3 s) is enough time to initiate a response, but not yet sufficient to formulate a comparison between the two stimuli as discrete parcels of experience. To make a comparison, like recognizing a melody, takes about three seconds. This is the fundamental "parcel of experience."

Like the poetic line, the parcel of experience is about three seconds – the length of the human "specious present" or present moment. (The eye is much slower than the ear.) Thus it is that a speaker will pause every three seconds or so to organize the next three seconds' worth of syntax; a listener will absorb about three seconds' worth of heard speech and then pause briefly to integrate what he has heard. This three second period to bundle information together to be sent on for processing to higher cortical centers constitutes a sort of pulse.

That the three second poetic line is identical to the three second pulse of the auditory information-processing system suggests a relationship between them: the former (a cultural universal) is tuned to the latter (a biological basic). It holds out the possibility of building an explanatory bridge between universally observed features of human verse and these latest findings about human audition.

The apparent identity between the three-second pulse of metered verse and that of the brain's fundamental auditory processing system may account for the easy memorability of metered verse as well as the subjective relaxation that commonly accompanies it.

Regarding the soothing effect of poetry, it is as if poetry is "natural nutriment." It appears to do much of the work that the brain must usually do for itself. For example, it has been suggested (Turner and Poppel, 1983) that poetic meter enlists the musical and pictorial power of the right brain to cooperate with the linguistic power of the left. In addition, poetry is concerned with "organizing information into rhythmic pulses, integrating different types of information – rhythmic, grammatical, lexical, and acoustic – into easily assimilable parcels and labeling their contents as belonging together. Like intravenous nourishment, the information enters our system instantly, without a lengthy process of digestion" (Turner and Poppel, 1983: 84).

On a more psychological level, how do poetic devices manage to stimulate and soothe at the same time? Through the simultaneous use of differentiation and integration: the former stimulates; the latter soothes (G.J. Rose, 1980).

Consider: Meter uses a fixed number of syllables, thus producing a rhythmic pulsation. Rhythm combines movement with constancy. Rhyme combines the same sound with different meanings – acknowledging as well as overcoming duality (Faber, 1988). Alliteration, the clustering of words beginning with the same consonant, is the mirror image of rhyme. All these devices – as well as simile, allusion and metaphor (Gorelick, 1989) – "tease" the psyche by "playing peek-a-boo" (Akhtar, 2000: 235) with its double task: to differentiate and integrate.

A final example of integration: onomatopoeia joins sound to sense (Siomopoulos, 1977). The sound of sense was important to Robert Frost. He believed it was inherent in every meaning and instinctively familiar to each individual. He set himself the task of making music out of it (G.J. Rose, 1980).

This brings us to music.

* * *

Just as humans everywhere appear to possess an innate (i.e. bodily based) competence to understand grammar and syntax in language, there is also an inborn competence to feel tempo and tempo changes. Musical aesthetic perceptions and judgments being closely associated with tempo and feeling, it would therefore seem that the emotional appeal of music comes largely from the body.

In music as in poetry we find a bodily temporal attunement in the phenomenon of proportional tempo or continuous pulse. This has been closely studied by Epstein (1988) and refers to the idea that all tempos in a work of music are intrinsically related to one another. This arises from a composer's conception of the work as a unified and coherent whole. These relationships of tempo can be expressed by whole number ratios of a low order (1:1, 1:2, 2:3, 3:4, or the inverse). They constitute a powerful integrating force both in the structure of the work and in its presentation to an audience.

In order to determine whether this is a universal phenomenon, tape recordings of seven cultures were sampled in a random order: two from the Pacific (New Guinea), two from Asia (Tibet, Nepal), two from Africa (Botswana), and one from South America (Venezuela).

One example is worth citing because it did not involve music, strictly speaking, but rather a long-winded, ritualized negotiating "bargain chant" of the Yanomami Indians of the Orinoco River,

Venezuela. During the course of almost 38 minutes, 143 tempo timings were measured. They all conformed to a ratio of either 2:1 or 1:2, confirming that tempo changes take place in relation to some governing pulse.

Epstein concludes that these data support the theory that tempos in musical performance change by low-order integral ratios and that this appears to be a universal phenomenon. The fact that this proportional tempo-keeping is so precise strongly suggests that it must be based on a biological foundation. Such a biological basis might well account for the constancy of proportional tempo in music of widely varying affect, purposes and settings, and even in rhythms and tempos accompanying ritualized bargaining.

* * *

The sensory qualities of consciousness of our subjective world are referred to as "qualia." These are the qualities of color, music, smells, and the other vivid sensations we value so highly. Specifying their neurobiological basis in terms of the location and character of the neurons whose firing determines these qualities of consciousness is of current interest to neuroscience.

Contemporary neuroscience appears to agree with earlier philosophers and Freud (1900), who wrote that consciousness was "a sense-organ for the perception of psychical qualities" (p. 615) whose underlying mental processes were themselves unconscious.

Some neuroscientists doubt that consciousness can be reduced to sensory representations only – whether imagined or remembered – and based on relatively few neurons functioning mysteriously as these so-called qualia. The internal modality of affects – degrees of pleasure/unpleasure – may constitute an additional dimension to the five basic modalities of sensory qualia (sight, hearing, touch, taste and smell) (Solms, 1997).

Elements of intentionality and action also play a role. Whenever we perceive or think of anything we always implicitly formulate a plan of achieving it through action. This further dimension has been termed "agentic qualia" (Humphrey, 2000).

Other neuroscientists suggest that the neural correlates of consciousness are probably located on some intermediate level further forward than sensory ones and involve attention, affective valuations, understanding and decision making (Jackendoff, 2000).

The perspective of evolution emphasizes the critical role of emotions in the construction of consciousness. Many of the affective experiences that human and animals have are said to arise from implicit knowing systems of the brain (evolutionary *equalia*).

> Emotions are fundamentally value coding mechanisms that emerged to provide organisms with an evolutionarily prepared motoric capacity to approach life-sustaining resources and to avoid the life-detracting pitfalls of the world . . . . The basic infrastructure of emotionality was a major force in the evolution of cognitive capacities.
>
> (Panksepp, 2000: 25–26)

A brief survey such as this might lead one to question the value of the term "qualia" for the sensory qualities of consciousness. If, for example, the neurobiological basis of the qualities of experience are as widely distributed as consciousness itself (Damasio, 1999), is the term little more than a linguistic trap, like the mythical ether of astronomy? On the other hand, are qualia more akin to the case of subatomic particles that were postulated before being discovered?

In contrast to the disputed status of qualia, language, at any rate, is no longer considered an essential key to consciousness. This is based on the findings from neurological conditions where individuals have lost all language capacity yet remain quintessentially conscious despite radically limited ability to communicate.

Returning to music: music is unquestionably a sensory experience, richly involving many sensory modalities and not merely auditory. A passive experience? Certainly not. Ordinary self-observation and introspection inform us how active an experience is listening to music, every listener an instrumentalist and conductor at the same time, inherently "performing" in concert with the music. It is worth emphasizing that the (mostly invisible) motor activity that accompanies the experience of music probably reflects and possibly generates and enhances emotionality.

* * *

Earlier I cited the young musician who expressed what it was like to try to begin therapy with someone he felt out of tune with. On another occasion he tried to put into words what it was like to

listen to the first eight measures of Nicola Matteis' (1650–1714)
Preludio of Ayr in D. I quote with his permission.

The *Preludio of N. Matteis' Ayr in D* starts in a horizontally
balanced calmly flowing quality (one could imagine that this
energy has started flowing a long time ago and only now
reaches the realm of perceptible sound). The calmly flowing
quality slightly expands, as if caught by a breath of wind and
collapses into a short, touched moment of dense, warm friction, resolves briefly and then gains a very similar friction
again, this time a bit longer and therefore more tense before
resolving longer and more fully.

In the meantime underneath the wind-like airy turbulences,
a line of thicker quality (like a thick, slow moving river on a
stream of lava) has joined in unspectacularly and initiates a
movement towards a wide expanded body. The inner space of
that body is expanded and open (empty); the borders are
stretched and create a certain tension – as if the two lines that
form the borders are in conflict and push each other away as
much as possible (while still relating). One can anticipate the
following collapse into hot inner tension, where the whole
body is connected again and vibrating.

That is in fact what follows and resolves, but only into
another body of hot tension with its own longing for
resolution.

As there is so much tension built up by now, the following
movement to resolution releases all of it – in an explosive
upward leap of the low thick line initiating an accelerating
delirious movement upward into the sky.

This energy condenses into an intensely burning high quality
(the highest so far) that carried forward as if caught by a
strong warm wind, lowering slightly only to find new hot
friction carrying it up again where the airy line is now hanging
in the air like a leaf in the wind – holding itself up against the
forces of gravity that appear to expand as the thick low line
descends. The tension increases to the point where suddenly
the leaf collapses and begins to descend only to be carried up
again by an almost imperceptible rising wind.

The process repeats a third time, only now the expanded
tension lasts longer and is almost painfully intense and
immobile. The airy line finally gives in and, more gradually

than in the quick collapses previously, resigns itself into a dark gray, foggy area of ambiguity. The tension is so high it feels like one is holding their breath. Intense colors appear in the foggy gray, snakelike and hesitatingly groping as if searching for the path.

Suddenly there is a release. The path and the light are found, the air is released in an exhalation and now the movement progresses calmly in a warm upwind, then descends and gains a bit of red-orange, glowing tension and calmly releases into the clear blue water.

Then my musician colleague supplements verbal expressiveness with harmonic analysis.

In musical terms, the basis of all this is the drama of tonality: the dominant area is one of density and contraction. It is a thick, hot, rich and colorful world of rednesses. The contracted, vibrating tension of the dominant longs to be released into the tonic – which is balanced, even-keeled, round. The subdominant area is one of expansion, thin air, open emptiness, airy–watery light blue colors. Characteristic is a lack of inside tension. It tends to collapse into dominant tension, but can be stretched for long periods of time; maybe at times it is a temporary dreamlike escape from the painfully short-lived intensity of the dominant world. When in that context the collapse into the dominant area takes place, it can be experienced as painful over-tension.

He concludes by expressing his doubts about the success of his experiment with translation.

I wonder whether the visual metaphors promote a physical tuning in to the described patterns of tension and release or whether they distract and disguise what is physically happening.

I recall an ear-training class some years ago: listening to the same Bach piece played by S. Richter and G. Gould. Richter's interpretation evoked a physical feeling in which tension and release seemed to be filtered out by many evoked metaphors. My body reacted calmly and the imagination shut down. Gould's interpretation did not allow me to have that slight

distance of metaphors but was physically immediately capti-
vating, like the experience of dancing.

In contrast to these two different reactions to actual musical
performance, my friend seems to suspect that his own valiant effort
to transpose music into words does not succeed. Despite his synesthetic imagery – of color (gray, red-orange, blue) and tempera-
ture (cold, warm, hot) – words only seem to defeat the experience
as music.

Like reducing literature to grammar? I agree.

Parodying such attempts is a possibly apocryphal anecdote
concerning a Harvard academic musicologist admonishing his
harmony class: "Remember, gentlemen: music is to be seen and not
heard!"

* * *

As music is *in* performance, so, too, I believe, is clinical
psychoanalysis.

My personal convictions are:

1 Its location is a one-to-one human relationship composed of
  equal parts conceptual precision of words and emotional
  attunement akin to music.
2 It stands or falls on the evidence of long-term clinical observations, honed on actual responsibility for real people, and
  hopefully tested and verified one day by neuroscience.

Chapter 2

On the shores of self

Samuel Beckett's *Molloy* – irredentism and the creative impulse

> A human being is a part of the whole, called by us "Universe,"
> a part limited in time and space. He experiences himself, his
> thoughts and feelings as something separated from the rest – a
> kind of optical delusion of his consciousness. This delusion is a
> kind of prison.
>
> (A. Einstein)

The irredentist principle in politics refers to the wish to restore
territory of which one has been deprived and reincorporate it
within one's own boundaries. In the psychology of the artist this
lost territory is the original dual unity with the mother. It is
characterized by fluidity of time, space, and sense of self. As each
did in the beginning, the artist resamples this undifferentiated state
and renegotiates a new equilibrium between inside and outside, self
and others.

While "rematriation" has long been a central tenet in the psychology of creativity associated with the British school of psychoanalysis, its reinterpretation in the light of primary narcissism and
early ego states seems warranted. This, and not an "explanation"
of art, is the aim of this chapter. It is taken for granted that there is
a far reach between the impulse to create and its fulfillment in
anything more than garden-variety growth processes like higher
levels of self-identity. However, while art is a rare outcome, the
creative impulse and the growth of self are interrelated in ways that
help to elucidate both.

When the artist destroys old forms and harmoniously integrates
new ones in the light of his ego ideal of perfection, he achieves a
temporary reconciliation between his ego and his superego. This in
turn gratifies an unconscious wish to recapture the original sense of

oneness with the mother. He may temporarily feel elated over the new aesthetic unity that has been achieved, or perhaps have mystical or religious emotions. The new unity, however, echoing the original oneness with the mother, soon threatens to return the artist to that loss of self inherent in the merging of self with mother. This is equivalent to psychological death. Sooner or later, then, he will be impelled to a fresh, perhaps irritable, anxious, or depressive need for a further delineation of self and world. This means he needs to do more creative work. The important point for our purpose is that the new irredentist sense of inner and outer balance carries with it its own imbalance and impetus for further change. In other words, it fuels a creative impulse that may be defined as an urge toward growth and differentiation via remerging and redefinition.

Creative work perpetuates the child's imaginative, restless searching for basic answers, his unwillingness to close the door on questioning. The creative person has a firsthand view of the constant variability of inner life and outer world, the endlessly shifting qualities of what we carelessly and monolithically refer to as self and reality.

Art is a projection of this delicate balance amidst the constant movement of inner and outer as well as between the continuously flowing regressive and progressive tides within the mind. This constant progressive–regressive flux reflects the current of life itself. Within the art-work this flux probably helps account for the work being experienced as "living."

In modern times Picasso, as well as particle physics, is partly responsible for having opened our eyes to the latent instability and mobility of seemingly solid forms. This permanent alteration of our perception of the world is the hallmark of authentic creativity. Having once seen the world through his recreated images, we find our reality has been transformed: "stable" forms can never appear the same; movement is everywhere. Picasso is quoted as follows:

> I'm like a river that rolls on, dragging with it the trees that grow too close to its banks or dead calves one might have thrown into it . . . . I carry all that along with me and go on. It's the movement of painting that interests me . . . . In some of my paintings . . . I have been able to stop the flow of life around me . . . . What I have to say is increasingly something

about what goes on in the movement of my thought . . . the
movement of my thought interests me more than the thought
itself.

(Gilot and Lake, 1965: 114–118)

One might say that Picasso has been able to concentrate more and
more on the movement of his thoughts and perceptions because he
could examine them through a unique analyzing, organizing, and
reintegrating aesthetic vision, thus enabling him to deal with the
Many through the One.

The problem of continuity amidst constant change, so central to
the analysis of identity, is as old as philosophy. While our senses
record that the world consists of an infinite variety of things, our
understanding is incapable of comprehending them, perhaps even
of recording them, without the aid of some organizing principle or
idea. Philosophers have long tried to reconcile the infinite variety
with the unity, the Many and the One, the endless forms of
becoming with the fundamental, indivisible being. The pre-Socratic
philosopher Heraclitus of Ephesus tried to solve the antithesis by
the proposition that change itself is the fundamental principle; it is
represented in his philosophy by fire as the basic element, since it is
both matter and a moving force.

The physicist, Werner Heisenberg (1958: 63), pointed out that
contemporary physics is extremely close to the ideas of Heraclitus:
"If we replace the word 'fire' by the word 'energy' we can almost
repeat its statements word for word." Energy is the substance from
which all elementary particles are made, and energy is that which
moves; energy is a substance since its total amount does not
change, and it is the fundamental cause for all change in the world.

Henri Bergson (1944) gave one of the most eloquent statements
of the view that reality is a perpetual becoming, that consciousness
is marked by successive births and rebirths of awareness, and that
living time is experienced as moments of choice:

> My mental state, as it advances on the road of time, is con-
> tinually swelling with the duration which it accumulates: it
> goes on increasing – rolling upon itself, as a snowball on the
> snow . . . . [p. 4]. The apparent discontinuity of the psychical
> life is then due to our attention being fixed on it by a series of
> separate acts: actually there is only a gentle slope . . . . [p. 5].
> Duration is the continuous progress of the past which gnaws

into the future and which swells as it advances . . . . [p. 7]. With regard to the moments of our life, of which we are the artisans, each of them is a kind of creation . . . what we do depends on what we are; but it is necessary to add also that we are, to a certain extent, what we do, and that we are creating ourselves continually. This creation of self by self is the more complete, the more one reasons on what one does . . . . For a conscious being to exist is to change, to change is to mature, to mature is to go on creating oneself endlessly [pp. 9–10]. Reality is a perpetual growth, a creation pursued without end . . . . Every human work in which there is invention, every voluntary act in which there is freedom, every movement of an organism that manifests spontaneity, brings something new into the world . . . . [p. 261]. The idea of creation becomes more clear, for it is merged in that of growth [p. 263].

Psychoanalytic findings lend substance and details to these philosophical–poetic intuitions. Psychological growth begins with the development of the sense of self from the primary unity of mother–child. In the beginning there is a coalescence of child with all that is, unbounded as to time, space, and sense of self. At first the boundaries between them are hazy, with constant remerging taking place. Little by little, satisfactions and disappointments repeat themselves; forms begin to emerge and acquire meanings. The idea of mother distinct from oneself begins to take shape and with it the idea of a self and one's separateness in the world. The sense of identity contributes to the growing sense of constancy and direction. The distinctions between thought and action, and time and causality, also impose order on things to build reality.

Reality itself, however, always remains somewhat fluid rather than static. Throughout life the boundaries of our separateness and identity keep being dissolved and recreated as we repeatedly dip back and re-emerge from looser and earlier arrangements of reality. We continuously fashion new syntheses between ourselves and the outside, creating areas of relative constancy and temporary balance in the midst of change.

It is from this pool of early fluid boundaries of self and reality that each person draws to "create" his own identity and construct viable forms of reality for himself. Growth is a form of self-creation.

The ego's coordinated functioning is a garden variety of creativity. And it is from this same pool of early fluid boundaries of self and reality that the artist draws to create imaginative forms. This is not to say that imagination is synonymous with the infant's efforts to distinguish himself from the external world. Imagination is the ability to make images and elaborate memories and combine them playfully with new ingredients as they are observed. The point is this: the greater the mobility of elements, the less sacrosanct the categories, the freer the imaginative play. And these conditions are most fully met in the flexibility of early boundaries of self and reality toward which the artist is drawn in his irredentist urge to regain the lost unity with mother and separate out anew (Rose, 1966).

* * *

In the novel *Molloy*, Beckett (1955) composes melodies of prose out of the flowing lines of time and space. His art explores what we may call the shores of the earliest sense of self. No less than scientific concepts, his aesthetic forms, acting as metaphors, effect new linkages and reorder the data of experience. Like analytic insight, his work accords a lasting reality to aspects of the world that would otherwise have existed only as traces of unconscious memory.

When he deals with time, it has little to do with the conventional wristwatch units that measure our workaday activities. It is felt time; it has the volume and cadences of music; it refers to the great reverberating circles of prescience and memory where past and future merge in a greatly expanded horizon of the present:

> My life, my life, now I speak of it as of something over, now as of a joke which still goes on, and it is neither, for at the same time it is over and it goes on, and is there any tense for that? [*Molloy*, p. 36]

Spatial dimensions, too, are elastic. Remote reaches of space feel intimately close, parts of the body seem remote, and the felt boundaries of the body are endlessly variable, sexually indeterminate, or even absent. It is unclear whether the stars seem to tremble or it is his hand upon his knee. The bodily boundaries are as fluid as the endlessly shifting, sometimes evanescent sense of self.

> Yes, it sometimes happens . . . that I forget who I am and strut before my eyes, like a stranger . . . . [p. 42]. Yes, there were

times when I forgot not only who I was, but that I was, forgot
to be . . . . You have to be careful, ask yourself questions, as
for example, whether you still are, and if no when it stopped,
and if yes how long it will still go on, anything at all to keep
you from losing the thread of the dream. [p. 49]

The thread of the dream is the sense of one's identity, and its loss is
death of the self and with it the absence of any meaning.

It is not you who are dead but all the others. So you get up
and go to your mother, who thinks she is alive. That is my
impression. [p. 27]

Is it mother who is alive and he who is dead, or vice versa? The
novel searches for a return to the oneness with the mother that was
in the beginning, and with it a taste of the oblivion of loss of self,
and then a rebirth of awareness of separate aloneness and renewed
longings for union.

There follows the mystery of beginnings. Not just biological
conception but the beginnings of self. For Beckett makes clear that
the self has not yet been born. Molloy cannot distinguish himself
from others, or memory from imagination. He imagined he saw
two men who looked alike, "but no more than others do" (p. 9)
who go down into the same trough, meet, and separate. One goes
back into town, the other out into the treacherous hills of the
world. He longs to follow both, be less lonely.

Are they both the same person on different occasions, or which
is which? And what is the significance of their different directions?
One out into the hills and the other into the town. Or are they, too,
really the same? Journeys into "all that inner space one never sees,
the brain and heart and other caverns where thought and feeling
dance their sabbath" (p. 10). Or could this be a dream of descent
into the primal trough of life, where the seed is flung toward its
union for new beginnings, and the sower departs to journey without, both sower and seed longing to return to oneness, through
death or conception?

The storyteller suddenly decides to go seek his mother. This must
be the common path for both travelers, if they are two – two routes
toward mother "in this world for you without arms" (p. 12).

After two transparently masturbatory sequences the author is
well along on his journey through the "mythological present," past

Oedipal and homosexual way-stations back toward a return, via sucking and sleep, to mother. On his bicycle he runs over and kills a little dog that was like a child to Lousse, the woman who owned it. She turns him into a substitute for the dog–infant he killed, and, unmanned, he awakens naked in her house in a woman's night-dress, locked up in a barred, dark room, perfumed and beardless.

The details of his loss of identity are now made more explicit. He cannot distinguish whether the room is moving from right to left. He listens to the voice of the frozen world collapsing endlessly to its death. He resigns himself to a dreamy torpor in her garden – lying on his back, side, stomach, fed and talked to and watched by her. His life becomes united to that of the garden. He hears words as sounds freed of meaning, his own sounds becoming like the buzzing of an insect. He can no longer understand language, judge distance, or discriminate smells and tastes. He remains in a waking sleep for vague months up to perhaps a year, eating hardly at all or, at times, voraciously; sometimes bounding into the air or col-lapsing without control.

Sexual stirrings commence. If, before, his journey returned him in imagination to some of the early fusions between himself and his world, he now ventures out from infancy through homosexual way-stations toward Oedipal ones. But not for long. When his mother's image intrudes in his sexual fantasies, he finds it intolerable and suddenly decides he must leave the woman Lousse's garden.

It might be autumn by now. He passes time in a blind, cloacal alley, full of rubbish, excrement, a meeting place for lovers, and crawls into a hole or cave by the sea, where he remains an indefi-nite time. He sucks on stones, has trouble breathing or retaining urine, and stumbles through the forest feeling, as he did in Lousse's garden, that he must get out or he will be powerless ever to leave.

It is now winter. He is crawling, flat on his belly, crutches out in front like grappling hooks. He crawls on his back, too. On his way to mother. All his imperatives bear on this relationship, as if all his life he has been going to his mother. Sometimes he says "Mother" to himself to encourage himself. Day and night toward mother. The day comes when the forest ends. He sees light. He opens his eyes and sees he has arrived. Will they roll him onto his mother's doorstep?

The forest ends in a ditch. It is the fall into the ditch which makes him open his eyes and see he is out of the forest. The plain seems familiar. He hears a voice telling him help is coming. It must be spring. He remembers the two travelers, one with a club. It is spring. He longs to go back into the forest, but Molloy can stay where he happens to be.

Where he happens to be is the trough where the men met and separated from each other. He has followed the path of one of them on his inward journey toward union, conception, germination through the apparent death of winter, life stirrings, growth and rebirth in spring.

What of the other traveler? He is Jacques Moran, and he has a son of the same name. He, too, is called to journey out in the treacherous hills, to see about Molloy. It is a Sunday in August, and his son is sleeping, thinking that he's on the threshold of life. Moran rudely rouses his son, ill with a fever, and departs from the house holding his son's hand behind him, toying with the idea of attaching his son to him with a rope or chain around both their waists to prevent his son from ever breaking away. As they walk out into the night, one behind the other, he wonders if people will imagine that he is a widower whose wife died in childbirth. His son, contrary to orders, is carrying his raincoat rolled into a ball on his belly, making it stick out.

As the homosexual imagery becomes more and more elaborated, reaching baroque proportions, Moran must, perforce, retreat from the obvious. He declares that both he and his son are innocent and retreats further yet by imagining himself a fetus or horizontal on mother's lap, incapable of motion, mute, memoryless, and deaf, and he almost swoons. When he sends his son away to the village and they part from each other, each masturbates alone.

Moran lapses deeper into passivity, surrendering himself to the scene, wondering if he secretly welcomes his infirmity and helplessness. His self-absorption increases as he gazes at his image in the stream and experiences homosexual hallucinations at night. When his son returns, he looks at Moran as if his fly were open. Rejoined with his son, astride the bicycle behind his son, his own testicles swinging low, he feels happy and well taken care of. But longings for a father of his own become stirred up, and he wishes he were one of the shepherd's flock of sheep, or Molloy's son. The wish for dependent passivity on a man leads to his being deserted again by his son, his masculinity, and he is robbed of his money as well as his bicycle. He lapses into deeper helplessness, growing weaker still, stretched out in the shelter, crawling out only in the evening, longing to lose consciousness in time.

Finally Gaber comes and orders him to return home. It takes from August or September till spring to get there. This is nine or ten months, a gestational period. He tells a farmer that he is making a pilgrimage to the Madonna, that he is going to mother, that he has lost his infant boy but kept his mother. Does this mean he has lost his masculinity and retained his identification with his mother? He skirts the graveyard and arrives home – to his mother's womb. But it is a dead womb, or she is dead: The house is empty, without light, the bees and hens dead. In the house he writes.

Moran is back where the story of Molloy started – in mother's room. In the opening pages:

> It's I who live there now. I don't know how I got there . . . . I'd like to . . . say my goodbyes, finish dying . . . . Was [my mother] already dead when I came? Or did she only die later? I mean enough to bury. I don't know. Perhaps they haven't buried her yet. In any case I have her room. I sleep in her bed. I piss and shit in her pot. I have taken her place. I must resemble her more and more. All I need now is a son. Perhaps I have one somewhere. [p. 7]

Perhaps, then, Moran is Molloy, reborn as his own son.

The strongest emotion this story conveys, aside from its black humor and ribaldry, is a longing for contact that is forever impossible. This note is also struck in the opening pages:

> It is a sorry sight to see him solitary after so many years, so many days and nights unthinkingly given to that rumour rising at birth and even earlier. What shall I do? What shall I do? Now low, a murmur, now precise as the headwaiter's . . . and often rising to a scream . . . I watched him recede, at grips (myself) with the temptation to get up and follow him, perhaps even to catch up with him one day, so as to know him better, be myself less lonely. But in spite of my soul's leap out to him, at the end of its elastic, I saw him only darkly, because of the dark and then because of the terrain, in the folds of which he disappeared from time to time, to re-emerge further on . . . . I felt the first stars tremble . . . . [p. 11]

Who are these two men, one small, the other tall, "who went down into the same trough and in this trough finally met . . . turned towards the sea . . . then each went on his way"? (p. 9). Are they father and son in a furrow of the earth facing the sea of birth before parting for their separate routes of conception and birth, death and rebirth, sower and seed? Or are they parts of the same man, his finiteness and his generativity, his past and future interlocked and separate? Part of himself goes forth as his own seed to fuse with the egg, live in the garden-womb or cave on the seashore, before emerging in spring from the blind alley and dark forest, to open his eyes on his mother's doorstep, still longing to go back into the forest.

Born without really wishing to be, how does a man live out his life while longing to return to the forest of his birth and the union with his mother? The two men we glimpsed in the beginning, small and tall, in the trough in the earth, together a few moments before separating, now return in the motif of Moran and his son. Or again, are they parts of each other, man and his past and future, or his body and his phallus?

They must stick together, but they keep separating and rejoining. If the son represents Moran's masculinity, Moran is constantly in danger of losing it. More than this, Moran is doing everything possible to get rid of his son while trying to attach him with ropes and chains. Is this conflict the consequence of longing to return to mother? One way to return to her is to become her, but this means emasculation, homosexual union, or death.

The alternatives are played out. His limbs atrophy, his knee feels like a clitoris, the hole of his hat becomes a slit, he kills a man who looks like himself and then feels better, no longer plagued with a stiff limb. But no sooner has he killed off his masculinity than he regains it in the form of his son, to whom he becomes joined on the frame of the bicycle. But again, only to lose him again. It takes him the period of a gestation to make his way home.

He has gained a sharper and clearer sense of his identity than ever before: he knows he has been reborn, but as a woman. He has averted death, at the cost of his masculinity. It is not the end. And he has learned to listen to an inner voice and to understand a new language. It tells him to write. It may even make him freer than he was.

This, then, is his salvation: his identity as a writer. Not a historian. The last lines of Molloy are: "It is midnight. The rain is beating on the windows. It was not midnight. It was not raining" (p. 176). So he must be a writer of stories. And this is something he told us in the opening pages:

> What I need now is stories, it took me a long time to know
> that, and I'm not sure of it. There I am, then, informed as to
> certain things, knowing certain things about him, things I
> didn't know, things I had craved to know, things I had never
> thought of. [p. 13]

His gift of imagination is where he lives. The opening lines of the
novel are: "I am in my mother's room. It's I who live there now . . . .
I have taken her place" (p. 7). He lives in his imagination in his
mother, in her dead womb. "Was she already dead when I came?"
(p. 7). Because he is joined to her, it is no longer clear that she is a
woman. Was it ever certain that Ruth, his first woman, was a
woman? Or Lousse, in whose garden he lived for almost a year? Or
were they the same? *Lousse* sounds like baby talk for *Ruth*.
"Perhaps I'm inventing a little, perhaps embellishing . . . perhaps
I'm remembering things" (p. 8).

His imagination lives inside his mother's womb. From her womb
his stories are discharged. Sometimes he shits his stories onto the
earth. Other times he speaks of the plant that springs from the
ejaculation of the hanged that shrieks when plucked.

And his mother? Of her, he says:

> I called her Mag, when I had to call her something. And I
> called her Mag because for me, without my knowing why, the
> letter g abolished the syllable *Ma*, and as it were spat on it
> better than any other letter would have done. And at the same
> time I satisfied a deep and doubtless unacknowledged need, the
> need to have a Ma, that is, a mother, and to proclaim it,
> audibly. [p. 17]

He reluctantly acknowledges the need to have a Ma. But Mag does
more than spit on Ma. It adds an appendage. He is the appendage.
By joining with her he has become added to her as a phallus. It is
as a phallic mother that he creates, shits, ejaculates his stories onto
the ground from her dead womb.

Who is Molloy? Molloy is Moran reborn with a son of his own,
an appendage. Molloy's mother is Mollose. Who is Mollose?
"After all perhaps I knew nothing of mother Molloy, or Mollose,
save insofar as such a son might bear, like a scurf of placenta, her
stamp" (p. 112). Mollose might be a contraction of Molloy and

Lousse, i.e. Molloy joined to his woman keeper, in the garden of his helplessness.

The world is a mother without arms. He goes into her furrow to join her, attached to her placenta, be born, die, and be reborn as a dual unity of mother and child, female with male.

The remote males who command him and bring him messages are Youdi and Gaber. Call them *y* and *g*. *G* is what he adds to Ma; *y* is what is added to Mollousse, or Mollose, to make Molloy. *Y* and *g* are male appendages. Problem: how does Molloy hang onto his *y*, his *g*, his youdi, his gaber, his son, his phallus, and still follow his longing to follow his imperative and return to his mother? He does it by returning to his mother's body from whence he creates and discharges his stories.

But why such a strong pull to return to unite with mother? His longing for a father is rebuffed with silence and distance. He wants to turn into a dog, a sheep, a baby, a fetus. His longing turns homosexual and paranoid. Because there is neither father nor mother, he cannot weep anymore in a world which is constantly raining down his own tears. It is this intensity of emotion that cannot be contained and ruptures the boundaries of his identity and his world again and again, until in imagination he reverts to the oneness of a hermaphroditic primal mother.

Before he regains and re-enters his dead home, he tells the farmer who accosts him that he is on a pilgrimage to the Madonna of pregnant women who took his infant boy but allowed him to keep his mamma. He confides to the reader that alas this never happened. What then is the truth? The truth might be the reverse: his own mother died in childbirth and he survived, longing to return to her in bodily fusion, spiritual identification, or death.

Was it during his own birth that his mother died or in giving birth to a sibling, a brother? Is the son, the sight of whom makes his blood boil with anger, the brother, the cause of his mother's death? When he looked behind him, he saw the boy with the raincoat rolled into a ball, carried on his belly, the stomach sticking out. This must be the image that enrages him. He demands his son's knife and takes it from him, attributing his own murderous impulses to his son. He wishes to kill the son, his unborn brother, and take his place – inside.

Both Molloy and Moran regain the intrauterine shelter for a time. Molloy accidentally runs over and kills Lousse's dog, who is like a child to her, and takes its place in her garden, before being reborn. His son's separate existence is acknowledged finally, and he manages, if barely, to control his murderous feelings. His son had been forced out of his bed and house, into the world at night, finally alone. Moran had his shelter to himself, but uneasily. Toward the end of the journey, whenever he is inside a proper shelter, he becomes obsessed with thoughts and images of his son's raincoat, that reminder of pregnancy. "I literally saw it, I saw nothing else, it filled all space" (p. 172). And thereafter he (phobically?) avoids being inside any shelter.

He returns home, skirting the graveyard at midnight, a place and time where, on setting out, the sight of his son's protruding belly made his blood boil. The hens are dead, and the bees only a light ball of dust in the hive. Martha nowhere. House empty.

Face the fact: it is mother who is dead, forever! Child is alive; not the other way around. "My son was well. He would be. Let us hear no more about him. He has come back. He is sleeping" (p. 175). Moran would write and submit his report about Molloy, the Molloy of the enquiry, or the Molloy he stalked within himself.

"How little one is at one with oneself. Good God" (p. 175).

* * *

If art is the instrument for refining the apprehending sensibility (Read, 1951), Beckett's art does this by providing the opportunity to resample the primary union of mother and child and separate out anew. We experience the rebirth of early forms of self and world out of the initial fluidity of time, space, and sense of self. The distinction between subject and object is dissolved, as in an undifferentiated stage of development, in order to be reconstituted afresh with our sensibilities refined.

Ideally, the child's emergence from primary narcissism should occur gradually, in its own time. The mother, in contrast to the nonhuman environment, reflects back to the child a configuration of its own presence, and the child experiences its existence as reflected by mother's libidinal attachment (Lichtenstein, 1964). If there is a disturbance of this "mirroring experience," there is the feeling of being negated in one's existence and perhaps the coercive unconscious demand for unconditional, total, and unrealistic affirmation (Lichtenstein, 1971). Such narcissistic personalities will develop idealizing or mirror transferences as efforts at self-repair through being echoed, approved, confirmed, attended to, and acknowledged (Kohut, 1971).

Where there is a psychotic outcome, such individuals may use actual mirrors to try to restore self-identity, as an infant does in a peek-a-boo game, trying to "retrieve" the ego, self, or boundaries they fear they are losing (Elkisch, 1957). An alternative result is premature ego development. A not infrequent cost of this is a grim and colorless reality that is succumbed to as a restricting cage rather than meeting and shaping a reality that offers possibilities for self-completion and liberation.

The irredentist urge to recapitulate primary narcissistic fusion with the pre-Oedipal mother corresponds to a partial merging of self and object representations within the ego and an expansion of ego boundaries between the self and the world (Rose, 1964, 1971, 1972). Whether reinforced by constitutional sensitivity, separation anxiety, developmental arrests, or the awareness of existential aloneness, it is far from a regressive defense only. The artist is explicitly engaged in a continual searching for harmony or balance between the heightened sensitivity to bodily sensations and to the outer world; the force of one's own body feelings, throughout the entire spectrum of sensory modalities, responds and causes a kind of amalgamation of body imagery with outer forms in the world and leads to a state of mutual permeability or sense of fusion with the outer world (Greenacre, 1957). From a philosophical domain the same has been expressed regarding sensitive perception in general: our sense organs bind, rhythmicize, and filter the world; where the function of the filter ends, a bodily element sends itself out to partake of a ground that otherwise would not be grasped, producing a unity (Buber, 1963).

The search for harmonious union with the universe (mystical, aesthetic, religious, empathic) is an essential recurrent phase in the development of a creative relation to the world (Milner, 1952; Rose, 1966). Again from the perspective of another field, the "aesthetic moment" has been described as:

> That fleeting instant, so brief as to be almost timeless, when the spectator is at one with the work of art . . . or with actuality of any kind . . . . Time and space are abolished and the spectator is possessed by one awareness.
>
> (Berenson, 1950: 93)

Ecstatic pleasure in music, likewise, relates to the loss of clear differentiation between oneself and the outside (Kohut, 1957; Margolis, 1954). The listener experiences the sounds as emotionally his own and feels his identity enlarged in an oceanic feeling of union with the nonverbal universe of sound (Kohut and Levarie, 1950). The reason why music invites such an experience of union is that its elements (rhythm, tempo, duration, pitch, tone, resonance, and clang) comprise many of the signs and signals that reach an infant in the first months of its life (Noy, 1968).

The image of seeking self-completion, rather than self-fulfillment, highlights the fact that Everyman has undergone separation from what was a primordial, unitary preself. Each is, so to speak, a single twin, bereft of his original partner. One version of the Narcissus myth, by Pausanias, has Narcissus gazing into the spring not entranced with himself only but in order to recall the features of his dead twin sister. Like other paired objects, twins unconsciously represent breasts. In dreams they stand for the dreamer and mother in an oral, pregenital union; this symbolism parallels the widespread belief in folklore that twins have a magical power to maintain union with the mother (Brody, 1952).

The artist searches for self-completion (Rose, 1972). His/her work is a shadow play through which one can better surmise one's substance. It is a projected part of the self with which one has a private dialogue, mirroring, smiling, frowning, approaching, and withdrawing, until the final completion and release. The motor aspects play a significant part in this dialogue (Rose, 1963). In the past they conveyed much of the emotional ambience between mother and child, the shifting ratios of distance and closeness, rapprochement and detachment, until finally a more or less separate existence was established for the growing person and, with it, the acknowledgment of outer reality. Now the artist's work takes on more and more of a separate reality until it is prepared to stand on its own. As in an earlier time, the artist may find that it remains fragile and never quite complete or, conversely, that it has "completed itself" before he was ready to let it go.

The intrapsychic processes involve a refinement of self and object representations, further internalization, and the acquisition of additional psychic structure. The work has discharged sexual and aggressive tensions. To the extent that it approaches the image of one's idealized self, the good parents will have been resurrected, guilt allayed, and self-esteem and secondary narcissism replenished.

With the passage of time, however, it turns out that the love affair with the world is not forever. Separateness and vulnerability go hand in hand. There may follow a gradual depletion of "confident expectation," a decrease in self-esteem, and an increased need for "refueling." As with the year-and-a-half- to three-year-old child, renewed rapprochement with the mother is necessary to protect him from acute deflation of his "omnipotence" and serious injury to his self-esteem (Mahler, 1966).

Here, as elsewhere, past experience is crucial. Where in the past the mother has represented an optimal (phase appropriate) balance of frustration and gratification, providing a resilient buffer against traumatic overstimulation and a precipitous deflation of omnipotence, the irredentist pull back to narcissistic fusion with her will be as essential and helpful as healthy sleep. It will, in addition, enrich with fresh impetus the supply of potentially creative ambiguities and paradoxes (Rose, 1971).

Where, however, the past has been unduly traumatic and the reservoir of oral craving remains intense, carrying with it an abundance of unmodified aggression, the wish to consume will be confronted with an equal fear of being devoured. A fear of loss of self in the mother, their mutual destruction and abandonment by reality, may generate anxiety on all levels – separation, castration, existential. The problem may be shifted to one of addiction or of object craving, each of which will represent an externalization of some essential psychic structure which is lacking. Or there may be an indefinite prolongation of the adolescent's moratorium on choice; a fashionably rationalized "alienation" will conceal the unharnessed orality lying behind a fear of drowning in lifelong "commitment"; or of becoming "enslaved" and "dehumanized" by "the establishment." The incapacity to love will show itself in its usual alternatives: hate, the wish to be loved, and a paralyzing indifference.

The artist's solution is to split, project, and externalize. One part is identified with the primal mother (Rose, 1961, 1972) and the other, identified with his infantile self emerging from narcissistic fusion, is projected onto the creative work. What was one is now the artist and his work in a narcissistic interaction of rapprochement and detachment, gradual correction in the light of reality-testing and the ego-ideal, refusion, and finally, again, detachment, redefinition, separation, and completion.

The creative worker's successive irredentist remergings, rebirths of self, and reconstructions of reality parallel individual development and growth. The completed work of art is the mask of one's inner life at a point in the flow of time. It marks a confluence of thinking, feeling, and action arrested in flight. If it is truly great, it captures a new aspect of reality and will live on – offering one the illusion that our time, too, is not passing.

Chapter 3

Whence the feelings from art: communication or concordance?

In the Beginning was the Word.

Words?

Not according to contemporary understanding of the development of communication. The first communication system is affective. The second communication system of words and language is based on the earlier one of affects.

At first the infant is "immersed in a word-bath," as Spitz (1957) put it, linking words and things into an inextricable network of emotional and perceptual experiences. Phonetic and musical elements of language become imprinted together in a context of meaning-laden intonations. Early on these come to center around the mother.

This was borne out by a series of experiments with newborns. Psycholinguists made use of the fact that a pleasurable event will cause a small baby to increase his sucking activity. Accordingly, a newborn baby is offered a pacifier connected to an electrode that makes it possible to record a graph of the variations in the sucking movements. Outside his field of vision different people speak various languages. It was possible to deduce that a four-day-old baby can distinguish his mother-tongue and, secondly, from among people speaking in this same language, show a "preference" for his mother's voice speaking in her usual tone and even without ever pronouncing his name or using her usual endearments (Eismas, 1971; Piaget and Chomsky, 1979; Mehler and Bertoncini, 1980; quoted by Amati-Mehler *et al.*, 1993: 139–140).

By the time the child is learning to walk he/she is also learning to speak. Thus, he/she enters and explores a new world of spatial organization at the same time as also discovering linguistic connections to the out-of-sight mother. Enter language and its symbolization function: words keep the child connected to mother while venturing out separately into the world and pending a welcoming return in accordance with the rapprochement phase of child development (Mahler, 1966).

At the same time, the world is beginning to become differentiated cognitively as well as linguistically: there are good and bad objects. The infant learns to distinguish them largely through the primary affective system – reading other people's *affects* through their facial musculature and communicating *affects* via one's own facial musculature. This is increasingly accompanied by language. Thus, the earliest affective communication system continues to work closely with later linguistic communication.

Language works well but far from perfectly. Modern philosophers have been rediscovering for some time what poets knew and complained about 2000 years ago: the improbability of conveying anything more than very partial truth by language. Facts, yes; the feelings about facts, no. This poses special problems for both psychoanalysis and art – specifically the scientific status of the former, and the inherent difficulty of describing in words the experience of the latter.

Words are flexible, meanings change, language is a living organism. As Wittgenstein pointed out, words are not crystal clear; they are nebulous with an aggregate of extensible, ill-defined meanings. Chomsky emphasized the limitlessness of human language; meanings press against and dilate the confines of each word. In short, linguistic meanings are indeterminate and "dilatative."

Here is a homely example.

The Five Mile River is the single most important feature of my town. It gives it a distinctive character. And its name gives it truth. It, is, in fact, five miles long.

Such a beautiful conjunction of language and truth! Or so I thought, until sailing out on it one day Crockett Johnson said, "Back then they didn't much care about it being five miles long – if that's what it is. It had five *mills* on it. That was important. So it used to be The Five Mills River. But nobody remembers that."

In psychoanalysis, the instrument for both psychological digging and reassembling of memory fragments is language. Following Freud's metaphor, we tell ourselves that through language we discover and reconstruct the subjective truth of one's personal past from fragments of memory – much as Sir Arthur Evans believed he was doing with the archeological fragments of the palace complex at Knossos. However, as any archeologist now knows, what Evans succeeded in accomplishing may be less a reconstruction of what was, than a new creation embodying old building blocks. He did bring intelligent, plausible, coherent "narrative" meaning to what had been fields of ruins. But "historical" truth?

Language, the second communicative system, is better designed to communicate the intellectual content of thought than its emotional coloration. When it comes to the world of one's personal past, cold facts without warm feelings about the facts will not do. However, in order to convey feelings through language one must resort to those qualities that are developmentally closer to its roots in the early affective system of communication. Those aspects of language are more like the tools in trade of poetry; while conveying feeling, they becloud the clarity of intellectual content. This undermines the claim of psychoanalysis to be a science.

There seems to be no way around this dilemma. If one wishes to become really businesslike (i.e. unemotional or scientific) about the organization of facts, one may invent mathematical signs to get around the muddy imprecision of words. Some philosophers express their ideas in this way and succeed in conveying ideas of quantity and dimension, relation and probability. This, however, places a mathematical stamp on the world and distorts it precisely to the extent that everything else has been left out.

Spence (1982) has been persuasive in demonstrating how this impacts on the scientific status of interpretation in psychoanalysis. For example, language is not only too coarse a rake to reproduce thought and feelings faithfully, but it is at the same time too broad and flexible in scope. It leaves out more than it includes, yet it includes so much that any number of connections can be made among the elements that are encompassed, especially given the wait-and-see analytic attitude and ongoing process of collecting more data.

This linguistic flexibility makes it possible for the analyst to create correspondences between the patient's material and the interpretation offered. By choosing the right words, a lexical overlap can be made between what the patient is or has been talking about and a given interpretation. The formal match or similarity, as by punning, is enough to convey plausibility, whether or not it is "demanded" by the material. If the given interpretation also includes a number of known facts that have not been otherwise accounted for, it gains in plausibility. Yet, even without the inclusion of facts, there is a need for closure and certainty that enables one to jump over the absence of facts. The greater the degree of anxiety present, the greater is this need for closure and certainty, other things being equal.

Even without the power of transference and the therapeutic alliance, the very fact that a proposition has been stated serves this need. If the proposition is plausible, familiar, and frequent, it becomes "true." It orders the data of the present and exerts a pressure on the anticipation of the future and the reordering of the past.

In this connection something further should be mentioned regarding the retroactive power of the present to discover or even create the past. Gestalt psychology has helped us understand the principles underlying our perception of formal line patterns. If transposed to cognition and recollection, these principles of pattern perception may help us understand the retroactive power of the present.

For example, in the perception of patterns, other things being equal, a shape tends to persist in its initial mode of operation. But the mind, continually striving for completeness, stability, and rest, tends to regularize irregularites and complete what was incomplete. Thus, a system left to itself tends to lose asymmetries and become more regular. Memory reinforces this tendency; less good shapes tend to be forgotten.

It is possible that these principles governing the perception of forms are applicable to the ways in which we tend to rework the past. That is to say, the tendency toward regularity, symmetry, and completion in our perception of formal line drawings might well be analogous to our tendency to rework the past in terms of our needs for narrative flow, plausibility, and certainty. In both areas, we might be dealing with the aesthetic need for "good shape."

Both the relevance of these gestalt principles and the "flexibility" of language touch on a fundamental *aesthetic* property: the plasticity of a medium, in this case the plasticity of words. Plasticity means that a medium can be treated as malleable and undergo many transformations while retaining its integrity and the interconnection of its elements. The plasticity of words is seen in the fact that their separate aspects of physical sound, intellectual content, and affective weight may be elaborated almost independently.

Poetry recombines their physical attributes, emotional overtones and semantic meanings. In poetry, words are the plastic, malleable medium, just as spatial forms are in painting and time is in music.

Another aspect of the problem for psychoanalysis is that the aesthetic plasticity of words that makes for dubious science can also make for effective interpretation. It can convey the essence of ambiguity, paradox, the coexistence in the mind of logical opposites. It thus makes it possible to correlate and link various dichotomies, objectifying them in order to make them available for conscious reflection, resolution, or, if necessary, at least a more peaceable cohabitation in the mind.

One such linking, fundamental to both art and science, is inner coherence amidst outer changeability. Conversely, the aesthetic property of plasticity makes it possible to experience that something familiar can now assume quite other aspects, or be in a different place, or take on an unusual character. The concern with an object not being what it was, and with its becoming something other than what it is, is a common concern of art and psychoanalysis. When analysts use words flexibly to show correspondences and suggest new connections between the familiar and the unfamiliar, they are, knowingly or not, exploiting the aesthetic plasticity of words and acting as artists.

In art, as in psychoanalysis, meanings depend more on affect than on words. Words struggle to shape cognitive understanding, but words alone, someone said, sketch only the contour of a river bed and not the flowing river of living thought plus feeling – unless, that is, they approach the status of poetry. In art, affect draws on the depths of the past and stretches from the rich sensuous modalities of the body towards consciousness and the world. It thus reaches beyond the self to a realm that surpasses mere cognitive understanding.

* * *

Since fantasy and language both appear at about 18 months of age, it was easy for psychoanalysis to assume that thought began with language and that fantasy would provide a key to early thinking. However, the study of severe language impairments due to neurological disease shows that thinking can remain essentially intact despite the loss of language (Damasio, 1999), suggesting that thinking takes place prior to the acquisition of language. There can be little doubt that language and verbalization can immeasurably enhance fantasy and thought, but it is also easy to imagine the possibility of simple fantasies in the form of nonverbal imagery.

Be that as it may, the capacity for feelings certainly precedes both fantasy and thought. Indeed, Melanie Klein and her followers insisted back in the 1930s, 1940s and 1950s that the psyche constantly endeavors to relate to feelings by concretizing them in the form of internal objects: fantasies and story-telling were primarily vehicles to articulate *feelings*. In other words, feelings come first and fantasies are elaborated in order to tell their story (Riviere, 1936; Isaacs, 1943; Klein, 1957: 88).

To put it a little differently, fantasy is a way of packaging affective tension *retroactively*; it imposes a cognitive structure of "explanatory" plausibility and narrative coherence onto otherwise unbound affect. Now that the developmental priority of affect over fantasy is once again coming into focus, nonverbal art may be viewed as representing ongoing attempts to bind intense perceptual and emotional stimulation that would have exceeded the capacity of the infant to contain. For the future artist, for example, aesthetic form offers a means of externalizing and transforming unmodified, emotional and perceptual intensity into highly elaborated, nonverbal structures of dynamically balanced tension and release.

In the moment by moment pendulum-like movement between primary and secondary processes – imagination and knowledge – affect normally enlivens knowledge as knowledge imposes realistic boundaries upon imagination in a smoothly working partnership. Less normally, affect becomes blocked, distorts thought and perception, and may find bodily outlets. In contrast to both, art may be thought of as a separate developmental path whereby affect becomes differentiated into novel expressive forms that help illuminate self and world.

Ironically, this illumination takes place despite the fact that at the core of art lies illusion. Picasso said: "Of course art is a lie. But a lie that helps one experience truth."

The question is, "Whose truth?" For psychoanalysis the "truth" in art consists of the "communication" by the artist through the work to the recipient. The fact of the matter is that the possibility of such communication retains little credit in the field of aesthetics (Dufrenne, 1953). Nevertheless, communication of regressive fantasies of infantile wishes embedded in the art remains the cornerstone of established psychoanalytic theory about the emotional appeal of art. What is at question here is not whether these same constituents may account for the power of neurosis, the nature of wit, the ubiquity of dreams, and the universality of religion and myth, but whether they are communicable from artist through art to audience.

A recent authoritative article on the aesthetic illusion claims exactly that. It bases itself on the clinical fact that we all have unconscious infantile fantasies and wish to regress to enjoy them with the least possible amount of guilt. Less guilt for more regression should yield most pleasure, the argument goes. The truth of art supposedly lies in the artist's specialized talent to "communicate" typical unconscious fantasies in such a way that we can have a guilt-free regressive ride. It exempts abstract art, dance and music from consideration because that entails unspecified "controversial issues" that are "profound" and "numerous," though my work is recommended (Balter, 1999).

It states:

> Typical fantasies are not only the emotional–instinctual foundations of the daydreams communicated through works of art. They also help to make that communication reliable . . . . [They] are the lingua franca of artistic communication . . . [that] allow beholders of a work of art to find personal relevance . . . . For example, Oedipal fantasies of rivalry and romance; "primal fantasies" of seduction, castration and the primal scene; rescue fantasies of the phallic woman; the fantasy of sharing a woman; beating fantasies; power acquisition fantasies, dismemberment fantasies; the fantasy of the maimed avenger; fantasies of intrauterine life; fantasies of dying together; three typical fantasies deriving from primal scene schemata: crucifixion fantasies, machine fantasies and banquet fantasies; oral incorporation fantasies; fantasies of having a double. This list could be extended.
>
> (Balter, 1999: 1299–1300; citations omitted)

The thesis postulates a regression of the ego function of reality testing back to the magical omnipotence of thought: we deny the reality of the artist as author of the art work, and sign on to accept his imaginary world as our own. The aesthetic illusion is said to involve an "emotional withdrawal from [one's] own immediate personal life . . . [and] from the social surround . . . . Art . . . is therefore fundamentally asocial and antisocial" (Balter, 1999: 1320). The author adds, parenthetically, "It may, however, secondarily take on social and socializing functions," but this later turns out to be "social regimentation" (Balter, 1999: 1328).

Among the difficulties raised by this grim and classic formulation are the following.

There is first of all a structural problem, both in the nature of language and in the nature of the aesthetic experience. The theory is based on fantasy. To the extent, however, that any but the simplest fantasy depends on language, language is deeply disadvantaged in dealing with art. That is because language makes a clear distinction between subject and object, while art and the aesthetic experience do not. As Marion Milner (1957: 161) wrote: "We are trying to talk about a process . . . in which the 'me/not-me' distinction is not important [art], but to do so at all we have to make the distinction."

Milner elaborates. In art and the aesthetic experience, subject and object interpenetrate within rationality. They are drawn into the experience of the movement of felt time in music, felt space in painting, and their mutually influential motion.

In formal, logical thought, on the other hand, subject and object are separate. Accordingly, from the point of view of formal logic the whole area of symbolic expression is irrational since the nature of a symbol is that it is both itself and something else.

But art and the aesthetic experience are not necessarily illogical or irrational; rather, they are nonlogical and nonrational; they follow other laws and yet the result is not chaos; it is another form of order: dynamic, harmonious, organic, simultaneously regressive and progressive, knowledgeable and imaginative, primary and secondary processes so balanced that unsuspected meanings may unfold in the course of time. (More of this later: see pp. 98–99.)

Another basic problem: the theory does not differentiate the structure of art from the other phenomena mentioned above – neurosis, myth, dream, religion, humor.

Thirdly, since the aesthetic experience of pleasure often involves a hyper-clarity of feelingful awareness rather than regressive instinctual gratification or defensive escape from reality, the regressive fantasy theory of art does not account for any *progressive* healthful aspect in the experience of art.

Nevertheless, if communication of unconscious fantasy does take place in art, one would suppose that the literary experience would be the most likely place to search for it. Reader response studies, however, appear to show that each reader uses the given narrative as material from which to form his own fantasy.

In an empirical study, Holland (1975) examined five advanced English-major undergraduates in regard to their understanding of Faulkner's story, *A Rose for Emily*. He found that each reader interacted with the story in terms of his own personality and intrapsychic life and in the light of this constructed something new which was most consonant with himself.

Through interviews and independently administered tests it was possible to delineate a characteristic identity theme for each of the readers. Each of the readers experienced and synthesized the story in the light of that identity theme. The reader who reacts in a positive way puts the elements together so that they tend to reflect his own lifestyle.

For this to occur, the defenses of the reader must mesh – in some subtle balance – with the work; from material in the work one creates wish-fulfilling fantasies characteristic of oneself. Finally, one transforms those fantasies into a literary interpretation that is also the product of personal style. In short, one takes from the work what is most consonant with oneself, rewrites it in one's own mind and becomes its coauthor.

This is in line with thinking going back to Descartes, Diderot and Kant, who held that art does not "communicate" meanings; it *generates* them in the receptive mind. It engenders much that is not contained in the object itself. Perhaps even better, T.S. Eliot said. The more it urges the mind beyond experience, the more it opens up the realm of the possible. And what is possible in one age is not possible in another. Which is why new generations will "bury" old art or rediscover it in the light of the current *Zeitgeist* and experience it in a new way.

There is one form of communication, however, that all artists engage in and that analysts generally tend to ignore. Van Gogh commented in his diary on the work of no fewer than 1100 artists. Other artists are one's critics, exemplars, cautionary signposts. Matisse and Picasso used each other's work as jumping-off points for their own. Matisse wrote that when either died there would be some things the other would never be able to talk of with anyone else.

If language arts do not "communicate" fantasies but rather stimulate the receptive reader to generate his/her own fantasies and then complete the work in his/her own way, it is even less likely that nonverbal, non-narrative, abstract art will succeed in transmitting the artists' fantasies. There is much anecdotal evidence in this direction.

In music: Hindemith (1961) commented that the second movement of Beethoven's Seventh Symphony "leads some people into a pseudo-feeling of profound melancholy, while another group takes it for a kind of scurrilous scherzo, and a third for a subdued pastorale. Each group is justified in judging as it does" (p. 47).

In painting: Gombrich (1972) pointed out that Van Gogh intended *Bedroom at Arles* (1888) to depict a haven of tranquility and in a letter to his brother stresses that there was no stippling or hatching, nothing but flat areas in harmony. Gombrich (1972: 96) concludes:

> It is this . . . that Van Gogh experiences as being expressive of calm and restfulness. Does the painting of the bedroom communicate this feeling? None of the naïve subjects I have asked hit on this meaning . . . . Not that this failure of getting the message speaks against the artist or his work. *It only speaks against the equation of art with communication.* [my italics]

Here is a final, semi-serious example of non-communication in art. I own a nonrepresentational oil painting entitled *Burning Sky*. It is composed of violent reds and oranges bursting out of a field of blues and blacks, securely contained by the compositional balance.

The artist, an old friend, said: "I was thinking of that violent volcanic eruption in Hawaii, but between you and me, this was also the first painting I did right after my open heart surgery and aortic valve replacement." I had known of his visit to Hawaii and of his aortic surgery. Now that he told me and linked them together, it was easy to imagine both the volcano erupting and his own fears of the aorta rupturing.

Then, after some more chatting: "Well, don't you see something else, perfectly obvious?" I admitted I did not. "Huh!" he snorted. "And you call yourself an old friend, let alone a psychoanalyst!" I squirmed.

> After knowing me for more than forty years don't you realize I'm still an Hungarian? Think of my accent – almost as fresh as when I came over before the war. Now look at those hot

reds: don't you know paprika when you see it? Can't you even taste it?

Whence the feelings from nonverbal art, such as nonrepresentational art and music unassociated with a verbal program such as opera or ballet? My thesis is: the concordance of formal patterns of virtual tension and release in the nonverbal art appear to be attuned to actual patterns of tension and release in the structure of affect, resonating back perhaps all the way to the earliest nonverbal holding environment.

Consider the following: A line is not just a line. "It is a certain *disequilibrium* [my italics] . . . within the indifference of the white paper" (Matisse, quoted in Merleau-Ponty, 1961: 184).

And this: A series of tones are not just flat acoustic sounds hanging in a void; they are dynamic impulses that strive toward completion (Sessions, 1950; Zuckerkandl, 1973).

It can be argued that neither statement can be literally true. Lines and tones are inorganic; they are not alive any more than a color, though vibrant, is really vibrating. It must be that they are so close in form to certain of our own living, breathing qualities that we automatically attribute our own vital qualities to the outside object, inspiriting it with our own. Enhancing it even, we may go on to feel inspired by *it*.

These few paragraphs will serve to thrust us into the center of the problem of how abstract art, and music in particular, conveys emotion. A summary of the relevant aspects of an excellent overview of the subject (Noy, 1993) will prepare the ground for outlining my own contribution (Rose, 1996).

While the discussion of the possible ways in which music may affect the listener's emotions is centuries old, two significant theories have emerged in the past fifty years: the theory of isomorphism by Suzanne Langer (1942) and C.C. Pratt (1952), and the theory of ego mastery by H. Kohut and S. Levarie (1950). Both are probably valid, but the former accounts for more instances.

According to Langer and Pratt, every affect has a specific form or shape; any message used in human communication that is isomorphic (i.e. similar in form) may activate this particular affect. The visceral organic patterns make emotion; the auditory contours evoke emotion *directly* by means of their formal shapes, which are similar if not identical to the visceral bodily patterns that are the basis of actual emotion.

Noy believes that a person's response to the recognition of the close similarity of visceral and auditory contours is based on a preverbal, constitutional, sensitivity and responsiveness to an other's emotions – a "primary empathy." (This receives support from current neuroscience: the infant early on learns to read and express primary affects through facial musculature.)

Kohut and Levarie (1950) claimed that music associated with frightening sounds stimulates the ego to deal with the resultant defensive anxiety by organizing and transforming it into recognizable forms; thus the pleasure of mastery *indirectly* becomes the pleasure of listening to music. This mode of receiving pleasure calls attention to how art provokes the recipient into being a participant and doing active work to deal with the stimulation. Noy is probably correct that all the higher arts provide pleasure in part by enticing the brain into more widespread organizational activity involving both primary and secondary processes.

In the light of clinical psychoanalytic experience and interdisciplinary readings, I came to adopt the Langer and Pratt theory of isomorphism and in the course of time have expanded it with psychoanalytic dimensions. To distinguish it from its antecedent in the philosophy of aesthetics, let us refer to my psychoanalytic elaboration as a theory of "concordance." Here is how it came about.

Where art had long shown that self and object interpenetrate in feelingful experience, this runs counter to long-standing psychoanalytic teaching: in the course of self-differentiating from the original psychological union with the mother, the infant comes to establish firm boundaries between Self and World. Where Id was, Ego shall be. Primary process gives way to secondary process, fantasy to reality, illusion to truth. So runs the canon.

My own clinical experience, however, taught me that there were a large group of individuals, often gifted and neither psychotic nor borderline, for whom reality and the sense of self retained a degree of sensitive fluidity. Reality was neither self-evident nor monolithic, let alone average or necessarily expectable; it could be refreshingly expansive. It is not a given; it is constructed. As one person said, "Reality is negotiable!"

I described a group of patients whose sense of identity depended in part on a sense of partial fusion with others, seeing themselves and others, for example, as extensions of each other, termed "narcissistic identity disorders" (Rose, 1963, 1964, 1966). Later, I came to appreciate Winnicott's description of the child's transitional object and expanded this idea into that of an ongoing transitional process related to creativity (Rose, 1978).

Instead of firm separation or fixed structures, more and more I saw ongoing fluidity and permeable boundaries as part of growth and openness to change. This was in accordance with Von Bertalanffy's (1968) thinking about the advantages of an open system theory over a closed one. I began to appreciate that behind our clinical predilection to see psychopathology there is also garden-variety creativity. One example is the gradual formation of one's self and identity from the original symbiotic unity with the pre-Oedipal parent. Yes, this may of course become a potential source of later pathology, but it may also be viewed as an early stage of a mundane creative process.

That is to say, "the creativity of everyday life" is the healthy counterpart of the psychopathology of everyday life. Not only long-term adaptation, but also each moment of perception – scanning, screening, affectively coloring and appraising each sensory datum in its everlasting mix of inner and outer – is the silent work of the ego maintaining homeostasis *creatively*.

As for major creativity, it perpetuates the child's imaginative, restless probing of reality, resampling early, less differentiated stages of imagination and reintegrating them with the realistic perspective of the adult in order, finally, perhaps, to recompose reality refreshingly. The artistic work, itself, highlights the shifting qualities of self and reality that went into its creation, projecting a delicate balance between inner and outer, regression and progression.

Another example of the fluidity of an open system is the constant interplay between primary and secondary processes rather than their isolation as separate entities. An example of this is the joining of primary process configurations such as condensation and displacement with the delayed discharge of the secondary process. In this way the terms of perception, itself, can be slowed down, magnified and made manifest. Primary process configurations can be rendered conscious and shown in the course of their unfolding. Think of the stretching out and unfolding of Bach's (based on primary process configurations) or Picasso's bold visual condensations of multiple viewpoints simultaneously. Transposing the terms "primary and secondary process" into everyday "imagination and knowledge" make their interplay inherently plausible.

As art helped to sensitize me to certain kinds of clinical experience and the awareness of the permeability of boundaries intrapsychically, it was analytic theory that allowed me to glimpse the possibility of a bridge between art and affect. That bridge was based on the idea of fluctuations of *energy*.

Freud's central idea about affect was that felt emotions are the conscious perceptions of an internal process which may be triggered by either external or endogenous events. Contemporary psychoanalysis and neuroscience agree that when an external event evokes affects, "the felt emotion is a perception of the *subjective response* to that event; it is not a perception of the external event itself" (Solms and Nersessian, 1999: 6).

In other words, the source is projected. When we listen to music we enjoy,

> We are not just emotionally moved by the music we enjoy, but the emotions actually appear to flow directly from the music. Even as we recognize that the information triggering the feelings is encapsulated within the well-interpreted score, the resulting mood changes arise from the dynamic responses of our brains . . . . In short, our brains are designed to project affect (as well as perceptions, of course) back into the world . . . . This is the way the brain generates its highly adaptive illusions of emotional realities.
>
> (Panksepp, 1999: 33)

What then, according to Freud, is the internal process? Affects are perceptions of "oscillations in the tension of instinctual needs [that] . . . become conscious as feelings in the pleasure–unpleasure series . . . [though] it is hard to say . . . by what means . . . these perceptions come about" (Freud, 1940: 198). He attributed the quality of the feelings to temporal factors: "the amount of increase or diminution *in a given period of time*" (Freud, 1920: 7–8). More specifically: "It is probable . . . that what is felt as pleasure or unpleasure is not the *absolute* height of . . . tensions [produced by stimuli] but something in the rhythm of the changes in them" (Freud, 1940: 145–146).

Though Freud tied oscillations of tension to instinctual needs lying behind conscious pleasure and unpleasure, we do not necessarily have to subscribe fully to instinct theory in order to retain the usefulness of the notion of energy.

Consider that, according to analytic theory, secondary process, logical cognitive thought entails a long-circuiting buildup of the tension of bound energy, until finally achieving delayed gratification. Primary process imagination, on the other hand, works with unbound, mobile energy pressing for immediate release of tension.

Returning now to the idea of a more open system of relatively fluid boundaries, intrapsychically we would expect a continuous interplay between primary and secondary processes: imagination stimulating knowledge and knowledge disciplining imagination. Such an interplay would involve a flux of energy; knowledge, increase of tension; imagination, release.

I speculate that this interplay of tension and release either generates affect, reflects it, or is otherwise closely related to the nature of affect. Thus, without dissociating ourselves altogether from instinct theory, the energic connotations of the constant interplay between the tension and release of knowledge and imagination offer an approach to Freud's question as to how the perception of affects comes about. (More of this later.)

If a dynamic of tension and release indeed lies at the core of affect, it is precisely that which is ready and available to respond to art, for central to each art there is a similarly dynamic balance of tension and release held together by formal means within a secure and sensitive frame (G.J. Rose, 1980). This is especially clear in nonverbal art like nonrepresentational painting and music, where the absence of narrative content highlights the abstract form.

In music, for example, one does not have to go back to eighteenth century formulations for the musical expression of certain typical emotions that characterized so-called *affectenlehre* of Quant and P.E. Bach. According to the music theoretician, Schenker (1935: 189):

> The highest principle that is common to all the arts: the principle of inner tension and its corresponding fulfillment . . . . If a differentiation is to be made between "classic" and "romantic", only the degree of tension and fulfillment should be considered.

While many others could be cited in all the arts, in music Hindemith (1945) graphically presents the rise and fall of tension in both the melodic and harmonic realms, with an almost mathematically developed thesis on the tension produced between various melodic intervals and between various harmonic permutations.

Few from the field of music have specifically explored how music conveys affect. The work of Epstein (1993, 1995) is an exception. After closely examining excerpts of Mendelssohn, Mozart, and Wagner, he concludes that the sense of *motion* unites form, structure, and affect. "It is the nuances of motion that effect, modulate, and ultimately control musical affect . . . . Affect is deeply and intrinsically wed to structure, and structure inseparably tied to motion" (Epstein, 1993: 119).

He joins his musical thesis relating musical motion to affect to my idea that art and affect share the common dynamic of tension and release:

> It is but a small and logical step from the dynamic buildup and release of tensions . . . to the factor of motion, as it operates in music as the carrier of these tensions and as the means through which tensions are controlled, modulated, and ultimately resolved. For our sense of musical motion is in part felt physically (muscularly) and psychologically in terms of tension and release. Tension/release may indeed be the essential factor, conveying the sensation of movement, of motion, in the absence of true physical motion in space.
>
> (Epstein, 1993: 99)

A composer knows that simple repetition, ornamentation, minor keys, modulation, remote harmonies, and dissonance may be used to increase tension. Conversely, returning to the central tonality of the "home" key, for example, after wandering in other keys, will always bring a relief of tension.

The foregoing discussion of tension and release in relation to affect in music is given substantive backing by the finding that motor areas of the brain are activated in the course of listening to music (cited in Benzon, 2001). The two come together in Nietzsche's remark somewhere that one listens to music with one's muscles.

Turning to tension and release in visual art, an artist knows how to highlight the dramatics of everyday visual experience and express them more energetically and clearly than is customary in daily life. How? For example, by knowing that oblique lines and rectangular or oval shapes are more tension-producing, and that horizontal or vertical lines or square or spherical shapes are more stable and tension-releasing. Knowing such matters, he can enhance the expressive qualities inherent in ordinary perception.

Now from the aspect of the viewer or listener and, more generally, perception itself, a perceptual sensitivity to the qualities of tension and release inherent in (or attributed to) any situation is at the root of that most basic aspect of perception, namely, affective perception. This is the capacity to have an immediate emotional gut reaction to any situation. It underlies the biological necessity that an organism be able to make an on-the-spot appraisal of the outside world's perceived hostility or friendliness in order to know how to respond: advance, withdraw, or wait. Needless to say, affective perception gives a first-alert signal. It must be evaluated and contextualized in the light of long-term memory and symbolization so that hair-trigger emergency actions may be aborted.

If there is a linkage in the tension–release deep structure of art and that of affect, their common dynamic of patterns of tension–release forms the affective bridge between art object and viewer. More precisely, the patterns of *virtual* tension and release in the artwork are concordant with the patterns of *actual* tension and release that constitute a person's capacity for nonverbal affective responsivity. It makes it appear that the artwork is *attuned* to the recipient, who thereupon responds with affective *resonance*.

By another route, starting in clinical experience, we have arrived at Langer and Pratt's theory of isomorphism. Note, too, that this has not required that the art-work communicate feelings; only that it generate them in receptive minds.

Does it matter? Yes, for reasons that are sufficiently significant to warrant calling it by a new name, "concordance." (1) It opens up a psychoanalytic developmental perspective on art; (2) it relates itself to neuroscience which may shed further light on our subject; (3) both points of view, psychoanalytic and neuroscientific, accord to art a weighty biological significance.

Regarding the first: The fit between virtual and actual patterns of tension and release can be so finely attuned that it can lead to a preconscious illusion that art is providing an emotionally responsive, witnessing presence. As in any intimately attuned encounter (like love or treatment) the aesthetic emotional experience may encourage one to feel more consciously what was always latent but inexpressible.

This mobilizes deeper emotional resonances from the past, perhaps even drawing upon the earliest nonverbal affective signaling that took place within the holding presence of the relationship between parent and infant. Ideally, this was geared towards the modulated buildup and resolution of tension in a finely-tuned dance of mother's attunement and infant's responsiveness. At that time it promoted a graded differentiation of feelings within the very beginnings of a sense of self.

Art, too, provides a holding presence of reliably balanced tension and release; it, too, allows affects to build up with modulated intensity to differentiate further. Thus, art continues a biological function of early mothering, namely, helps elaborate transformations of affect on higher, abstract levels of the same resonating emotional responsiveness that existed in the beginning.

The foregoing provides a theoretical rationale for a fundamental role of the arts in accessing affects blocked by trauma, and facilitating their differentiation irrespective of whether they eventually achieve verbalization.

Art theorist and therapist Dr Ernest Zierer pioneered a related line of thinking to art therapy in the 1950s. His work was largely unrecognized, perhaps because there was as yet no body of theory to receive it. (For a first-hand personal account, see Finn, 1992.)

Believing that the task of integrating a painting paralleled overcoming situations in daily life, he applied his ideas of art theory to art therapy. He deliberately imposed obstacles ("push marks") onto the canvas that a patient was working on. The patient's task was (1) to integrate the imposed obstacle into a finished art-work, which at the same time (2) achieved a high level of aesthetic tension. The level of tension (he developed a scale of fourteen different levels) was determined by the size of a color area, the degree of color contrast, and skillful brush work. Success in the task indicated an improvement in both creative ability and coping capacity.

Just as art therapy is directly related with the ability to cope, music has an intimate relevance to socialization. Ethnomusicologists note that dance and music probably evolved together; in almost all premodern societies members of the social group dance and make music for and with others (Feld, 1974).

The social action of singing and dancing together can lead to an altered mental state characterized by increased malleability, and trusting, cooperative group behavior. Rhythmic behavioral activities that are induced by the beating of drums and music can lead to altered states of consciousness. In extreme form, trance states help to break down established habits and beliefs.

Thus, far from being a private individual matter, originally the action of dancing and singing together served an opposite function, namely, socialization. It probably played an important and perhaps primary role as a wordless means of bringing about deep emotional social bonding (Freeman, 2000).

Returning now to the isomorphism or concordance of patterns between art and affect, a bridge toward current brain neuroscience begins to appear possible.

According to Damasio (1999), from whose text the following is abstracted, there are six primary emotions: happiness, sadness, fear, anger, surprise, disgust. They are associated with a repertoire of facial expressions and varied temporal profiles. Some tend to "burst" patterns of rapid onset, peak of intensity and rapid decay.

There are also secondary or "background emotions" that reflect the organism's ongoing physiological process or interactions with the environment, or both. These consist largely of reflections of body-state changes associated with musculoskeletal changes like body posture and movements. They are practically inseparable from the continuously generated "pulses" of core consciousness. Their patterns are more "wavelike" and are present continuously like an ongoing *melodic line* (Damasio, 1999: 93; my italics). They are: well-being/malaise, tension/relaxation, fatigue/energy, balance/imbalance, harmony/discord.

It is worth emphasizing at this point that one of the background emotions, tension–relaxation, appears to be a common attribute or underlying feature of all. This conforms to the central dynamic we have postulated regarding both aesthetic form and affect, namely, a pattern of interplay between tension and release in their virtual and actual forms. Further, musculoskeletal elements play an important role in the affective response to art – as they do in background emotions.

When the organism interacts with an object, Damasio continues, neural images map the organism, the object and the interaction between them. The maps pertaining to the object cause changes in the maps pertaining to the organism, which in turn enhance the object. All these changes can be re-represented in yet other, non-verbal, second-order maps. The neural patterns of second-order maps can become mental images describing in wordless but feeling stories of how all this came about. While these can be converted immediately and automatically into language, it is again worth emphasizing that they exist initially in nonverbal form.

The experience of feelings is achieved in two ways, either a "body-loop" or an "as-if body" loop. May this correspond to the distinction we have made between the actual tension and release of affect and the virtual tension and release in the formal structure of art?

The experience of feelings through a "body-loop" is achieved through neural and chemical signals which change the map of the body landscape. It is represented in somatosensory structures of the nervous system on many levels.

In the experience of feelings by an "as-if body" loop, the representation of body-related changes due to feelings is represented in changed body landscape maps via direct sensory body maps under the control of other neural sites such as in the prefrontal cortices. They bypass the body proper, partially or entirely, indicating "as if" the body has really been changed but it has not; they bypass the body and create "as-if" body states based on empathy, mirroring, fantasy.

"As-if body" loops are important for *internal simulation* (Damasio, 1999: 281; my italics). Further, "The brain can get direct neural and chemical signaling from organism profiles that fit background emotions" (Damasio, 1999: 293).

Either route – body maps registering body-state changes or simulated "as-if body" loops – gives rise to a full gamut of feelings. Again, while these exist initially in nonverbal form, they can readily be converted into language. They include, for example, the emotional "chills" induced by music (Panksepp, 1995; Blood and Zatore, 2001; as cited by Damasio, 2003: 137).

Let us extend this in a way that attempts to approximate psychological discourse. The stimulating yet secure "holding environment" of balanced tension and release inherent in aesthetic structure is a profile that fits "background emotions." As such, it provides the brain with direct neural and chemical signaling. The experience of feeling evoked by nonverbal art like music would be registered via an "as-if body" loop involving "internal simulation."

This interdisciplinary exercise offers a lure and a limit. It offers a neural basis for the power of imagination – "as-if" loops and "internal simulation" – but it also highlights a limit. For a neural map of the power of imagination encompasses both the benign illusion of an empathic presence lying embodied in aesthetic experience, and the intensity of non-organic hallucinatory imagery and animistic fetishism, for example. So-called "reality testing" remains to a significant extent on the uncertain ground of judgment which, as we all know, is captive to the transient spirit of an age.

In other words, the interactive nature of mental contents in the form of body-based neural maps induced by real or simulated body-states necessarily involves an irreducible element of subjectivity. Hence, the nonveridicity of perception, the inevitability of ambiguity: a potential formula for pathology – and art!

All of this suggests an offering to Music as Metaphor:

> My mind is my piano,
> playing and played upon by a sentient world,
> its co-creator.

> Identity themes and internalized chords:
> resonating pulses
> of cumulative Time.

Chapter 4

The music of time in Faulkner's *Light in August*

Jean-Paul Sartre (1951: 180–181) wrote that "The novelist's aes-thetic always sends us back to his metaphysic . . . . And it is obvious that Faulkner's is a metaphysic of time." He went on to state that, like other great contemporary writers – Proust, Joyce, Dos Passos, Gide and Virginia Woolf – Faulkner tries to mutilate time; his technique arrests motion in time and reaches real time by negating clock time. The nature of this "real time" and how his technique attains it are matters we will examine in this chapter.

Faulkner's style has perplexed, fascinated and infuriated critics from the beginning. One of the principal complaints registered against him has to do "with his 'perverse' maneuvering of syntax, his reckless disregard of grammatical 'decency', and the exorbitant demands he has made upon the reader's attention" (Hoffman, 1951: 28). Some have been troubled by the fact that by combining contradictory elements in oxymoron he makes logical resolution impossible, and his synesthetic images make precise sense localiza-tion impossible. It has been charged that although these devices are admirably suited for depicting inner mental states, they enable him to deliberately hold elements in suspension. Some claim that this avoidance of "commitment" seriously limits his stature (Slatoff, 1963).

Aiken (1960) described Faulkner's style as "strangely fluid and slippery and heavily mannered prose" (p. 135) with passion for over-elaborate sentence structure: "trailing clauses, one after another, shadowily in apposition . . . parenthesis after parenthesis, the parenthesis itself often containing one or more parentheses" (p. 137). He went on to point out that these constituted in a curious and inevitable way "an elaborate method of *deliberately withheld* meaning of progressive and . . . delayed disclosure" (p. 138). Aiken compared the repetitiveness to a kind of chanting, a living pulse, and used such musical terms as *fugue-like* and *symphonic*. Beck (1951) called attention to the contrast between the irresistible rhythm of Faulkner's prose and the sense of suspension brought about by lengthy sentences and a full vocabulary. Abel (1969) compared Faulkner's images of time and found that they were essentially those of Bergsonian duration.

Our discussion will begin by providing a synopsis of the plot of the story. Then the various circles of time represented by the characters in *Light in August* will be described, largely in Faulkner's own words. Imitating his style of writing will serve as a general illustration before discussing it in some detail later. For it is through his style that Faulkner evokes an early time of life and conveys a sense of endless recurrence or timelessness: fluid boundaries between the genders and the tenses, images of fusion, reworkings of the "primal scene" and use of rhythm are the powerful stylistic devices he employs. Counterpoising these intimations of timelessness there is a manifest insistence that time is also non-recurrent and its consequences irreversible. This contrast results in a sustained uncertainty. A system of reverberating tension is set in motion, mirroring the mind's own task of maintaining a dynamic balance between objective events and subjective needs. The recognition of the concordance between the tensional system in the novel and in ourselves may be a key to the aesthetic experience and will be discussed in the following chapter.

Synopsis

Lena, a young, unmarried orphan in the last stages of pregnancy, has been deserted by Lucas Burch, the father of her child. She has been seeking him by hitchhiking wagon rides for four weeks from Alabama to Jefferson, Mississippi. She is mistakenly directed to Byron Bunch, an older bachelor. He realizes that the man Lena is looking for is going under the alias of Brown to avoid being found by her. Brown now has a bootlegging partner, Joe Christmas, a wanderer of unknown origin and rumored to be part Negro. Christmas has been carrying on a secret affair with Joanna Burden, a middle-aged Yankee spinster who lives alone on the old farm. While Byron Bunch and Lena are talking we learn that the Burden farm is on fire; Joanna Burden has been murdered. A drunken Brown is taken into custody and, to claim the reward, accuses

Christmas of the murder. Christmas eludes the posse, running in circles for seven days; finally he is apprehended walking brazenly on the main street of a nearby town.

Doc Hines, a Negro-hating religious fanatic, and his wife are convinced that Christmas is the bastard son of their daughter who had run off with a part-Negro circus worker thirty years before. Doc Hines had killed the man and refused to allow a doctor to attend his daughter's delivery. After she died in childbirth he had taken the newborn boy on Christmas night and left him on the orphanage steps. The young doctor there found the child and he and his mistress, the dietician, took him in and named him Joe Christmas. Doc Hines took a job as the orphanage janitor. At the age of five Christmas was adopted by a sadistic, religious fundamentalist, Mr McEachern, and his wife. When he was a young adolescent he ran away, living as an itinerant worker until he returned to Jefferson and struck up a bootlegging partnership with Brown (Lena's Burch) and an affair with Joanna Burden. Doc and Mrs Hines go to Jefferson where Christmas has been jailed. There they meet Byron Bunch, who has them installed in the cottage where Christmas and Brown had been living and where Lena is awaiting the birth of her child. The next day Lena is delivered of a baby boy by Byron's friend, Reverend Hightower, a recluse and a minister without a congregation. Mrs Hines imagines that the baby is her lost grandchild and Brown, brought to see Lena and the newborn, flees and thus forfeits his reward for the capture of Christmas. Christmas escapes from jail; he runs to a Negro cottage and then to Hightower's. He strikes Hightower on the head with a gun and is himself gunned down by a vigilante group and emasculated by their leader. Although Lena refuses to marry Byron Bunch, they and the child set out for Tennessee together. The entire action takes place in only ten days. When we last hear of them they are reaching Tennessee and Lena is marveling at how far she has traveled since she left Alabama just eight weeks before.

Characters and time

There are a number of circles of time which Faulkner orchestrates through the plot: dead, detached time; moralistic, vindictive time; wishful, undoing time; instinctual, appetitive time; a dawning time of cause, consequence and personal accountability; and natural, amoral, cyclical time. These circles are embodied in the lives and thought processes of the principal characters.

Reverend Hightower's time is dead time, detached from present life. He identifies with his dead grandfather who was shot from his horse and, instead of having an identity of his own, he dozes in his daydreams or sleeps in his canvas chair until Bunch wakes him to take a responsible part in the events unfolding around them. Until then his life had been defined by resistances to the life around him: he would not resign from the Church, would not leave Jefferson, would not deal with the townspeople's needs, would not tell who beat him up. He did not see his own name on his signpost, nor did he hear the music he waited for each day to signal nightfall and the return of familiar dreams of the past. Unlike Bunch, he uses neither watch nor clock, having needed neither for twenty-five years. Although he lives dissociated from mechanical, contemporary time, he could know at any moment where he would be and what doing in his old life in relation to Wednesday night and Sunday church services. He could know almost to the second when he should begin to imagine the distant music from the church to begin.

Mr McEachern and Doc Hines live in moralistic, vindictive time, each believing himself the instrument of God's punitive will. McEachern wore a heavy silver watch chain across his vest. From before breakfast on Sunday mornings the thick silver watch would lie face up on the table. Exactly on the dot of each hour McEachern rose deliberately, without haste, took up the watch, closed it and returned it to its pocket, looping the chain again through his suspenders. Then he took the boy, Joe Christmas, to the stable, had him drop his pants and administered ten strokes of the strap. Each hour he would strike him ten times for not learning his catechism. Then he would kneel and pray for the boy.

Doc Hines believed that his daughter's pregnancy by a non-white was the devil's punishment for his own former drinking. Doc Hines acted as God's punishing agent when he killed the man responsible. His daughter's death in childbirth was her punishment. The illegitimate mulatto baby was to be the instrument of other people's punishment. And Doc Hines, with his wide open, blind, fanatical eyes, was to be the witness of the slow, inexorable working of God's unhurried will.

Mrs Hines represents wishful time, time that can be undone and repaired. She wished that just for one day it could be as though the murder had not been committed; if it could be like that for just one day, after that she would not interfere. When Lena's newborn son cried it was like thirty years were obliterated by wishful thinking; she imagined this to be her dead daughter brought back, and this the grandson she had not seen since birth.

Brown and Christmas, part-time bootleggers, were outside the law and time. Theirs was the amoral time of appetites, governed by recurrent instinctual need for food (drink) and sex. Brown hollered that he did not know what time it was since he was not rich enough to own a watch, but with his new car he had only to drive past the courthouse often enough to see the clock in order to keep up with the time.

As for Christmas, time, sex, violence and orality were all tied together. The first time he bought a watch was before his first date and sex. He had forgotten to wind it so the watch was dead, for which he blamed Mrs McEachern. But he knew it was late without having to look at the watch. In adolescence he had learned about women's monthly time; when he heard that his waitress girlfriend was having her period, he struck her, walked into the woods and vomited. In his affair with Joanna Burden he began to see himself sucked down into a morass of her insatiable nighttime appetite. At first it was a torrent, and then it became a tide with an ebb and flow.

When he fled after killing her he ran in circles for seven days. While he was trying to remember how many days since he had eaten, a strange thing came into his mind. The name of the day of the week seemed more important than the food. At last he felt a need to keep track of the time spent toward some goal (p. 317). "I am tired of running of having to carry my life like it was a basket of eggs" (p. 319).

When he woke in the dawn it was still too dim to see his face clearly in the water. But now he goes in a straight line. He is like a man who knows where he is and where he wants to go and how much time he has to get there. He is not sleepy or hungry or even tired. In the past seven days he has traveled further than in all the thirty years before. And yet he is still inside the circle.

What circle? He has always been driven solely by instinctual needs and, lonely and alienated, has almost drowned in them. Now for the first time he discovers that he is also part of another circle – one of cause and effect and accountability: "I have never broken out of the ring of what I have already done and cannot ever undo," he thinks quietly (p. 321).

Accepting cause and consequence, he waits for more light to see his image reflected in the stream. Now he no longer runs in circles but goes in a straight line to the nearest town and walk up and down the main street until he is recognized and, finally, apprehended.

The messenger through whom these various circles come to intersect as the dramatic action unfolds is Byron Bunch. A middle-aged bachelor and Sunday choir master, he may be said to live in mechanical, impersonal time. He works six days a week in the wood-planing mill, keeping his own time to the final second of an imaginary whistle as well as on his huge silver watch, not leaving out even the minutes he stops to rest. He has managed to remain uninvolved, hidden from the chance to harm anyone, largely outside of human-relational time, until he falls in love with Lena. Feeling that there is a price for being good the same as for being bad, he makes himself responsible for Lena, finds a place for her to stay and gets Hightower to deliver her baby. In the process of engaging themselves with her need, these two men are reborn into life from their own mechanical, dead time spheres. Thus, while they rescue her, she rescues them.

But, with typical Faulkner irony, Lena remains outside of human-relational time. The steady, creaking wagons she travels on take her to a place not very different or worse from the present one or the last one. Hers is the recurrent time of Nature's unchanging cycles of seasonal rain and fertility. As the carrier of life, she has attracted the constructive force of the community; it gathers itself around her while neither condemning nor approving her illegitimate pregnancy. She conventionally accepts the sacrifices made on her behalf and, unreflective throughout, remains as unchanged through the catastrophic changes around her as Nature herself. She comments in the last paragraph of the book, as in the last sentence of the first chapter, "My, my. A body does get around" (pp. 26, 480).

As Brooks (1969) points out, the characters form many contrasting pairs. Lena and Joe Christmas stand in obvious contrast. They are both orphans who escape from home by crawling out the window. Betrayed by their first loves, they both come to Jefferson; but Joe Christmas repels while Lena attracts the community into which they come as strangers. Christmas' alienation and isolation from the community is similar to that of his executioner, Peter Grimm. That is why the wounded Hightower sees their images blurred together. Christmas' rootlessness, knowing nothing of his origins, living only in present appetites, is contrasted with the absurd, historical rootedness, which is alienated from the present, of Joanna Burden, Hightower, and Grimm. Joanna's sterility is a stark contrast to Lena's fertility.

Regarding a fertility theme, it happens that the same day Joe Christmas is killed, Lena's baby is born. In the mind of Mrs Hines the baby is little Joey, her daughter's baby of thirty years ago, reborn. Both the death of Joe Christmas and the birth of Lena's baby, the new Joey, take place on the ninth day after Lena's arrival in Jefferson.

Of particular psychoanalytic interest (and this has not escaped literary critics; see Brooks, 1969) is the likelihood that both Christmas and Hightower are latently homosexual. It is thus no wonder that Hightower, having earlier refused to provide an alibi, now tries to protect Joe by saying that he was with him the night of the murder, and Grimm accuses him of having taken his pants down to Christmas.

This ambiguity in their gender identification merits further examination for, as we shall see, it is paralleled by the particularly slippery way in which Faulkner handles time and mode, in describing these characters at crucial times. The tenses move back and forth, the active and passive modes alternate with each other, and time is cut off and flattened out until distinctions are almost obliterated.

It may be asked, "How is the issue of bisexuality related to that of time?" The characters' bisexuality and the stylistic device of letting tenses and modes "hang loose" both have the effect of returning us to a much earlier time of life, a phase of development in which the knowledge of sex differences has not yet registered, gender identity is unformed, and the boundaries of time are similarly fluid. Thus, we are referred back to a time when reality itself is little more than a playground for the imagination, the realm of the storyteller's once-upon-a time.

First, then, let us look at the temporal and gender ambiguity of Hightower; then at that of Christmas.

If there is a "musical" theme associated with Hightower it is his waiting for the end of each day for the moment of night to hear the distant choir music, waiting for twilight to cease, for the time to begin to say, "Soon, now. Now, soon." Between the "soon" and the "now" and back again, the "now" and the "soon," he can "feel the two instants about to touch: the one which is the sum of his life . . .

and the suspended instant out of which the soon will presently begin" (p. 160).

This hinge of time swinging back and forth between the "Soon, now. Now, soon" future–present–present–future signals the moment for Hightower's fantasy to return to the past: "The only day he seemed to have ever lived in – that day when his grandfather was shot from the galloping horse . . ." (p. 57). It was as though he had been killed too. Time had stopped for him, and his own life and time had ceased before it began twenty years before. He lived in the present as though dead, declaring that he is not in life anymore. He listens as though "in a cathedral to a eunuch chanting in a language which he does not even need to not understand" (p. 301).

The movement is from obliviousness of the living, active present to passively listening to a eunuch chant in a lost tongue. The imagery is consonant with a slightly earlier description of Hightower being transformed into a woman, and a pregnant one at that: "His obese stomach is like some monstrous pregnancy . . ." (p. 291). And later, when he sleeps in his canvas deck chair, his mouth open, "loose and flabby flesh sagging away from the round orifice, [it seems] as though the whole man were fleeing away from the nose which holds invincibly to something yet of pride like a forgotten flag above a ruined fortress" (p. 343). And still later, after Hightower acts as midwife and delivers Lena's child, he thinks, "If I were a woman now [I'd] go back to bed to rest" (p. 383). He does so, and dreams of the newborn child as his namesake.

Is the unknown language chanted by a eunuch in a cathedral perhaps that of an early, unconscious longing for a time, not far removed from the cathedral of the womb, when the boundaries of time, gender, the sense of separateness from mother, and the sense of reality itself, are equally fluid? However intriguing that possibility, we are on firmer ground if we limit ourselves to the claim that there is an intrinsic connection between Hightower's conscious wish to return to the past and an unconscious wish to keep his gender options open or to renounce his masculinity.

Toward the close of the book, we learn that Hightower's grandfather had not lost his life in a gallant cavalry charge but in a raid on a henhouse. What are we to make then of his lifelong obsession with the heroic myth? The recurrent image of his grandfather dying in battle magnifies his masculinity and unmans him at the same time, thus emphasizing the loss. His compulsive repetition of this particular scene in his imagination suggests that Hightower is repeatedly killing off the male part of himself in the shape of his grandfather. It also suggests that cutting off time at precisely this point is, for Hightower, a symbolic emasculation.

If Hightower killed off the man within, stopped the clock, and stood still, Christmas killed off the woman within, tore her hands off the clock and ran in blind circles. One character only remembered and hardly acted; the other only acted and hardly remembered. Both are incomplete men and both, being outside the flow between memory and action, are timeless.

The woman within Christmas is represented by Joanna Burden, who, Faulkner emphasizes repeatedly, is a woman who seems like a man. "'My God,' he thought, 'it was like I was the woman and she was the man'" (p. 222). When he mentally watched himself making love with her he could have been looking at a sexual struggle within himself, one which threatened to leave him feeling unmanned (like Hightower): he watched two creatures in one body.

The day that Christmas murdered Joanna Burden began just after midnight with a fight with his bootlegging partner, Brown. He stooped astride Brown and struck him repeatedly in the face. But he did not reach for the razor. The oral imagery keeps highlighting the underlying homosexual tension. Brown's mouth was open, snoring; Christmas went outside, lascivious, naked into "the cool mouth of darkness, the soft cool tongue" (p. 100). The imagery then moves from male-oral to female-oral, then back toward the male: "to smell horses because they are not women . . ." (p. 101).

The bisexual struggle still unresolved, he finds himself by afternoon in Freedman Town, surrounded by the smell and voices of invisible Negroes equated with the "hot, wet, primogenitive Female" (p. 107). Blackness is equated with female, and whiteness with male. He began to run towards the light – "cold hard air of white people" (p. 107). And he goes on to murder Joanna Burden who, being a white, masculine, barren female is suitable to represent both elements in himself.

While the sexual struggle between his own shifting identifications is being thus described, the conflict is transposed to the Time element. The tenses shift back and forth as well as between active and passive voices: He thought "something is going to happen to me [future-passive]. I am going to do something [future-active]" (p. 97). When he awoke he wondered, "maybe I have already done it [past-active], maybe it is no longer now waiting to be done [past-passive]" (p. 104).

Later, standing in the lonely, empty road, he heard the bell-tower clock tolling ten o'clock. The road for Faulkner is a symbol of time and memory. The ten strokes of the clock are the same ten strokes that McEachern used to deliver to the bare bottom of the boy Christmas exactly on the hour as he stood passively in the stable, and took his punishment, preferring this stern, male justice to the unpredictable softness of females.

Time recedes and is halted in past memory. A series of negatives, in both active and passive modes, indicates that time has stopped: "When he heard eleven he was not thinking . . . thinking had not begun now; the voices had not begun now either. He just sat there not moving until after a while he heard the clock strike twelve" (p. 110). To the negatives arresting time, and the interchangeability of active and passive modes, is now added the reversibility of the tenses. After a while he heard the clock strike twelve. "Then he rose. He didn't go fast. He didn't think even then, 'Something is going to happen'" (p. 110). "He was saying to himself, 'I had to do it,' already in the past tense" (p. 264).

The conflict within himself between active and passive, male and female, black and white, the wish to resolve the struggle into peaceful sameness has been depicted by Faulkner by stylistic devices centering on time that finally emasculate it. They parallel Christmas' murder of Joanna Burden and his own death. When he mounted her stairs the last time he heard her praying. Before when he had been sitting in the shrubbery outside hearing the last stroke of the far clock die away, "the dark was filled with the voices out of all time that he had known, as though all the past was a flat pattern . . . tomorrow night, all the tomorrows . . . that had ever been was the same as all that was to be, since tomorrow to-be and had-been would be the same. Then it was time" (p. 266).

Time having been transformed into a flat pattern by Faulkner, Joe now mounts the stairs the last time and confronts his secret double, Joanna, who is found to have a hidden gun pointed at him. He disarms and perhaps decapitates her, loses his memory, runs in circles for seven days, and then deliberately gets himself caught.

If Faulkner's style of interchanging tenses and active–passive modes parallels an oscillation in gender identification, certain imagery suggests also a purposeful blurring of other distinctions that are first made in early life. The merging of self with outside objects rolls time back to the earliest period, before the establishment of a sense of reality. Similarly, when various sensations are confused and condensed, memory is returned to its origins in raw sensory date. In both experiences there is obliteration of separateness and a return to early fusion states in which the rudimentary sense of time is scarcely discriminated from the ebb and flow of physical needs. If an unconscious memory of these early states comes close to consciousness it imparts a sense of uncanny foreboding as of impending truth. The feeling of conviction that accompanies it precedes and outlasts conscious understanding, actual recollection, or imagining.

Faulkner puts it this way: "Memory believes before knowing remembers. Believes longer than recollects, longer than knowing even wonders." He continues in a sentence a third of a page long which, abstracted, reads: "Knows remembers believes a . . . building . . . surrounded by smoking factory purlieus and enclosed . . . like a penitentiary or a zoo, where . . . orphans . . . in and out of remembering but in knowing constant as the bleak walls, the bleak windows where in rain soot from the nearly adjacenting chimneys streaked like black tears" (p. 111).

In this passage, Faulkner is describing the experience of Joe Christmas in his earliest years in the orphanage. Christmas knows, remembers, and believes the black tears of rain soot on the bleak windows. This image forcefully fuses Christmas' face with the window, his tears with the rain, the sense of his blackness or perhaps a dirty face with bleakness and soot. The black tears running from his eyes down his face are like the rain running down the sooty windows of his orphanage and are scarcely distinguishable from them. This is an imagist picture of the feeling of early childhood depression; depression that occurs before the establishment of the sense of separateness from the outside world.

Many years later Joe Christmas hears the far clock strike nine and then ten, and enters Joanna Burden's window like a cat, perhaps remembering how he used to leave the McEachern's window and the rope he used to climb out. He moved unerringly towards the food and ate something from an invisible dish, with invisible fingers. "His jaw stopped suddenly in midchewing and thinking fled for twenty-five years back down the street . . . I have eaten it before, somewhere. In a minute I will memory clicking knowing I see I see I more than see hear I hear I see my head bent I hear the monotonous dogmatic voice which I believe will never cease . . . and peeping I see the indomitable bullet head . . . and I thinking How can he be so not hungry and I smelling my mouth and tongue weeping the hot salt of waiting my eyes tasting the hot steam from the dish 'It's peas,' he said aloud. 'For sweet Jesus. Field peas cooked with molasses'" (p. 217).

Here Faulkner is describing how Christmas struggles to reconstruct a memory from bits of raw sensory data buried alive years ago and now stirred up; it is just barely teased out, and now finally linked to the smell and taste of the unseen food in his fingers, his mouth; at last it is given a name and identified by the words on his tongue as field peas. The interminable sentence tells us physically that waiting to eat them must have felt like an eternity. Weeping with his eyes, and waiting to taste with his tongue, he smelled the steam from the dish of peas: "I smelling my mouth and tongue weeping the hot salt of waiting my eyes tasting the hot steam from the dish" (p. 217). Weeping and waiting to taste, tears, saliva, and hot steam merge, and eyes and tongue become fused, so that tears might as well be coming from a weeping tongue, and saliva from drooling eyes. In the experience of waiting, weeping, smelling the steam and wanting to taste the field peas, the senses merge. All the while McEachern's voice, monotonous, dogmatic and not hungry coming from his head bent over the food, drones on interminably saying grace. Taste, smell and the sound of McEachern's voice come together like wet watercolors without clear boundaries. In trying to match the present taste and smell with lost memory, all these old sensations come up at once with their confused registration and organs of origin. Past and present are joined together till Christmas speaks the words, "It's peas," and probably simultaneous with hearing himself speak, identifies the food and re-enters the present.

Thus, painting and over-painting with words, the senses are mixed and spread and stroked over the canvas until a feeling experience is made to emerge from the depths of past body memory and freed to live again in the present. This condensation of Christmas' senses in a kind of synesthesia which is sorted out and made into a recognizable sense which he can label finally and communicate to himself resembles some of the minute stages in the process of perception, thought, and memory.

We will discuss this further later, but now let us repeat: like gender uncertainty and loose boundaries of time and mode, images of synesthesia and of fusion between self and outside objects all have the effect of returning us to an early, relatively undifferentiated phase of psychological development, and thus evoke a sense of timelessness.

A particularly forceful image of fusion is that of sexual coupling, the "primal scene." Observed in childhood, as Joe Christmas did at age five, it puts special demands on the mind to master the experience. This often takes the form of total repression of the memory and sometimes lifelong compulsive repetition of it with its details altered for disguise. The very act of repetition transforms an experience which was originally endured passively into one actively perpetrated. This turning of the tables represents a step towards psychological mastery. Beating and rape, for example, may often be unconscious attempts at active mastery of earlier experiences of having been beaten and raped, although both the original and later acts may be consciously disavowed. Thus, when Joe Christmas, having raped Joanna Burden, saw her calm, cold face by day he could think that he dreamed it and it didn't happen.

Such repeated working through of an early primal scene is necessary because, as is commonly pointed out in analytic literature, it may appear to be a mortal battle; it floods the observing child with a confusion of sexual and aggressive stimulation. Moreover, as is rarely pointed out, it threatens his fragile sense of the integrity of his own bodily boundaries to imagine, or view, in Faulkner's description (p. 246) two creatures appearing to struggle in one body, drowning in the abyss, merging into each other. Before the sense of self is fairly developed, such overstimulation and apparent melting of bodily boundaries threatens to overpower both the sense of reality and of self, that is, to return the individual once more to that early, undifferentiated stage of life when reality and self are first being formed and there is little sense of time.

Faulkner's style deals with these boundaries in their early fluid state. Nonetheless, he disavows their exclusive authority and, sometimes, even their existence. We have noted how tense, gender, and separateness are dealt with as flexible entities. But throughout the book the disavowal of sight seems particularly insistent. Indeed, as Millgate (1969) has pointed out, many of the major events have already taken place before Lena's arrival in Jefferson. And even much of the present action of the novel is not observed directly but reported by witnesses not themselves involved in the incidents. For example, Gavin Stevens interprets the events that led to Christmas' death; the traveling furniture dealer recounts to his wife what happens to Byron and Lena at the end of the novel. The story of Christmas' arrest is also told by an anonymous "they."

Hightower no longer sees the sign in front of his house. He sits like an Eastern idol with his eyes closed. Doc Hines, working as a janitor in the orphanage, looks directly into the dietician's face with his wide open blind fanatical eyes. Joe Christmas, after being beaten up, arises like a blind man and enters the fifteen years long street. When he entered Joanna's window he ate something from an invisible dish with invisible fingers. In the final murderous encounter between them, the last thing we see directly is her right hand reaching out holding an old-style revolver. Then our view is shifted to the shadowed pistol on the wall and its cocked hammer when it fires. We see no more of what happened and never really know.

Even the murdered body of Joanna Burden with its nearly severed head is described ironically in terms of the disavowal of looking: "[Miss Burden's body] was laying on her side, facing one way, and her head was turned clean around like she was looking behind her, [like] if she could have done that when she was alive, she might not have been doing it now" (p. 85).

All the careful looking away, not seeing at all or seeing only the shadows of preliminary actions, is suddenly dispelled and everything turns to an emphasis on looking, even endless gaping, when the people crowd around to look down at her body. When the body is taken away there is only the fire to look at. They stare and stare, imagining the sexual scenes that must have led up to the killing and the final flames. All the frustrated sexual looking now becomes concentrated on the symbolic substitutes – fire truck, rising ladders and hose. They stared at the flames "as if all their individual five senses had become one organ of looking" (p. 275).

This careful looking away or hearing without seeing, together with this sudden avid staring at the flames which consume everything and consummate the affair of Christmas and Joanna Burden, reminds us of Joe's first sexual experience at age five, which led to his life-long tragedy. He had heard footsteps in the empty corridor and did not wait to see, but he heard without listening and hid in the closet among the woman-smelling garments and saw by feel alone the worm of tooth paste he squeezed into his mouth and ate; and the dietician and the young doctor coupled on the bed – and Joe vomited, and was discovered. The recurrent disavowal of looking may refer to this original trauma in the life of Christmas. The unconscious repetition of this scene in various forms may well have determined his life and death and is perhaps a key to the novel. Such a sweeping hypothesis cannot be made lightly, but, as we will see, there is much to support it.

In this early primal scene trauma at age five there are, besides hearing and not seeing, three elements that should be noted and traced through his later sexual life: food, money and punishment. The woman who was being forcibly taken in sex while Joe crouched behind the curtain eating toothpaste was the dietician of the orphanage. In Joe's mind she was associated with the dining room. Ordinarily, he would have eaten only one mouthful of her toothpaste. But now, hiding and waiting, he had squeezed the entire tube into his mouth and swallowed it. Suddenly he vomited and was discovered.

The punishment which was not forthcoming, and which young Joe needed to strike the balance and be able to write it off, came later in full measure at the hands of Mr McEachern: on Sundays, every hour on the hour, ten strokes to his bare bottom, and Joe took it stolidly; he even welcomed it as one of the few dependable things in life.

As for food, after dark on a Sunday when he was beaten, Mrs McEachern had brought him a tray of food to his bed; and he had dumped it on the floor. And he stole Mrs McEachern's coins and told her to remember that he took them without asking because he was afraid she would give them to him if he asked. (The relationship with Mrs McEachern is heavy with sexual elements: the rope, which he uses to get out of the house at night to visit his whore, he hides in Mrs McEachern's secret hole – the same one in which she hides the coins he steals from her. And there are many similar details.)

The same three elements of food, money and punishment are present in his first sexual affair. The girl (Bobby) is a waitress; he eats at her counter and is meticulous about paying for it; and he is beaten into insensibility.

And finally, the fatal affair with Joanna Burden begins with stealing her food and raping her. Eating her food remains constant throughout. The affair comes to an end when she wants him to take charge of her money and he refuses. Whether he kills her or not we never know because we are not allowed to see. But after fleeing he allows himself to be caught; and when he escapes and his executioner corners him he does not fire his gun but again allows himself to be caught; and this time he is castrated and killed.

Undoing what we have called the original trauma, the primal scene, appears to have been a determining, if unconscious, theme in Joe Christmas' life. He does so by repeating it and changing the essential elements: eating food when and how he wills, or voluntarily refusing it though starved, rather than involuntarily vomiting; paying for food or sex, stealing money, and refusing to be given money, rather than accepting a bribe to keep quiet; and seeking out punishment and enduring it rather than having the strain of expecting it and not getting it.

Repetitiveness is inherent in mental life and is not limited to the undoing and mastery of trauma. In the smallest stages of perception, thought and memory, there is a moment-by-moment recapitulation of the development of these functions from distant past to present, a rhythmic alternation between blurring of boundaries and their redelineation. This melting down and recasting goes on subliminally. In perception it involves the merging of figure and ground and the re-emergence of forms and boundaries into the more or less familiar shapes of inner and outer, subject and object, self and other.

Faulkner's style slows down and makes explicit these split-second recurrences in mental functioning. He makes the clear, hard boundaries of conscious discrimination and separateness once again negotiable, blurred, and flexible. The senses merge, self and objects fuse, the tenses are flattened out and become inseparable, active and passive modes alternate, and the genders struggle within the same body. And then order is restored, reality is reconstituted with experience replenished, and the moment expanded. Faulkner's style mirrors the rhythm of the mind which, like music, follows recurrent time.

In perception and thought there are (primary process) rapid subliminal oscillations between global, scanning, condensing operations on the one hand, and (secondary process) discriminating, abstracting, focusing ones on the other. Both go on simultaneously and recurrently; the first one draws on levels of memory and symbolism, the second of shifting angles of attention. Their harmonious matching and sorting results in formed perception and conscious thought, against a matrix of latent personal meaning.

In music, vertical harmonics and horizontal melody lines synchronize two kinds of time: simultaneity and succession. Moreover, the statement of a theme is usually followed by variation on it and, finally, by a restatement and resolution. In both music and mind, recurrence in time permits the changing material to be worked through into patterns on the one hand of aesthetic form or, on the other, of meaning. Changing thematic material in music may be worked through many elaborations, while other elements such as tempo or key maintain constancy in the midst of change. And in emotional life, endless personal vicissitudes may be worked through and navigated successfully as long as a reliable sense of identity provides inner stability in spite of change.

Faulkner's style of rhythm, recurrence, and progression is peculiarly satisfying, both musically and psychologically, and it merits further examination.

Faulkner's sentences often appear to flow forward and to ebb back: "so often our deeds are not worthy of ourselves. Nor we of our deeds" (p. 382). As in music, an idea may be stated, then restated with a partial inversion that elaborates the theme: "He will have no more shame than to lie about being afraid, just as he had no more shame than to be afraid because he lied" (p. 407). In addition to employing the restatement with inversion, this example begins with the future tense and moves back to the past.

Sentences may overlap in describing an action, ebbing part of the way back, then driving further forward. As in perception or thought as well as music, there may be a first, fast scanning and summarizing sweep, then a series of fragmented, discerning examinations from various angles, until feelings are mobilized and reflections gathered, and then action moves forward again.

In the confrontation between the scoundrel Lucas Brown and the pregnant woman he had abandoned, Faulkner describes his eyes darting around the room; Lena is watching him, until he brings himself to look at her, then he breaks off the contact and flees. "Ceaselessly here and there about the empty room went his harried and desperate eyes. She watched him herd them . . . like two terrified beasts and drive them up to meet her own" (p. 406). We first see the action, then we observe Lena watching the action, then we examine the scene with the help of a metaphor. His eyes are like two terrified beasts herded together and forced against their will in her direction.

The metaphor sets up an anticipation. How might two terrified beasts behave when herded? The action is repeated, the anticipation is made explicit, then broadened: "She watched . . . his eyes

. . . like two beasts about to break, [and he] . . . would never catch them . . . and that he himself would be lost" (p. 406). The metaphor of the darting eyes and the herded beasts who break and flee is turned back upon their owner: "He himself would be lost." The owner of the beasts, the two wild eyes, finds this thought intolerable and his observation of the unwelcome scene is immediately disowned, attributed to his eyes only, and then moved even further away: "His eyes watched her . . . as though they were not his eyes" (p. 408). Then he fled.

In this confrontation between Brown and Lena and her child, we are once again back to a reworking of the primal scene. Instead of the child, Joe Christmas, being trapped while the dietician and her lover are in bed together, it is Lena and her sleeping newborn who are in bed together, and it is the former lover, Brown, who looks and flees out the window.

Indeed, there are a number of images in *Light in August* that could be taken as symbolic allusions to the primal scene. For example, Hightower nurtures his own obsession, the image of his grandfather being shot from a galloping horse; the figure of horse and rider unconsciously often stands for coitus. Freezing it into a silent, statuesque monument is one way of undoing the frightening impression made on the child by the movements of parental intercourse, and of dealing with the tumultuous affects observed and stimulated thereby. The significance is muted and distanced somewhat by transferring it from parents to a grandfather on horseback. On the other hand, its symbolic meaning is further betrayed when we discover much later that the "cavalry charge" was, in fact, a glorified cover for setting fire to a henhouse, raiding it, and being shot ignominiously with a fowling piece.

The symbol of horse and rider reappears in still clearer form when Joe Christmas, after striking down McEachern and stealing his wife's money from her secret hole, leaves on McEachern's galloping horse. He strikes it rhythmically across its rump with a heavy stick taken from Mrs McEachern's garden. When the horse will move no more he batters its head until the stick is reduced to a fragment. He then proceeds on foot to his whore where he, in turn, is beaten into insensibility.

The primal scene, as indicated by these few examples, encompasses so many confused affects and anxieties, it comes to stand as an example of recurrent time and the reworking of the past. So, when Faulkner finally succeeds in transforming it from rape, death and mayhem into a scene in which Lena's former lover, Brown, abandons her and her sleeping infant, it is – from the infant's point of view – a happy dream of pure wish fulfillment and total mastery: father–rival has been excluded and infant is in total possession of mother by merging with her in sleep. This represents an Oedipal as well as a pre-Oedipal triumph. As we shall see later, it prefigures yet another, and final, reworking of this theme.

"If only we could repeat time, change it, set it back," the various characters of the novel keep repeating. The dietician feels blind fury at the impossibility of turning back time just for an hour, a second. Hightower lives out the denial of time every day as though living in his dead grandfather's life. Mrs Hines asks for just one day like it hadn't happened (p. 367). Joe Christmas thinks he only dreamed it and it didn't happen (p. 226).

Against this recurrent wish for the undoing or negation of time is the insistent beat of inexorability of causal time and accountability. It reaches Hightower, who says to Lena about Byron: "You are probably not much more than half his age . . . . That, too . . . is . . . irremediable . . . . He can no more ever cast back and do, than you can cast back and undo" (p. 389). Christmas, too, finally reaches it: "I have never broken out of the ring of what I have already done and cannot ever undo" (p. 321), he thinks quietly. And he sets out to let himself get caught and enter the circle of judgment time.

The insistent beat of God's judgment time, which can be neither hurried nor delayed, sounds through Doc Hines, speaking as though with the voice of a ventriloquist in the next room, puppet-like, without inflection. Instead of inflection there is the drum-beat of unchanging rhythm: "And old Doc Hines went when God told him to go. But he kept in touch with God and at night he said, 'That bastard, Lord,' and God said, 'He is still walking My earth,' and old Doc Hines kept in touch with God and one night he wrestled and he strove and he cried aloud, 'That bastard, Lord! I feel! I feel the teeth and the fangs of evil!' and God said, 'It's that bastard. Your work is not done yet'" (p. 365).

The next line tells us that the sound of music from the distant church had long since ceased (p. 365). There follows the scene in which Mrs Hines wishes that time could be set back for one day; then Byron asks Hightower to alibi for Christmas and Hightower refuses. The chapter ends with the observation that the sound of insects beyond the open window had not faltered (p. 370).

Time and Fate do not falter. Moved by an unseen Player who acts through them, the characters speak words that do not signify anything (p. 380). Just people playing their parts, and now they were played out. In Byron's mind they are just like discarded toys gathering dust in a closet (p. 416).

What remains is natural time and the cycle of unchanging seasons and perpetual recurrence; and human time with the linear progression of cause and effect and certain death. But for the author who has been orchestrating recurrent and non-recurrent time with devices of plot and style, there is yet one final word. He brings us the gift of a "happy ending" and the news that human time is also circular and not linear. Perhaps it can be undone after all and played backward in memory and forward in hope and made to feel right, just as the tenses can be used interchangeably and the feeling of being of both genders can be experienced instead of being separate, alone, and finite.

The novel closes as a furniture dealer tells his wife how he had picked up a man, woman and newborn in his wagon: Byron, Lena, and her child. Within the safety, convention, and good humor of their marriage – and between two acts of intercourse – the furniture dealer recounts that Byron tried to have sex with Lena but she refused since it might wake the baby (p. 477). (A speech that Faulkner later referred to in an interview as "one of the calmest, sanest speeches I ever heard"; Stein, 1963: 80.) Byron left but he returned the next day to remain with her and the baby, saying that he had come too far now to quit.

So Joe Christmas' original trauma was again repeated and again corrected. The baby, little Joe of thirty years ago, continued to eat. He did not have to weep or go unheeded or be interrupted by his father; his virgin mother never had sex; no need for money nor cause for punishment. There never was a primal scene or original sin.

Conclusion

We would like to believe that time recurs, that through little changes, people do progress. But the flow of an individual's time is linear and irrevocable. Nor is it at all certain that people progress in the light of events. Faulkner doubts it. The characters in *Light in August* progress little. A few begin to accept that what is done is irrevocable, and begin to enter human-relational time. They become less alienated, more accountable. But then they suffer the despair that may go with love, one's own limitations, and finite time. Before dying they persist in doing what they do because they believe that's what they have to do. All their words, in the meantime, "were not even us, while all the time what was us was going on and going on without even missing the lack of words" (p. 380).

We would like to believe that because the generations renew themselves and because the rhythm of the season recurs endlessly we do too; and because each day dispels the night, what is done can always be undone, or at least somehow mediated. But while Nature is cyclical and the mind too functions according to the principle of mastery through repetition and adaptation, the relation of cause to consequence is inexorable and cannot be rescinded.

While learning the harsh lesson that all things have their price, and that the consequences of the flow of time cannot be undone, we have to think, act, and feel as though they might be undone. Faulkner's style, like human mental processes, resembles recurrent time. He evokes timelessness by recalling early periods of one's life; by interchanging tenses and modes, by treating the genders as ambiguous, and by using synesthesia, oxymoron, and images of fusion between the self and outside objects. Timelessness is also conveyed by numerous reworkings of the primal scene in the latent content of the novel. Finally, his "musical" rhythms express endless recurrence and thus stimulate the illusion that the individual, like Nature herself, is timeless. There is an ebb-and-flow, statement and reversal, image and inversion, as if an individual's time, like his mental rhythms or phrases of music, could be reversed; as if it were not "irremediable."

Faulkner presents us with no solution, no synthetic interpretation, but the universal dialectic between man's finiteness and his imagination. It corresponds with the task of the mind in accommodating, not necessarily reconciling, two intrinsically discordant streams of mental activity – and accurate registration of objective events and subjective needs – and is reflected in the orchestration of time with timelessness in *Light in August*.

Chapter 5

Music as temporal prosthesis

Reflections from the Sundown Syndrome

Music is the temporal art form *par excellence*. It is meaningful primarily through time. It projects a temporal process by offering aural images of temporality. Yet, surprisingly, music as a primary image of time has been little studied even by specialists in music (among the few exceptions are Greene, 1982; Kramer, 1988; Epstein, 1995).

It is the temporal element of music that is the focus of this chapter. My license to enter an area where few musical specialists dare to tread is the nocturnal delirium referred to as the Sundown Syndrome and its often remarkable response to music.

Since pathology often highlights a phenomenon that otherwise remains seamlessly invisible, this response of Sundowning to music may have something to tell us about the nature and function of music itself. This is the intended thrust of this chapter – *not* a reductively simplistic contribution to clinical neurology. Since the organization of the central nervous system is hierarchical, when there is damage the resulting impairment depends on the location of the insult, the systems involved, the loss of higher functions, the "release" of lower ones, and the degree of restoration and reintegration. Reductionism is inappropriate.

Sundowning is a general phenomenon of nocturnal delirium most commonly seen in the evenings in elderly persons with nonspecific cerebral damage and resultant dementia. The clinical picture is one of confusion and agitation, reduced ability to maintain attention to external stimuli, and disorganized thinking and speech. Perceptual disturbances such as illusions and hallucinations, and emotional disturbances such as anxiety, fear, anger, and paranoia, are common.

While those affected may demonstrate little or no dementia during the day, the change toward the evening can be dramatic and escalate rapidly so that it becomes clearly evident to those around them. Advanced age and cerebral damage predispose one to delirium from a variety of contributing causes such as intercurrent infection, dehydration, and cardiovascular disease. Sundowning has also been attributed to increasing fatigue and stress during the afternoon, medication side-effects, poor sleep, sensory deprivation and, because the compromised brain cannot handle novelty, the change of routine prior to the evening meal and preparations for bedtime.

As mentioned, the response to music can often be dramatic even when major neuroleptic (antipsychotic) and/or tranquilizing medication is ineffectual.

- A room full of restless, bickering, demented patients calmed down rapidly when the TV was turned off and replaced by soothing, orderly, and graceful music on the stereo like that of Handel or Bach.
- Another resident's crying and screaming stopped instantly when a Walkman was placed on her head and tuned in to an FM "soft-rock" station. With this technique it became possible to reduce her psychotropic medications.
- Playing country music made it possible for another patient to take regular five-hour car trips to a distant city. She sat up in her seat clapping her hands until she became sleepy. When she awakened and became irritable, increasing the volume of the music would always calm her.

Sacks (1973, 1985, 1995, 1998) has written eloquently about the dramatic effects of music on conditions other than Sundowning. The broken speech patterns and jerky movements of Tourette's, like the stiltedness and skewed posture of autism, can instantly normalize on singing; Parkinsonian crises and abnormal EEGs can disappear on *imagining* rhythmic music.

Tourette's and Parkinson's, however, are motor illnesses with specific timing problems (autism is a more profound matter) and do not necessarily speak toward dementia and Sundowning. Perhaps the most that can be said is that, whatever the contributing causes of the agitation and delirium of dementia in general, the temporal regularity of the Sundown Syndrome reflects a disturbance of the temporal sense of experience at some fundamental level. Since the biological circadian rhythm roughly follows a twenty-four-hour periodicity in phase with changes of light to dark, this is one likely site of the temporal desynchrony, *probably among others*.

Supporting this idea is the well-established sleep–wakefulness disturbance in dementia and its relation to delirium, as well as the observation that the diastolic blood pressure has been found to fall in the afternoon instead of its expected normal rise (Evans, 1987). The ensuing delirium may be viewed in part at least as an escalating panic or catastrophic reaction to a premonition that the perception of time flow is slipping away and threatening an imminent and disastrous loss of control. This will be my focus.

In essence, we have here a disorder of major temporal deregulation calmed not infrequently if only temporarily, by a temporal art form, namely music. The Sundown Syndrome, highlighting, I believe, the threatened loss of the experience of time flow, suggests that one normalizing function of music is to support the illusion that time "flows" in an ultimately orderly way. Thus, when needed, as in cases of temporal desynchrony due to organic damage to the nervous system, music can act as a temporal prosthesis. When not so needed, it silently supports our notion that our world of reality is as we experience it. And, to be sure, since we have so created it, so it is.

The illusion of time flow

Time is variously defined from different aspects: philosophical, physical, psychological and biological. The physical aspect of time will not concern us since from the point of view of physics, time is not an independent entity like space in a Newtonian universe; rather, time and space are inseparable aspects of a four-dimensional universe.

A neurophysiological basis for our experience of time will be discussed later in connection with the bodily basis for the shaping of time in music. Briefly, our experience of time may lie in a hierarchy of biological clocks in the nervous system, ranging from the vastness of circadian rhythms of sleep and wakefulness that synchronize with rhythmic phases of environmental change, down to regulators of periodicity in the metabolism of cells.

Philosophers debate the reality or unreality of time: is it an objective datum or a subjective projection? The popular view is that it is a real entity that flows uniformly. For Heraclitus the flow of time is of the essence of reality and cannot be grasped by reason. Henri Bergson, like Kant, held that the flow of time, by which he meant human advance through time, can be grasped only by non-rational intuition. He even held that the scientific concept of time as a dimension misrepresents reality. Alfred North Whitehead, too, believing it to be an important metaphysical fact, referred to time flow poetically as "the vivid fringe of memory tinged with anticipation" (Whitehead, 1920: 72–73).

The perception of time flow depends on our awareness of change. In Western societies time is conceptualized as linear and the experience of time flow is based on our awareness of sequence and duration. Sequence is the sense that one event follows another. Sequential events are separated by more or less lengthy intervals called durations. In other words, succession of mental events and their duration together constitute fundamental aspects of what we in the West perceive as change and project onto the external world in order to create the sense of time flow.

William James (1892) described the present moment as the "specious present," or "intuited duration." It consists of extending duration and succession back from the present into the past and forward into the future:

> A sort of saddle-back of time with a certain length of its own, on which we sit perched, and from which we look in two directions into time . . . with a bow and a stern, as it were – a rearward- and a forward-looking end.
>
> (James, 1892: 280)

> Its *content* is in a constant flux, events dawning into its forward end as fast as they fade out of its rearward one . . . . Meanwhile, the specious present, the intuited duration, stands permanent, like the rainbow on the waterfall, with its own quality unchanged by the events that stream through it.
>
> (James, 1892: 286).

A number of factors influence the perception of time flow. Especially interesting in the present context is the fact that the ear is particularly adapted to the awareness of change on which the perception of time flow depends. Thus, the ear is more sensitive than the eye in this respect. Other factors affecting the experience of time flow: stimulants make the experience of duration appear much longer; depressants, sensory deprivation and aging make the experience of duration seem shorter.

Psychoanalysis has contributed to our knowledge of disturbances in the experience of time flow, beginning with Freud (as quoted by

Bonaparte, 1940), in implicit agreement with Kant (the perception of time flow is a projection of our inner perception of the passing of our own life), Schilder (1936) (whatever negates the sense of self interferes with the sense of time), Orgel (1965) (time difficulties may sometimes be traced to early overstimulation and abandonment), Hartocollis (1976) (the experience of time should be seen as an inherent dynamic of all affective experience, especially in relation to need frustration and the integrity of the self), and Arlow (1986) (intrapsychic conflict influences how time is consciously experienced, e.g. *déjà vu*, timelessness and premonition; recurrent early patterns of need frustration and/or frustration set up enduring future expectations). Anthropology and linguistics have taught us that the experience of time is culturally relativistic. It is a Western idea that time is linear with duration and sequence as its basic constituents. There are many cultures that have nonlinear or cyclical concepts of time: Tibetans, South Indians, many tribes in Africa, the Hopi and Coeur d'Alene Native Americans, the Quiche Indians of Guatemala, the Javanese.

One example will suffice. The Trobriand Islands do not have a language for past, present and future. There are few words to communicate ideas of process, change, becoming or continuity. There are neither tenses nor words corresponding to our words for causality or comparison. Trobrianders value patterns of sameness, and draw no inferences from the past or predictions about the future. Time is part of a holistic pattern that accounts for events rather than one event leading to the next. Objects are named and identified by the state in which they are found.

From all this we may reasonably conclude that the *experience* of time – contrary to newer conceptions from quantum theory – serves us subjectively as an ordering principle. "Time does not flow or stand still, it does not expand or contract, it neither brings nor takes away, nor does it heal or kill" (Arlow, 1986: 514).

And the everydayism, "time flies" is a facile projection to ease an insufferable insult to immortal narcissism that it is not time that passes but we.

Musical images of time

Thanks to music, we have a man-made virtual image of time, just as plastic art creates virtual images of space (G.J. Rose, 1980). In music we may manipulate sequence and duration – each culture and era in its own way – to create an illusion of control over time flow; even to destroy the sense of its passage.

Motion is the central element of time flow. Rhythm, as organized movement in time, plays a large role in creating the effect of organic motion in music rather than merely endless undifferentiated time flow.

An overview of European music reveals that different concepts of rhythm prevailed at different times. In the thirteenth century there were strict rhythmic modes. During the Renaissance free oratorical speech rhythms predominated; in Renaissance polyphony there was almost a stressless flow. Strong body rhythms came to the fore in the Baroque era, and primitivistic rhythms in the twentieth century.

Greene (1982) offers a closer look at the different aural images of temporality projected by music. According to his analysis, Bach's music is an aural image of Newtonian time unfolding with lawful, inexorable necessity. The course of the music entails considerable uncertainty, but by the end it appears that everything has happened for a completely sufficient reason; everything that needed to happen has taken place in an enduring order that stands outside the temporal process, subordinate only to the supraordinate rationalistic principles of the Newtonian world-view.

In contrast, Baroque music contradicts the basic premise of Newtonian rationalism that the human mind can grasp the world's fundamental rationality. In its image of temporality it is the past that determines the future.

Romantic music portrays an inner self struggling with its own yearnings as well as a resistant world. Greene (1982) claims that it tells us as little about the external world as classical music tells about the self. While this may be disputed (Beethoven, Mozart), it is undoubtedly true that each style highlights what the others pass over.

Yet another perspective on musical images of time is provided by Kramer (1988). He summarizes the two different ways in which the dominant and non-dominant cerebral hemispheres program time, referring to them as linear and nonlinear styles respectively. Having made the important point that linearity and nonlinearity coexist and are complementary in all music, he goes on to correlate them predominantly with Western "horizontal" music and Eastern "vertical" music.

Western language and thought are linear and typical of the dominant cerebral hemisphere. Being eminently utilitarian, they have made possible the development of scientific thinking. Linear concepts of time are sequential and goal-directed; in the linear mode of time, time is a directional, durational *flow* from the past into the future with the present always falling behind us. In line with this, Western horizontal music is imbued with progress and change; it requires teleological listening; its tonality always strives for a return to the tonic, unchallenged by other keys.

Nonlinear thinking is more dreamlike, timeless, holistic and characteristic of the nondominant cerebral hemisphere; in the nonlinear mode of time the present is all that seems to exist. Eastern or oriental vertical music deals with consistency and persistence, stasis and eternity. There is little apparent flow. It does not build or release tension, it starts rather than begins, ceases rather than ends. There are no implications or expectations, no symbolism of referential meanings. It requires cumulative listening.

In addition to the revolutionary changes that have transformed the modern world in all respects, nonlinearity became more prominent in twentieth-century music more specifically because of the impact of recording technology and of non-Western music, especially the influence of the Java gamelan orchestra on Debussy (Kramer, 1988).

This deserves the following brief digression (summarized from Becker, 1979). The underlying assumptions of Javanese gamelan music, played by ensembles of from five to twenty-five instruments, mostly bronze gongs and bronze xylophones, have little in common with Western music. In Java, the fundamental governing principle in gamelan music is the cyclic recurrence of a melodic/temporal unit, which reflects the way in which the passage of time is also ordered. Time is represented as several concurrent cycles running simultaneously. Important days are reckoned as those points of coincidence between the different, continuously ongoing cycles: the five-day-week cycle, the seven-day-week cycle, the lunar-month cycle divided into halves, fourths and eighths.

The basic unit of gamelan music is a cycle marked off by a gong, subdivided into halves, quarters, eighths, etc., by instruments playing at successively greater levels of density, or at successively faster rates of speed. In the gamelan tradition, melody or tune was originally the result of a process of subdivision applied to a concept of cyclical time. Thus, while melodic variation is highly relevant to most Western music it is rather insignificant in Javanese music.

Kramer notes that, under such influence, some recent pieces of music in the West are totally undifferentiated temporally to produce unchanging consistency without progression, goal direction, movement or contrasting rates of motion or phrases. "The result is a single present stretched out into an enormous duration . . . that nonetheless feels like an instant . . . . Whatever structure is in the music exists between simultaneous layers of sound" (p. 55).

As Kramer further notes, such vertical music experience is consistent with the aesthetic articulated by Stockhausen as "moment time": each moment is independent and individual, centered in itself, existing on its own, thereby cutting across horizontal time perception into a timelessness and an eternity present in every moment. The sensuous present is favored over memory.

Vertical music is a radical cultural stretch. The ability to listen to it is usually suppressed in our dominant hemisphere-centered society; like a foreign language of time, listening to it – should one wish – requires learning, or a creative act.

It should be mentioned that many conditions – meditation, dreams, certain mental illnesses, hypnosis, psychedelic drugs and sensory deprivation – can create feelings of timelessness by diminishing linear thinking and goal orientation. The crucial difference between vertical time experiences and the common assumptions about schizophrenic time experiences (now being challenged) is the continuing availability of reality testing in the former – the temporal continuum is not destroyed (Melges, 1982). (Some examples of the time experience of dementia will be deferred till later.)

Bodily correlates of musical temporalities

Elsewhere (G.J. Rose, 1980), I have shown that the structure of aesthetic form – literary–poetic, visual art or music – has to do with orientation. It harmoniously accommodates the two fundamentally different frameworks with which the mind concurrently processes the data having to do with orientation for time, place, and person as well as with the many gradations in between.

The two different styles may be succinctly subsumed under (primary process) imagination and (secondary process) knowledge of reality: holistic merging as against delineated separateness; similarity versus difference; simultaneity as against change. The last is especially applicable to music, for example by synchronizing vertical harmonics and horizontal melodics, duration and succession.

I pointed out (G.J. Rose, 1980) there that the characteristics of imaginative as against knowledgeable processing of data appear to conform to the different cognitive styles of the two cerebral hemispheres. Put simplistically, the dominant hemisphere speaks, the nondominant one sings. As far as the creative process is concerned, it was suggested that a collateral integration of differently styled information coming from each side with as wide an access as possible to both seemed a better explanation than postulating a special cognitive process or regression in the service of the ego.

While the foregoing citation deals globally with the structure of aesthetic form including music, with special attention to the body in relation to creative imagination, the following material chiefly having to do with neuroscience focuses on music as the temporal art form. It is abstracted from Epstein (1995) and reflects a vast interdisciplinary literature.

Many biologists believe that oscillation, based on periodicity, may be the fundamental mode of living systems. There are biological clocks throughout the nervous system on various hierarchic levels precisely regulating bodily activities. The nervous system itself functions by way of periodicity: it sends out intermittent firings which result in a continuous movement, sensation or state.

A pacemaker in the hypothalamus, in the same area that receives visual information about day and night, controls circadian rhythms of wakefulness and sleep. The length of neural loops is another basic element for estimating time: the larger the loop, the longer is the interval of time, thus enabling the nervous system to entertain various time cycles concurrently.

The electroencephalogram registers "brain waves" but there are also many non-nervous-system organs that contribute rhythmic information that is integrated by the nervous system, for example, the cardiovascular, cardiorenal, alimentary, and glandular systems. Metabolic processes control rhythms in nervous and muscle cells. Chemical pacemakers control the speed with which oxygen is metabolized in some cells of the brain on which the time sense of human beings depends.

The fundamental premise of Epstein's argument is that

> Our biological mechanisms are . . . a major basis by which we make music and control time and timing in music. The periodic manner in which our biological timing mechanisms function is seen as the quintessential factor that controls our

sense of [musical] pulse. And pulse is the prime aspect of tempo. (p. 136)

While these are not universally accepted by specialists, Epstein finds direct reflections of coordinated biological timing mechanisms in two musical phenomena: proportional tempo and the cubic curve description of rate changes in accelerando and ritardando.

Proportional tempo was mentioned in Chapter 1. It refers to the idea that all tempos in a piece of music, whether made up of single or multiple movements, are intrinsically related in ratios of a low order. This helps organize the whole work into a coherent whole. Epstein writes (1995: 105): "The implications of proportional tempo . . . involve not music alone but neurobiology as well, and thereby our psychological perception of our biological response."

Concerning cubic curve, there appears to be an innate tendency of the nervous system to control changing time series in a manner that can be described graphically by an S-shaped cubic curve. Smooth changes of velocity of limb and joint movements, for example, conform to such a curve. The same curve also describes the trajectory or shaping of ritardandos and accelerandos in music when performed with maximal smoothness.

Musical performance, according to Epstein, thus has to do with playing musical proclivities with and against innate neural ones. Take tempo rubato, for instance:

> Rubato seems the ultimate degree of playing with time. In its stretching and compression of phrase it tantalizes and dares us, exerting a kind of musical brinkmanship . . . . Done well, it rescues us from the edge, falling back into phase with our expectations . . . . These various modes by which our innate sense of periodicity is played with . . . deal with . . . our need to organize the passage of time . . . [in accordance with] a physiology that has evolved in a way that makes this organization possible. (p. 482)

Music as "prosthesis" for time flow

(The following is abstracted from Melges, 1982.) An intact brain is necessary for the temporal organization of the mind. The human brain as a whole may be considered to be a highly specialized, time-binding organization since no one brain center is primarily involved with timing and temporal processes. Different areas contribute to the temporal processing in different ways. The parietal lobe, for example, has to do with the sequential ordering of events; its impairment makes tasks like dressing and undressing oneself nearly impossible.

Once a time distortion takes place, whatever its cause, it alters the psychological organization of time flow. When mental sequences become even mildly disconnected, present experiences seem to last longer and are relatively isolated from past and future events, seeming to "stand alone."

In addition, the inability to sustain a continuous train of thought leads the person to attend to a variety of present stimuli that would ordinarily be screened out of consciousness. Perhaps it is the incipient breakdown of sequential thinking that gives rise to the prolongation of the present which, being focused upon, enhances one's awareness of current sensations, seeming to heighten them.

As the fragmentation of sequences becomes more pronounced, past, present and future become telescoped. Past and future collapse into the present which is experienced as a "timeless now" – "awash in a sea of immediacy" (Gray, 1993: 91): a succession of moments strung loosely together, all present and immediate with little yesterday and still less tomorrow.

Memories and expectations seem as real as present perceptions. For example: "I think I hear [present perception] A—— [daughter] in your mother's parlor [reference to forty years ago]. Before your folks [long deceased] come home [future expectation]. My mother is dead [sobbing about a distant event as though it had freshly occurred]."

Fantasy and reality are confused with each other. Example: "I saw my brother. It was wonderful! But he looks so much worse since he died!"

Conversing with a person in this situation has been described as "creating . . . an . . . island together in the ceaseless flow of time" (Gray, 1993: 42), especially as the person may revert to a native language. Example:

Resident: *Je suis morte.*
Visitor: What did you say?
Resident: I'm dead. I've been telling you that for six months [impatiently].

Visitor:	What's it like?
Resident:	Not bad . . . Compared to here.
Visitor:	What's it like here?
Resident:	The people. Not exactly my genre.

Several years later the inexorable course of the disease had destroyed most of the resident's capacity for spontaneous speech, motility, responsiveness or affect. Nevertheless, a core of identity was tenaciously preserved. It was elicited by an attendant *singing* to her to rouse her from her almost continuous dozing.

Resident:	*(with pleased surprise)* I'm not dead!
Attendant:	No, dear. You're alive!
Resident:	*(tentatively, but with the terse, stubbornly objective clarity that had always been her trademark)* Maybe . . . .

When the whole brain becomes impaired, as in the Sundown Syndrome, all components of psychological time – duration, sequence and temporal perspective – become chaotic and behavior becomes markedly disorganized. Being unable to locate oneself in the context of time flow of previous happenings, any event like a door slamming seems jarringly unfamiliar; it readily triggers panic that all controls are failing – one is at the mercy of random events. As mentioned earlier, when the Sundown Syndrome escalates into delirium, this represents a classic catastrophic reaction based on the premonition of disastrous loss of control due to organic deficiency.

Music, a man-made acoustic microcosm of controlled time flow, would appear to function as a temporal prosthesis for such a damaged system of temporal regulation. The resident cited above would often peacefully "keep" time with recorded music, literally and concretely, torso and shoulders rhythmically swaying "in" time with the music. This bodily gesture was uncharacteristic of her before her illness. Music had always been important and she readily acknowledged that it was more important now, but she could not say why or how.

This behavior is a surface manifestation of the fact that music can *entrain* vital functions of the body, i.e. cause the body to fall into synchrony with the music. Such entrainment represents a coupling between external periodicity and the innate periodicity –

in this case flawed – within the nervous system. Entrainment by music has been traced to heart rate, muscular activity and respiration (Harrer and Harrer, 1977). Some experimental subjects tended to synchronize with the music primarily through heartbeat; others through breathing. (Animal experimentation succeeded in entraining periodic oscillators in various aspects of the nervous system to the periodicity of an external driving force provided it was within the range of the living system's periodicities.)

The often remarkable response of the Sundown Syndrome to music would appear to be based on a neurobiological entrainment of the person to the periodicity of the music. This in turn provides needed support to temporal regulators throughout the nervous system. (A later chapter discusses the psychological dynamics of the affective response to music.)

Two other issues are relevant in the present context. The first has to do with the earliest stages of perception and reality testing. Freud (1895, 1925a) speculated that early perception seeks not to find an object as much as to *re-find* it. He suggested that primitive perception and thought aim at establishing an identity between outside and inside, and so we tend to perceive that which comes close to what is already inside in the form of a presentation. Freud guessed that the original one was mother's breast.

Some early infant observations suggest a modification of this speculation:

1 Severe head-banging in infants may be stopped by a metronome at the same or a slightly greater frequency than that of the heartbeat (Lourie, 1949).
2 Newborns cry less and gain more weight when a normal heartbeat is played continuously in the nursery (Salk, 1965).

Perhaps the internal periodicity of neurobiological mechanisms responds preferentially to concordant, i.e. identical or proportional, external periodicities. Thus, returning to Freud's speculation, primitive reality testing may be seeking not the mother's breast, literally, but rather the rhythm and motion that is recognized as one's own milieu and the identification with that.

This leads to a second psychological issue relevant to the present context: self-recognition. Rhythm and motion are crucial to how adults come to recognize themselves. Allport (1937: 487–488) quotes a 1931 German study by W. Wolff. Experimental subjects frequently failed to identify their own voices, styles of retelling a story, pictures of their own hands, sometimes not even their own profiles, but were better at recognizing these corresponding features in their friends.

In order to study the significance of *gait* upon one's self-recognition, subjects were dressed in loose-fitting garments, heads covered or blocked out to control all extraneous cues, and they were filmed walking. All subjects recognized their own gait, but subjects failed in seventy per cent of the trials to identify the gait of friends. This is a curious finding since one often sees the gait of friends yet seldom sees one's own. Allport concluded that, in addition to a number of measurable specific attributes of gait (regularity, speed, elasticity, etc.), the most important and non-measurable one was *rhythm*, probably created by the sum total of all of them.

One might say that these experimental subjects recognized themselves kinesthetically, i.e. from within. If this is so, it is perhaps related to Sacks' observations (previously cited) on the dramatic response of some neurological conditions to music: music transformed individuals for the moment into their former selves, making manifest the healthfulness behind the disease.

How did music allow them to rediscover and recognize themselves anew? Describing the Parkinsonian crises of obstructive–explosive behavior of a particular patient, Sacks writes:

> This power of music to integrate and cure, to liberate the Parkinsonian and give him freedom while it lasts . . . is quite fundamental, and seen in every patient . . . . With this sudden imagining of music, this coming of spontaneous inner music, the power of motion, action, would suddenly return, and the sense of substance and restored personality and reality . . . . But then, just as suddenly, the inner music would cease, and with this all motion and actuality would vanish, and she would fall instantly, once again, into a Parkinsonian abyss . . . . Music serves to arouse her own quickness, her living-and-moving identity and will, which is otherwise dormant.
>
> (Sacks, 1973: 60–61)

As to what kind of music would be effective:

> Rhythmic impetus . . . "embedded" in melody. [Neither] shapeless crooning [nor] raw or overpowering rhythm . . . . The only music which affected her in the right way was music she could

enjoy; only music which moved her "soul" had this power to move her body. *She was only moved by music which moved her* [original italics]. The "movement" was simultaneously emotional and motoric, and essentially autonomous.

(Sacks, 1973: 61–62)

The possibility presents itself that music – because of the periodicity, motion, and tension and release at its inner structure – taps into our capacity to recognize our unique identities from within. It becomes an external mirror for the temporal, motional and affective workings of our mind.

The Sundowning response to music, as in Sacks' patients, may have to do with self-recognition, union, reinforcement. Inner, neurobiological periodicity, rhythm and the tension and release of affect find mimetic reflection and become seamlessly integrated with the external periodicity, motion, and tension and release of music. And by dint of this union, there may be sufficient reinforcement of one's own identity to transcend organic and affective limitations. (This will be discussed further in a later chapter.)

What further implications may we draw regarding the nature and function of music itself?

From the point of view of physics, space-time is an inseparable dimension of the universe; time, in and of itself, is not a given. From anthropological studies we know that the experience of time flow – as distinct from time itself – is not a universally shared concept but rather a socially constructed form of order imposed on experience (Seeger, 1987).

Some form of music, however, is universal. It would appear that all music is a temporal mirroring of our innermost neurobiology; on a psychological level, such mirroring would also have to do with self-recognition.

Just as music itself is universal, so is some kind of experience of time flow – far-ranging though it may be in all its cultural diversity, including playing with its absence.

Psychologically, music exploits the experience of time flow. This supports, as by a prosthesis, the necessary illusion that we shape time itself.

Why "illusion?" Because music creates virtual time, as art does virtual space.

Why "necessary?" Because both, though illusional, are underpinnings of the constructs of our "reality." We create music and art in our own image. They are mimetic images, as Leonardo wrote of painting, of "the motion of mind."

For the neurologically maimed, music may act as a psychobiological temporal prosthesis. For others it acts, like other arts, to support the illusion that reality is self-centered. They are all self-created "witnesses" in our own image – no less than religion – to "verify" oneself against ultimate solitude.

Chapter 6

In pursuit of slow time
Modern music and a clinical vignette

The creative artist is often fine-tuned to currents of unconscious thought and feeling in inner and outer worlds. This being so, the arts may not only reflect the times but also prefigure them.

Music, the art of time, may mold the perception of the flow of time in such a way as to balance defensive with creative purposes. It may, for example, represent the wishful illusion that the flow of time is controllable – that time is cyclical as well as linear. Perhaps in this way it can serve as an unconscious defense against the fear of death.

The argument of this chapter is that this may be, at least in part, what some music of the modern era is "getting at" – and foretelling. Juxtaposing a clinical vignette to some innovations in the musical approach to time suggests that some of this music, like some traumatized patients, responds to the anticipation of imminent yet unpredictable violence by altering the perception of time itself. Creative and defensive aspects of mastery unite to transform and expand the perception of this temporal dimension of contemporary reality through the means of music.

The art of the novel treats the stuff of personality as a malleable medium. The novelist reaches into himself/herself to discover the raw material of memory and imagination, therein fashioning characters and narrative possibilities. They reflect the potential and the limits of the "multiple personalities" within each of us.

Music, too, treats its material as a malleable aesthetic medium. However, its material being time, and nonverbal, we are confronted with especially formidable problems – problems regarding the nature of time, and the need to use language to discuss a nonverbal art-form.

The Greeks used two different terms, *kairos* and *chronos*, to refer to different modes of experiencing time and organizing behavior in relation to it. The term *kairos* remained in classical Greek only and did not come down through Latin into the Romance languages. It denotes the human and living time of intentions or goals. It is episodic time with a beginning, a middle, and an end. It has to do with the flux of Heraclitus – a confluence of past memory, present perception, and future desire. These coexist in the ongoing human experience, along with preconscious awareness and unconscious motivation.

Chronos, on the other hand, is clock-time. It refers to the measurable time of succession, before and after, earlier and later. It has to do with the static atomism of Parmenides, the discontinuous world of fixed and constant entities in empty space. Instead of a range of preconscious awareness and a whole field of unconscious motivational forces, there is a conscious, focused perception of the passage of units of time.

This is not to say that there are two types of time, one real and one unreal. Nor, for that matter, are there three types of time – past, present, and future. There is only one time. It is a mental abstraction, not a thing. It does not do things, such as "flow" in any direction, either linear or cyclical. There are cyclical events, like the seasons, day and night, and serial events, like growth, aging, and death. Whether one experiences time as primarily cyclical or serial depends partly on one's attitude toward death. The cyclical experience of time denies death; the serial experience of time accepts it.

Chronos and *kairos*, in other words, are different ways of *experiencing* time as well as of expressing certain truths about the relations between events (A.N. Whitehead). For Newton, "true" time was absolute and mathematical time in a uniform flow. For Bergson, this so-called true time of Newton was a fiction as opposed to Bergson's *durée réele*. For Cassirer, neither concept sufficed; each represented a partial view into a whole – a particular standpoint of consciousness. Both must be understood as *symbols* that the mathematician and the physicist take as a basis in their view of the outer world, and the psychologist in his view of the inner one.

The conception of the physical world requires only the chronological aspect of time. Both views, however, are necessary for a conception of the human world. Furthermore, while the world is both atomic and in flux, continuous and discontinuous, static and flowing, objective and subjective, concrete and abstract, universal and particular, one cannot experience both of these awarenesses of time cognitively at the same time. Instead, there is an oscillation between the two, organizing our experience of the world (Jacques, 1982).

The dual experience that the cognitive mode cannot accomplish, the aesthetic mode makes possible. By treating time as an aesthetic medium, music is able to bridge two different dimensions of time and harmoniously accommodate diversity and unity, change and constancy. Just as the novel treats the constituents of the person as having the plasticity of an aesthetic medium suitable for shaping into new, self-consistent characters, music deals with time as being infinitely flexible while retaining its inner integrity.

Through the use of various devices (ornamentation, the minor key, moving from one key to another, dissonance) it causes delay and arouses the tension of anticipating what will come next (Meyer, 1956, 1967). At the same time, many of the melodic, rhythmic and harmonic variations introduced for the sake of apparent variety are actually repetitions and recurrences in disguise (Bernstein, 1976). Being experienced as returns to the familiar, they are associated with the reduction of tension. Thus, in music, one may experience the tension of change together with the release of tension that comes with the return to constancy (G.J. Rose, 1980). Moreover, since the built-in delays and concealed recurrences act as a steady stimulus to memory as well as an anticipation of what will come next, there is a conflating of past and future. In music, past and future coexist with the present as a dynamic whole. This whole is built up in an accumulation of wave after wave of intensification. In other words, instead of being viewed as a static measure – divisible into equal parts – of the transient events that give *form* to experience, time is revealed as a dynamic force, reflecting the complexity, volume, and variability of the *content* of psychic life (Zuckerkandl, 1956).

How else may one account for the widespread impact of a "simple" musical structure such as the famous first movement of Beethoven's "Moonlight Sonata" (no. 14 in C-sharp minor, opus 27/2)? One of the most popular pieces of keyboard music, it has inspired at least two novels and several paintings and poems. It has even been arranged for chorus and orchestra with the words of the "Kyrie" as a text. According to Czerny, Beethoven himself resented the popularity of the work. Nor did he have anything to do with its programmatic title. The phrase, "Moonlight, or a boat passing the wild scenery of Lake Lucerne in the moonlight," was applied to the sonata by the poet-musician Rellstab thirty years after its composition.

The three-note melody is itself only a slight variation of its three-note accompaniment. The accompaniment figures gradually become an end in themselves as they rise from the middle to the upper registers of the piano and back to the role of accompaniment. The original melody then returns. The brief coda is based on the rhythm of the melodic motif, which was itself derived from the rhythm of the accompaniment.

Obviously, this structure is devoid of any referential meaning to things outside itself. It has nothing to do with either moonlight or other scenes from nature, let alone abstract concepts such as courage or longing. Rather, the accumulation of three-note wave after similar wave combines near-constancy with minute differences, and this gradual intensification of focused attentions is associated with mounting feeling. Such feeling, in fact, is associated with the same physiological changes that occur during emotional experience: changes of pulse, respiration, blood pressure, electrical conductivity of the skin, delay in the onset of muscular fatigue (Mursell, 1937).

This emotion, according to Langer (1942, 1953), is the "meaning" of music; it is a representation of the emotional quality of subjective, lived time made audible – an auditory apparition of felt-time. Instead of vaguely sensing time as we do through our own physical life processes, we hear its passage. But it is not a trickle of successive moments as it is in the conceptual framework of classical physics with which we usually operate in practical life. "Musical time is not at all like clock-time. It has . . . voluminousness and complexity and variability that make it utterly unlike metrical time" (Langer, 1957: 37). Music sounds the way feelings feel, mirroring their ups and downs, motion and rest, fulfillment and change.

Langer's distinction between discursive and presentational symbols is a helpful one. *Discursive* symbols are readily translatable and have fixed definitions. Music, on the other hand, like all the arts, expresses the quality of emotional life through *presentational* symbols. Presentational symbols are untranslatable; they are understandable only through their relations within the total structure of the work. The meaning of a piece of music lies entirely within the work – that is, in its own formal structure and inner relations. Unlike ordinary language, presentational symbols capture the flux of sensations and emotions.

For example, music can express opposites simultaneously and so capture the ambivalence of content better than words or language. In addition to such simultaneity, the linear unfolding of music in the course of time also mirrors the "shapes" of emotions. Music sets up expectations, interposes delays, and grants hidden recurrences before reaching a final resolution. The frustration of expectations is associated with rising tension, its gratification with release of tension. Tension–release embodies feeling. And it is precisely this element – the balance between tension and release – that has been called the specific dynamic of musical form (Toch, 1948: 157).

Artist-analyst Marion Milner's *On Not Being Able to Paint* (1957) and musician-philosopher Victor Zuckerkandl's posthumously published *Man the Musician* (1973) provide important insights into the relationship of language to nonverbal art. Both make a clear distinction between formal, logical thinking, on the one hand, and creative or aesthetic thinking on the other. According to formal logic, all thought which does not make a total separation between what a thing is and what it is not is irrational. Thus, according to formal logic, the whole area of symbolic expression is irrational, since the point about a symbol is that it is both itself and something else. Formal logic, then, gives a false picture in aesthetics; this false picture is avoided, Milner writes, only "if we think about art in terms of its capacity for fusing . . . subject and object, seer and seen and then making a new division of these" (p. 161).

Similarly, Zuckerkandl spells out the differences between objective hearing and musical hearing. The "I" that hears music, he writes, is different from the "I" who is the subject of a sentence, who is going to attend to outside signals in order to react to them in one way or another. The listener to music is more like the swimmer who allows himself to be carried by the water as he swims. Language, being firmly tied to subject–object predicate structure, fails us here. The "I" that listens to music is no longer something that "does" – that is, hears and now "has" the results of what it has done; namely, the sensations of tones. Hearing music involves hearing not only tones but also their direction, tension, motion, organic structure. It is the kind of hearing that moves with the tones and draws the hearer into their motion. Thus, it involves an interpenetration of subject and object, within rationality, drawn into the experience of the movement of felt-time (Zuckerkandl,

1973: 160–162). The similarity to psychoanalytic listening is so striking as to require no comment.

Both Milner and Zuckerkandl make it clear that aesthetic hearing or viewing is more like creative, nonlogical thinking; also, that both are quite different from objective perception and cognitive, logical thinking. The difference lies in the opposition between subject and object (their separateness) in the case of cognitive, logical thinking, and in the togetherness of thinker and thought (their mutually influential motion) in aesthetic, creative thinking.

Milner summarizes the problem neatly:

> Clearly the great difficulty in thinking logically about this problem is due to the fact that we are trying to talk about a process which stops being that process as soon as we talk about it, trying to talk about a state in which the "me/not-me" distinction is not important, but to do so at all we have to make the distinction. (p. 161)

Turning now from the psychological to the cultural pole, perhaps nothing less than profound scholarship is able to show satisfactorily how a musical style is part of the expressive life of a culture. For example, Charles Rosen (1980) considers the evolution of sonata form out of eighteenth-century arias and concertos. In the late eighteenth century sonata form changed from being music for the court or church into music for a new concert audience, the rising middle class; musical themes took on the dramatic roles and tensions found in opera and were resolved with classical order and proportion. In the nineteenth century sonata form became something else again: it provided prestige, respectability, and constraint for the romantic impulse and a vehicle for the virtuoso's performance.

A comparable study is yet to be written for music of the modern era and contemporary times. In the meantime, two considerations seem obvious. First, the experience of time has become drastically different from what it was previously. As during other disturbed periods in history, our era is characterized by pervasive, random violence, meaningless death, and bankrupt faith. Man has long known dread of total extinction, of course, but never its actual feasibility through instruments of destruction of unprecedented speed, range, and scope. While previous ages had a wider margin of time to buffer the unpredictability of life and powerful religious ideologies to rationalize the seemingly senseless, our own age is largely lacking in both. Secondly, while it would be impossible to prove that such a profound change in our temporal experience is reflected in contemporary music, it is plausible to assume it.

As representatives of music in the modern era, if not the most recent, I have arbitrarily selected Charlie Parker's bebop jazz and Arnold Schoenberg's twelve-tone atonal music. Both, in reflecting a new experience of time, also contributed significantly to altering the musical experience of time. A clinical vignette that throws some light on the psychological meaning of this altered sense of time is shown by the case of a woman who thought her appointment was one hour earlier than it was, at 3:00 p.m. instead of at 4:00. She then came fifteen minutes late for the imagined appointment (at 3:15), slept in the waiting room, and left fifteen minutes before the actual appointment was about to begin (at 3:45). As I hope to show, she was uprooting time from its usual matrix in a way somewhat analogous to certain aspects of modern music. But first to Charlie Parker and Arnold Schoenberg.

At the end of the Second World War, highly educated black people were coming into the mainstream of American society. Even Duke Ellington was not sophisticated enough for their taste. Hindemith and Stravinsky were becoming known to innovative jazzmen. Hindemith's own instrument was the viola, but he had played drums in jazz bands in European hotels before coming to the United States in 1940, and his "Symphonic Metamorphosis on Themes by Weber" has a strong jazz flavoring. But it was Stravinsky who was the main hero to jazz musicians because he was pushing beyond conventions. The great bebop innovators in America – Charlie Parker, Dizzy Gillespie, Thelonious Monk, Art Blakey, Kenny Clarke, Max Roach – looked on him almost as a god. (As did the pioneers of modern jazz, like Miles Davis and John Coltrane, who later took their music even further out.)

Despite these connections to the past, however, bebop of the 1940s and early 1950s represents a startling break from preceding jazz styles, and one that still causes some discomfort among today's listeners. Ron Rose (1980), in an unpublished ethnomusicological paper, maintains that the musical changes brought about by the bebop movement strongly reflected the changing black self-image in America. I am indebted to him for what follows on bebop.

Dixieland had its childhood in New Orleans. It became refined into the smoother and more "literate" styles in the years to follow, reaching its height of polish under the rule of the big band style where improvisation (the original tenet of jazz) became the exception rather than the rule . . . . Bebop . . . appears to be a clear and unsubtle black rebellion against the white dominated swing scene, as well as the historically established caricature of the black entertainer as mindless and officiously amusing . . . . The bebop musicians were intent upon creating a music which would allow a complete break from its "illiterate" black predecessor, and their white competitors. The music itself . . . with its difficult chord changes and rhythmic bridges, often executed at breakneck speeds, helped keep the movement "pure" of musicians not entirely competent, as well as create a new standard for the white establishment.

The leader of the bebop movement was Charlie Parker. (While he was considered one of the major innovative forces in the history of jazz, he himself said that if he could take a year off he would go to Yale to study with Hindemith.) Perhaps his major contribution was his conception of the musical phrase as tied to, yet at the same time free from, limitations of meter. Specifically, while the musical phrase had previously been restricted to the bar-lines, he extended it through the bar-lines. This means that, as soloist, he would sometimes speed up, sometimes slow down, to bring the melodic line "out of sync" with the underlying metric foundation, which was all the while being provided reliably by the other instruments. The relationship between the melodic line and the rhythmic pulse was thus rendered much more ambiguous; that relationship was no longer bound to the downbeat. Instead of classic syncopation, with its stress on up or downbeats, melodic emphasis could now be placed on any division of the beat on a sixteenth- and thirty-second-note level. This led other jazz musicians to experiment with unorthodox meters, fragment the beat until the meter became indiscernible, or blur the distinction of the downbeat much as a twelve-tonist avoids the concept of a tonic.

In short, Parker's restructuring of pulse into what might be called a fluid meter superimposed on a metric foundation turned the rhythmic conventions of Western popular music on end. One far-reaching effect was to shift the functions of the other instruments. The beat could now be displaced to the lighter cymbals, freeing the drum to become a most articulate instrument on its own. Similarly, the pianist's left hand was freed to pursue a different path.

Just as Parker's rhythmic innovations loosened the relationship between the melodic line and the underlying beat, Schoenberg's twelve-tone scale had already freed musical harmonics from the concept of the tonic. This also had far-reaching effects on the musical experience of time. A brief excursion into musical theory is necessary to show how.

It is possible to consider that the most important fact about music – its basic ingredient – is not so much sound as movement (Sessions, 1950). Music embodies, defines, and qualifies movement. Each musical phrase – that portion of music that must be performed in a single breath – is a unique gesture that moves constantly toward the goal of completing a cadence. Everything else – the appropriateness of harmonies, melodic intervals, the details of rhythmic elaboration – depends on it. Hearing music is hearing the dynamic quality of tones – that is, hearing their direction, their movement. (In the same way, seeing a picture involves seeing the force, direction, intention in form and color.)

A musical scale is one of the main ways of organizing the current of motion. The scale is a system of order among tones. It describes the relationship among the tones making up the musical organization of a culture. The scales are based on the physical phenomenon of overtones making up the harmonic series. (It is said that using the overtone series for musical theory actually dates back to the ancient Greeks and Chinese, who found the overtone series useful in establishing the norms of pitch relationships, scale structure, and so on.) The starting point or tonic tone in the key of C is C; the tonic tone in the key of G is G, and so forth. The main or dominant overtone of the tonic is five tones away and is called the fifth. The main overtone or dominant of C in the key of C is G. One may move from the key of C to its main overtone, G, and then take that as the starting point, or tonic, of the key of G. One may move in the key of G to its main overtone or dominant, D, and the key of D; thence to its main overtone or dominant, A, and the key of A; thus on to the keys of E, B, F#, and ultimately back to C, completing the circle. This moving from one key to another, from tonic to dominant, makes possible a circle of fifths. It is based on the underlying organization of the scale, namely, a stable relationship of tonics and dominants based on the universal *physical* phenomenon of the harmonic series of overtones.

A second point: because of the tonal organization of the scale, the tones strive in certain directions. They have driving qualities.

This accounts for one of the main ways in which music sets up a current of motion, a system of expectancies. For example, the tonic tone of any key is the one of ultimate rest and stability toward which all other tones tend to move. The octave and fifths and fourths were already binding forces for the ancients. They were relationships so fundamental that they became decisive points of reference around which to organize tones. Together they defined the space within which melody could coherently move.

In the West, other intervals were gradually incorporated into the service of musical expression – thirds, sixths, sevenths, seconds, and finally, augmented and diminished intervals. Each new conquest was associated with a new struggle. The use of these intervals led eventually to the use of chords and a new dimension in music – namely, tonality – and the modulation from one key to another, as well as major and minor modes. "Tonality implies a kind of perspective in sound, sometimes compared rather shrewdly to perspective in visual art. For it makes possible a system of relations which are unequal in strength, in emphasis, or in significance" (Sessions, 1950: 40).

Thus, because of a combination of the universal physical phenomenon of the harmonic series and cultural evolution, tones that come before lead the Western ear to expect that certain tones will come after. This is so even though, in order to build up tension, this motion or expectancy may be delayed in various musical ways already mentioned.

Tonal music feels like the natural experience of time flow to Western listeners because it is *learned* so early, but it is far from universal. Training and culture are important factors. For example, a Western listener interprets the vibrato (a slight fluctuation of pitch often less than a semitone) as a constant pitch with a rich sound. An Indian musician, however, whose native music is based on microtones – intervals smaller than the semitone – may perceive the Western vibrato as a significant fluctuation of pitch probably meant to express agitation. Even the basic ability to distinguish the octave – so basic that it is shared by white rats (Winner, 1982) – may be lost if one is immersed long enough in another culture where such an interval is unimportant (the music of Australian aborigines).

Now, if we could set up a series of tones which was lifted out of the gravitational pull of tonics and dominants, the overtones of the harmonic series, we would no longer be in a secure circle of fifths, going from one key to another in an orderly way. Any single tone would no longer carry implications of where it came from or where it was going. In other words, we would be taken out of the ordinary flow of time – from past to expected future.

Essentially, this was what Schoenberg did with his twelve-tone scale. It represents a whole system based on rootlessness from the harmonic series. The twelve tones and their sequence are selected in such a way that no tone has any implications regarding the tone that preceded it or the tone that may follow it; much of the directedness of tones has been rendered inoperative. Each of the tones can be played forward, backward, in mirror-image, or backward *and* mirrored. Since there are twelve tones in the Schoenberg system, we now have forty-eight possible sequences. All of them alter the ordinary experience of time as we know it in the West – not, it must be stressed, by tampering with time directly (for example, through rhythmic changes) but through changes in the tonal system, setting up ambiguous expectancies.

In addition to these changes in tonality that modify our expectancies of what will follow what musically, in much of the music of the twentieth century there is a deliberate dissolution of the sequential flow of music events as we have come to know it. Instead of a musical event in a composition depending on at least one previous musical event in order to build up to a climax or resolve tension, each musical event arises independently. For example, the sections of a piece of music may be put together in any possible sequence from one performance to the next with no set beginning or ending. Instead of development and recapitulation as we know them in sonata form, for instance, a piece of music in so-called vertical time does not purposefully set up expectations or fulfill any that might arise accidentally. The listener is forced to give up any expectation, any implication of cause and effect, antecedents and consequents. The sounds are unhampered and also unhelped by referential meaning. The experience has been compared to looking at a piece of sculpture: each viewer is free to walk around it, view it from any angle, in any possible sequence, linger long or briefly with each, leave, return, whatever. In "vertical time" there is nothing to direct the way time passes (Kramer, 1981).

In other words, in the new temporalities in music, past and future have been collapsed into a present moment which floats in uncertainty. There being no impulsion from the past, the overarching present leads to no-future. More than this: the bond tieing

cause and consequence together has been loosened and meanings
are cast adrift.

However, having stated this boldly for the sake of clarity, it must
be noted that experienced listeners to contemporary music insist
that while at first it may sound random, expectancies inevitably
emerge and order the musical experience – even that of John Cage.
Thus has it ever been with innovation. What is at first disturbingly
new becomes even comfortably familiar. The dialectic between new
and strange and good old familiar is inherent in any organically
evolving process.

Not only music but art and literature for decades have been
foretelling and mirroring a world unhinged from the conventions
of time, space, and causality that had traditionally supplied order.
Take art: if discontinuity is the key to the new temporalities in
music, fragmentation describes much of art history after the turn of
the twentieth century and before the Second World War. Cézanne
fragmented the image; the cubists fragmented shape; the impres-
sionists and pointillists, light and color; the surrealists, reality itself.

After the Second World War, abstract expressionism and then
minimalist painting rejected the illusion of three-dimensionality as
well as all imagery of symbolism which might permit any conventional meaning to be read into these paintings. Instead, oversize
canvases and large expanse of color draw the viewer "inside" the
canvas, "enclosing" him. Describing a painting by Robert Natkin,
art critic Peter Fuller (1980: 179) wrote:

> It is almost as if at this level of your interaction with the work
> the skin had reformed by this time *around you* so that you,
> originally an exterior observer, feel yourself to be literally and
> precariously suspended within a wholly illusory space which,
> like the unconscious itself, contains its own time.

One is drawn through the skin of paint between successive gauze-
like veils of color so that the viewer feels suspended within some
interior, timeless space.

Such sense of enclosure and oneness is the visual counterpart of
auditory immersion into the "vertical time" of some contemporary
music. Just as in the painting there are layers of color and light
which draw one into a timeless space, in some "vertical time" music
there are layers of dense sound: relationships take place between
layers of simultaneous sound rather than between successive events,

as in conventional music. "The result is a single present stretched out into an enormous duration . . . that nonetheless feels like an instant" (Kramer, 1981: 549).

In some recent literature, one finds analogous discontinuities and fragmentations, resulting in a similar prolongation of the present moment lifted out of the flow of past-to-future. In the years since her work first began to appear in *The New Yorker*, Ann Beattie has become for many readers the representative young American writer. Here are some of the things she said in an interview with Joyce Maynard (*New York Times*, May 11, 1980):

Beattie: I don't know how to write a novel . . . . I would like to take a course on that some time, if I ever take another course . . . . It's very hard for me to work on Monday and Tuesday, and on Wednesday I wonder what I said on Tuesday, let alone what I'm moving toward . . . . That's why all the chapters jump around. I can't think how somebody would move from one to the next, so I have to take a breather and hope that I come up with something . . . . I certainly listen to records a lot. But if I write a story I tend to put on what my husband is playing on the stereo at that moment . . . just what's on the turntable . . . . I really love the notion of found art. Warhol soup cans – that kind of stuff. When I write something, I like to look out the window the night I'm typing and see what kind of moon it was on July the 15th and put it in . . . .

Maynard: Do you write about the relationships between men and women?

Beattie: I just assume that there are going to be moments. But when I start to write it isn't with the thought that I want to communicate about the relationship between men and women. I think, "I'd really like to work that interesting ashtray I just bought into a story about men and women . . . ." I read a lot – mostly modern fiction, nothing before 1960 if I can help it. I'm a great time waster. See what a shiny coat my dog has? I go buy him vitamins. I rap with him. I brush him.

Maynard: And did you actually know somebody who did what the two lovers in *Falling in Place* did, during the early

Beattie: days of their relationship – hold hands uninterruptedly for two days?

Beattie: Yes – four days. They've split up now.

Does a clinical perspective give us an inkling as to the significance of these shifts away from the usual principles of sense and sequence? Let us turn to the woman who came late for an appointment she did not have, slept, and left before her actual appointment was due to start. While not "removed" from the flow of time from past to future, this was surely a slippage – whether one thinks of it as backward or forward – a slippage in the ratcheting of the cogs of time. Here is more about her and the clinical situation.

I had seen her years before in analysis. Now forty-seven, she had asked to come in for a few sessions. We greeted each other warmly. She sat down and smiled. I asked how she had been. She struggled with her features and said, "Since Nancy was killed it hasn't been the same," and burst into sobs. Shocked, I blurted, "What?" Nancy was her daughter, and she would now be about twenty-two. As we shall see, the way she broke the news was not incidental.

Indeed, her twenty-two-year-old daughter had been killed instantly in a car accident a year earlier. The patient had managed to continue all her activities but experienced a numbing disconnection from her feelings. Not mourning her daughter, she felt, was like holding onto her, not letting her go. She had only recently begun to weep, and this brought some relief from the sense of deadness.

She had entered analysis originally saying that she rarely knew what she was feeling; whenever she was under stress she would disconnect herself from her feelings and hide inside. In this way she could fight off depression and "keep moving and smiling." Convent upbringing had taught her that it was more important to maintain a prayerful attitude than to seek to understand many things. She had cultivated a vague fogginess as a defense against sexual and aggressive impulses. This was modeled partly on her mother. Mother was remembered mostly for her bland smilingness and the way she cultivated stereotyped responses to handle any situation. Father was a powerful political figure whose family life was characterized by towering rages and emotional withdrawal. Neither parent ever exchanged a single word with their daughter after she married outside the Church. She had been temporarily expelled from the family in adolescence for always getting into "trouble," though she was not sure what the trouble had been. She of course knew there was a past, but the quality of herself in it was not available to her, and when it was it was like remembering the feeling of having had a nightmare but not knowing what it was about.

She had married a driven man who became very successful. She married him to get herself "organized" by him and play out the roles he assigned her. She did this very well and became known as a sophisticated hostess, a responsive friend, a generous volunteer worker for good causes, and a natural athlete. A few close friends also knew that she was very bright, had a discerning literary and musical taste, and had graduated with high honors from a top college. She experienced modified analytic treatment as the only calm relationship she had ever known and the first time she had allowed herself to feel that she was taking something for herself instead of being selfless.

The clinical vignette relevant to our discussion has already been related. It was easy to imagine that it represented a conventional resistance of ambivalence to talking about painful matters, but the form it took seemed unusual.

At the next session, when we discussed what had happened, I asked, on the basis of what I knew about her from the past, whether having come late for an imagined appointment and having left before a real one was a way of expressing something about wanting to reverse what was real and unreal. Whether this was wrong or irrelevant, her answer in any event led elsewhere. She said that repeatedly when she met someone she had not seen for some time, the other person would "surprise" her by asking innocently and casually about her daughter, that the patient would then have to say her daughter had died, that this would always come as a shock to the other person and the patient would have to soothe *her* down. I said it seemed surprising that it always came as a surprise to her that someone should ask innocently about her daughter. Why did she not anticipate this and somehow try to cushion the news and shield both of them from the shock? She replied that everything seemed to come as a surprise to *her* nowadays; *she* was just never ready for anything. For example, although she had been an excellent tennis player, now every time the ball came to her it seemed to come from the blue; because she did not keep her eye on her opponent's movements she could not anticipate where the ball would land, and as a result her return would always be late.

I wondered if she might be turning every moment into a kind of shock and a surprise, ripping each moment out of its context in the flow of time, and in this way perhaps continuously repeating, actively, the traumatic moment when she was informed of Nancy's death. As for coming early and leaving before her appointment was due to start, we might speculate that this was a way of dislocating time in order to correct and master it, a way of saying, "If only it had been an hour earlier, or later, Nancy would be alive now." (It has since been shown (Terr, 1984) that, following trauma, disturbances in all major aspects of time functioning serve adaptive and defensive functions.)

Any analyst would wish for more data regarding this vignette, particularly the role of unresolved transference. But since the episode of the missed appointment arose out of a brief contact many years following the termination of treatment, this is not possible. This unavoidable omission, however, helps direct our attention to a recently revived area of early psychoanalytic interest: the role of reality and the effect of trauma.

We know that random, meaningless violence can destroy both the sense of self and reality. A less drastic result of trauma is that its reality may be denied and disavowed in various ways. Uprooting the connection between cause and consequence by altering the flow of time from past to future may be one means of blunting the impact of trauma. One may attempt to master past trauma by reliving it in an endless repetition compulsion, transforming the present into that past, thus effectively halting the flow of time.

But what mechanisms help to master and defend against a reality that is not denied or disavowed – that remains well recognized, in other words – and yet flies in the face of common sense and logic? The patient of course understood very well that a head-on collision led to her daughter's death, but this bears so little relation to sense that the mind recoils from such "meaning" as absurd. If it cannot totally sever cause from consequence, past from future, it can at least defensively *modify the experience of time flow* – sometimes slowing it down and at other times speeding it up. Is this what the patient was doing in coming late for an appointment she did not have and leaving early for one she did? Or in being too slow in meeting her tennis opponent's return, too slow in preparing the ground for breaking the news of her daughter's death, too quick in blurting out the news?

If this seems tenable, we might ask: have the fragmentation, discontinuity, and "timelessness" – so pervasive in art of the modern era for so long – been all-too prescient imaginings of an unthinkable future?

As previously discussed, some of the still newer temporalities of music represent even more drastic attempts to cool the flow of time – actually to separate each moment from its historical context, deal with each like rootless tones, without implications, in the discontinuous Now. Thus, in the words of the folk ballad: "We'll make a space in the lives we've planned/And here we'll stay,/Until it's time for you to go. Don't ask why,/Don't ask forever,/Love me now" (Buffy St Marie).

If we were to accept the hypothesis that it was the sudden shocking death of her daughter that led the patient to modify defensively her experience of time flow, could we make a parallel hypothesis about some contemporary music? In short, the question is: should some aspects of modern music and of current clinical phenomena be bracketed together as defensive alterations in the experience of time – attempts to modify and thus "master" its inexorable passage?

The immediate musicological answer might be: "No. The new temporalities in music represent (1) experimentation, (2) reflecting the gradual absorption of music of different cultures (for instance, the Javanese gamelan), (3) making use of technological innovations like radio, records, electronics and tape-splicing" (Kramer, 1981: 543–544).

Yet, if all this were true it would not negate one possible meaning of this musical experimentation: like the patient's reaction to sudden, random death, the new temporalities in music may still represent a deeply felt need to suspend time, to deal with the possibility that any succeeding moment might fracture conventional sense and flood the self. In other words, just as my patient experienced a defensive alteration in her sense of time in response to the life-threatening unpredictability of daily life, some contemporary music (and art), perhaps in similar response to shared anxieties of the age, dissolves familiar temporal (and spatial) frames of reference.

Whatever the cause, it would be misleading to dismiss such apparent dissolution of familiar structures as simply regressive. It is a frequent analytic finding that a temporary dissolution of structure may be a prerequisite for further development. Thus, in the case of my patient, if what she went through were to lead to further growth, or in the case of music or art if it is to be an aesthetic experience, such partial dissolution will be followed by a rediffer-entiation of the self (G.J. Rose, 1980).

This two-phase process – partial dissolution and reintegration – occurring in rapid oscillation appears to be central to creative experience. Much slowed down, it also describes the process of growth. We observe it, too, in that particular form of growth we call psychoanalysis and refer to it there as an alternating movement of therapeutic regression and working through, losing and refinding the self, emotional reliving and thoughtful reflection.

Or so we hope.

Chapter 7

The birth of music in the context of loss

Music and affect regulation

It is said that music was given to mankind by the God Shiva six thousand years before our era. With the help of music, Orpheus (son of Apollo and the Muse, Calliope) went to rescue Eurydice from the Underworld. And he nearly succeeded, until he turned back to see her. Then she faded away. Was Orpheus' mission only a dream – a memory – woven through music?

The ancient Maori are said to have navigated over three thousand miles of open Pacific Ocean aided only by Song. One wonders what data, inscribed in Song, guided *their* journeys. That they succeeded was no mere dream. That they thus became masters of their fates lay surely in themselves. But perhaps also in the stars – their constellations encoded in the structure of Song?

Australian aborigines have complex songs that map their terrain acoustically. Rising and falling arpeggios trace mountain paths; monotones denote flat plains. Songs mimic different footsteps on particular kinds of soil.

What dreams, memories, or maps go into the body of Song to orient one in an uncertain reality? We begin with a child humming to himself to maintain his courage while snorkeling. We will return via his grandfather, dreaming music while struggling with the trauma of loss. *En route* we will touch on early development, some neurobiological roots of music, and trauma theory – with the aim of helping to build a psychoanalytic aesthetics.

* * *

Adam, age eight, has the self-confident spirit and sunny nature of the family pet. Brave but not a maritime hero particularly, sociable but also introspective, he is never far behind even when the whole family goes snorkeling together in tropical waters.

Equipped with flippers and mask, breathing tube clomped between his jaws, face immersed in the water, he was overheard to be humming. Later:

> I heard you humming while snorkeling. How come?
> Sometimes I sort of comfort myself.
> What do you mean?
> Well, when I come across a whole bunch of fish – big fish – I don't feel alone.
> So what do you hum?
> Oh, like mummy would sing to me.
> Like?
> Like, "You are my sunshine." Things like that.
> Do you ever make up your own songs?
> Sure. When I come across a little fish all by himself. I sing like, "You never had a friend like me."

Adam said it: music reaches back and reaches out. Music has long been associated with the need for hope and comfort, prayer and the wish for rescue. In the modern era, nowhere was the need for music better evidenced than in the experience of Jews under Hitler. The following are two examples.

Herbert Zipper was an inmate of Dachau and Buchenwald between May 1938 and February 1939 while they were still only forced labor camps. (The following account is abstracted from Cummins, 1992.) On the second or third night he and a friend began to recite lines from Goethe's *Faust*, going back and forth between them trying to transcend their hunger and the dirt and stupidity around them and forget the exhaustion of a day's work pushing cartloads of stone back and forth.

> I have no explanation for what urged me . . . to start in a loud voice reciting [these] passages . . . while scores of other inmates were scattered on the ground, exhausted, mute and hopeless . . . .
> Soon the inmates on the ground grouped themselves around us listening with obvious intensity. The dramatic change of mood that happened to all of us is still vividly in my memory. The following evenings an ever-increasing crowd urged us to

continue . . . and we obliged with the best of German poetry that we could remember. *Poetry did its intended work*. (p. 84)

Many of the prisoners who gathered around were simple, uneducated laborers, poor farmers, criminals – for many their first exposure to poetry.

This led to the seemingly preposterous idea of making music. He composed in his head and memorized it while at forced labor. He came across two good instrument makers in the wood shop and set them to working with stolen wood. A sympathetic guard (who turned out to be a Communist spy) provided violin strings. He was able to enlist about a dozen players with a peculiar assortment of instruments, some of them only hollow boxes bound in tight string.

On Sunday afternoons when the guards were often off-duty, and with a couple of prisoners standing guard, they held "concerts" in an unused latrine. Twenty to thirty prisoners at a time listened in absolute silence in shifts of fifteen to thirty minutes for two to three hours. The music was written in the margins of Nazi newspapers that had been cut and pasted together by the listening audience. The ensemble was never discovered.

Zipper learned first hand in Dachau that the arts are no mere adornment, but essential to life.

Not in a concentration camp, but herded by the Nazis into the Ghetto of Lodz, Poland, 1940–1945, the miserable inhabitants sang for their lives.

In the evening there was not enough light for reading. So we sat in the darkness and sang. We sang and sang . . . for its own sake . . . . I think it was one of the things which helped us to survive.

(Flam, 1992: 156)

They sang in their homes, for the family, in public, in private, in youth groups, on stage, during work.

The songs contained everyday events and ironic commentary. The content ranged from despair, anger, hope for freedom, call for revolt, group solidarity, even to humorously poking fun at some of their own. However serious or light, the content of the song was always secondary to the music.

Why the necessity for song in particular? Art philosopher, Victor Zuckerkandl (1973) writes that people sing in order to melt their

separateness into "authentic togetherness" (p. 42). "Music . . .
provides . . . the most natural solvent of artificial boundaries
between the self and others" (p. 51).

A woman of the Lodz ghetto describes how listening to herself
singing helped her to feel less isolated. "Only singing could help.
When one sings, even when he sings a sad song, his loneliness
disappears, he listens to his own voice. He and his voice become
two people . . . and afterwards you feel free" (Flam, 1992: 107).
Drawing comfort from being both singer and listener – single but
not "alone" – permits an analytic inference: it likely taps into the
primal *safety* of an early precursor, namely, the infant–caretaker
pair. In that dual unity, mutually responsive cooing and expressive
vocalization between the two partners long antedated verbalization
and being able to distinguish oneself from a loving Other.

* * *

What can developmental psychology say about this ancient time of
life? Studies of prenatal and neonatal responses to auditory stimuli
suggest that musical development and responsivity may start even
prior to birth. The anatomical wherewithal is present. In contrast
to the eye and the visual areas of the brain, the cochlea and middle
ear are fully developed by the fifth month of fetal life, and the
sensorimotor cortex and cerebellum are active at birth.

Fetuses respond to music, probably depending mostly on tempo
(Olds, 1984). When musical stimuli were applied directly to the
abdominal skin of pregnant women in five to ten minute periods, in
ten out of thirty subjects the fetus responded with sharp, rapid or
agitated movements to stimulating music, and with rolling, soft or
muted movements to calmer musical selections (Shetler, 1988).

From birth onward, newborns produce sounds that have melodic
structures and rhythms related to neurophysiology and breathing
(Ostwald, 1988). Up to three months of age perception is "amodal,"
i.e., sound may be seen or *felt motorically* as well as heard. This
results in "global affects" or undifferentiated emotions (Stern,
1985).

Pending elaboration later, we should note here that more differentiated emotions evolve from a matrix of sensations of pleasure/
unpleasure. As need tensions accumulate, delays intervene, and
anticipations rise, muscles contract; as needs are satisfied, muscles
relax. This is not to suggest that tension is equated with unpleasure

and release with pleasure as formerly believed; tension is related to the long-circuiting of secondary process (cognition) and release with the short-circuiting of primary process (imagination). Rate and contour of stimulation are also highly relevant.

The motoric patterns of *actual* tension and release that accompany emotions are the kinesthetic, bodily end of the bridge that later connects with the *virtual* tension/release that is built into the structure of art. My contention is that their concordance triggers the emotional response to art.

Returning to music, the aspects of speech that most compel the neonate's attention are the musical ones: first, rhythm and timing; by six months, the variations of intonation and a tonal range at a particular pitch (Panel, 1980). Between five and eight months the infant can discriminate pitch differences of less than half a tone.

Is it a coincidence that parents across cultures exaggerate the musical features of speech in sing-songing to the infant (Emde, 1983: 171–172)? Repetitiveness and rhythm, fine-tuned like a dance, are important features of this interplay. The baby responds in kind well before six months of age and matches pitch, intensity, melodic contour and rhythmic structure of mother's songs. It leads to a growing attachment between them and this becomes the central growth-promoting factor and the basis for the baby's well-being (Stern, 1985).

Thus, from early on there is an open system of responsive affective signaling between the preverbal infant and its caretakers. This reciprocal emotional signaling becomes a self-reinforcing dyadic system of affect–feedback and becomes consolidated by the first year of life.

* * *

Since Penfield and Perot (1963) were able to show that precise and vivid memories, coupled with the emotions of the original experiences, could be evoked by delicate electric stimulation of the cerebral cortex, it seems likely that the sum total of experience remains perfectly preserved. Of this total, music makes up a generous portion – orchestral, vocal, piano, etc.

Nothing seems to be lost, music least likely of all. Oliver Sacks (1985) presents a case of an eighty-eight-year-old woman with a sudden onset of stroke due to a thrombosis of her temporal lobe. She first became aware that something was wrong when she suddenly felt herself drowning in an ocean of sound which she took to be due to a loud radio playing old Irish songs deafeningly at night. She said to the doctor, "I know I'm an old woman with a stroke in an old people's home, but I feel I'm a child in Ireland again – I feel my mother's arms, I see her, I hear her voice singing" (p. 130).

With gradual recovery in the course of four months she gradually lost the songs, was unable to recall them, and missed them. "It was like being given back a forgotten bit of my childhood again" (p. 127). On questioning it was determined that her father had died before she was born, and her mother before she was five. Sent to America, she had no conscious memory of her first five years of life.

The music had brought her profound joy, like the opening of a door that had been closed all her life. As she recovered she said,

> The door is closing. I'm losing it all again . . . . I'm glad it happened . . . . It was the healthiest, happiest experience of my life. There's no longer a great chunk of my childhood missing. I can't remember the details now, but I know it's all there. There's a sort of completeness I never had before.
>
> (Sacks, 1985: 137–138)

Sacks presents a number of other cases illustrating the power of music, dance, narrative and drama to re-access motor sequences and programs that appear to be otherwise totally lost due to neurological damage. Apparently art provides forms that may remain intact and reliably available despite otherwise extreme motor incompetence and bewilderment. This suggests that the capacity for aesthetic form (like one's identity/style) is so diffused, embedded and organized as to hold an overall design together.

In musical perception, for example, tunes are immediately felt and recognized as indivisible wholes involving warmth, emotion, even personal relation. They are like "faces," Sacks writes, in that normally we do not recognize familiar faces by "piecemeal analysis or aggregation." With a lesion in the right occipital (visual) cortex, on the other hand, one may have to resort to analysis of separate features (Sacks, 1985: 198).

An example of this pathology is the case of a distinguished musician who had lost the ability to visually imagine, represent or remember faces as well as his own body-image. Instead, he used his musical sensitivity to take the place of image. He took the world in through his hearing. His wife said:

> He does everything singing to himself. But if he is interrupted and loses the thread, he comes to a complete stop, doesn't know his clothes – or his body. He sings all the time – eating songs, dressing songs, bathing songs, everything. He can't do anything unless he makes it a song.
>
> (Sacks, 1985: 15–16)

Like this patient, a man who was severely retarded due to meningitis in infancy also managed to relate himself to healthful aspects of life through music. The *spirit* of music evoked his musician father with whom he had lived all his life on affectionate terms until he died when the patient was in his thirties. Especially when singing in church, this spirit could transform him from a pathetic disabled creature to a vibrant one.

His father had also read aloud to him all nine volumes of *Grove's Dictionary of Music and Musicians*. They – all of them – remained "indelibly printed upon his son's limitlessly retentive, if illiterate, cortex. Grove, thereafter was 'heard' *in his father's voice* – and could never be recollected by him without emotion" (Sacks, 1985: 180). Apparently it was his father's voice that acted as the personal affective medium through which music was able to exert its beneficent effect. Or was it that music was the medium that facilitated the internalization of his father and activated the benevolent effect of that relationship? We do not have to decide between these alternatives. They may both have been effective, as in early development where the musical interplay is inseparable from the relationship.

How are we to understand these observations attesting to art's effectiveness in reintegrating the performance of neurologically devastated individuals? In other words, how do aesthetic forms help hold the design together?

Consider that the cerebral hemispheres in their moment-by-moment activity process data differently. It is the task of the ego to correlate and integrate the different ways the hemispheres deal with the successiveness and constancy of time, the separateness and wholeness of space, as well as the person's thoughts and feelings. These constitute the coordinates of orientation – time, place and person.

Art reflects what the mind attempts in its moment-by-moment activity, and does it ideally, slowed down and magnified: *integrates* diverse data to aid psychological *orientation* in an inconstant reality. At the same time, all the arts reinfuse feeling into thought and perception and make it more like it was in the beginning. It is as though painting, for example, were a visual model of the mind, and music an acoustic one, while all the arts reinvigorate personal experience with feelingful thought and perception (G.J. Rose, 1980, 1987, 1996).

Therefore, when the ego's integrative function is deficient because of neurological impairment and, as we will discuss later, in the case of traumatic stress, the arts may act as prosthetic devices to lend support where deficiencies exist.

In short, art acts as an external auxiliary ego to aid the continuous task of integration.

* * *

Modern trauma theory goes back more than a century to Pierre Janet, who described hysterical dissociation of memories from consciousness and ascribed it to congenital disability and the impact of intense emotion. For Freud, the "failure of mental synthesis" under emotion was due to intrapsychic forces and repression (1913: 207). In modern terminology, a dissociation between the observing and the experiencing aspects of the ego has often been described in traumatized individuals (Fromm, 1965).

Whether we prefer "dissociation" or "failure of synthesis," it is useful to make a distinction between two different types of "splitting off" of ego states: "horizontal" and "longitudinal." The former characterizes neurosis; unconscious conflicts lie buried by repression while remaining dynamically active. In the latter, characteristic of traumatic splitting, there is an inability to reflect and observe oneself objectively while experiencing thoughts and feelings subjectively. In both, the integrity of the self is compromised.

Traumatized people may act and feel disturbed without knowing why, or know what has happened but have no feelings about it. Flashbacks and nightmares of traumatic experience occur with undiminished intensity and, in some people, without any accompanying verbal (narrative) recall; the memory may be entirely organized on a perceptual level. In short, emotional, sensory, cognitive and behavioral aspects of the traumatic experience are not integrated; sensations and feeling states having achieved little verbal or symbolic representation, they begin to lead a life of their own.

Various nuanced degrees of fragmentation reflect the degree of psychological distance that the traumatized person has been able to take, in respect to the originating massive psychic trauma; how much the person "knows" or "doesn't know" – the ratio of acknowledgement to negation – describes the various forms of traumatic memory (Laub and Auerhahn, 1993). Another way of stating this is that it is also a measure of the relative intactness of the observing ego in respect to the experiencing ego – both within the overall context of a weakened sense of self.

The degree of functional partnership between the observing and experiencing ego and thus the intactness of the sense of self may account for the fact that trauma comes in all sizes. It ranges from what might be experienced as a challenge to resiliency for one person to the other end of the spectrum, of undeniable vulnerability and massive psychic trauma for anyone. In between there is a complemental series of challenge/trauma combinations.

The emotions accompanying trauma are a complex mixture. Rage and helplessness are central, including rage at feeling helpless and unable to trust one's own body and mind to see one through and continue to feel whole. The various ways in which the ensuing crisis are expressed are unique to the individual.

One person's silent rage at chronic childhood neglect and abuse was aggravated by its always being turned against herself as having caused it. It took the form of compulsively tearing her hair out, thus also expressing the assault she experienced on her bodily sense of wholeness. For this she was further blamed and shamed – and was even less able to stop. Ultimately, with the help of analysis she was able to reassemble herself and convert her repressed wish to scream in outrage into voice training and a professional musical career.

At the core of trauma is a breakdown of adaptive mental functioning and consequent flooding – whether triggered by a loss of trust in a functioning external "other" or to the incapacitation of a part of oneself, namely, the observing ego. Without the observing ego's capacity to reflect on what one is experiencing on a primal, often somatic, level there is no possibility of representing the trauma to oneself. Indeed, the sense of self itself is fractured.

Without self-witnessing and self-representation, the massive overstimulation that the individual has undergone can only exist as a wordless emptiness, or else as chaos that at best can only remain sequestered. The experiencing ego has been flooded, its connection to the observing ego disabled, and thus the possibility of self-representation and subsequent reintegration ("mental synthesis") of these two aspects of the ego destroyed (Laub and Podell, 1995).

Hence the relevance of the illusion provided by music (and art) for the therapy of traumatic stress. By enabling the person to recognize and feel what had been unformed and therefore inexpressible, as if by a responsive empathic presence, it helps repair the loss or damage to a reflective inner "other." As we will discuss later, like mourning it facilitates internalization. By enhancing mindfulness it helps to "create symbolic representations of past traumatic experiences, [the better to] tam[e] the associated terror and desomatiz[e] the memories" (van der Kolk *et al.*, 1996: 205) and reunite the self.

The interplay between the experiencing and observing ego lends itself to cautious correlation with data concerning the factual (declarative/explicit) and emotional (procedural/implicit) memory systems (cf. Damasio, 1994; LeDoux, 1996; van der Kolk *et al.*, 1996; Yovell, 2000).

The hippocampus and the amygdala are bilateral structures deep inside the medial part of the temporal lobe, connected to the orbital frontal cortex. The factual memory system is hippocampal-based and primarily neocortical; the developmentally older amygdala-based system is subcortical.

Building a bridge between psychoanalysis and neuroscience, the significant point has been made that, while neurobiological findings are incompatible with the structural model of ego–id–superego, the hippocampal-based system is congruent with the earlier (prestructural) theory of the ego; and the amygdala-based system is congruent with the dynamic unconscious. Further, "the prefrontal cortex is the crucial locus of interplay between intellect and feelings" (Slap and Brown, 2001: 113).

Normally the two memory systems synchronize intellect and feelings. This suggests that they are, in part at least, also neuroanatomical loci underlying the observing and experiencing aspects of the ego; like the hippocampus, the observing ego is able to moderate emotional triggering.

The amygdala triggers rapid response survival reactions such as hyper-vigilance (by releasing ACTH – adrenocorticotrophic hormone). These emergency reactions can be modified or aborted by neocortical and especially frontal lobe systems as well as the hippocampal system. By processing comparable events cognitively and relating them to each other in a spatial and temporal context, the hippocampal system provides a more objective and narrative understanding of emotional experience and enables one to discriminate and learn to avoid danger rather than have hair-trigger responses to each perceived "danger." Thus, in the presence of emotionally alarming data, it evaluates and is then able to abort or slow down emergency reactions (by regulating the amount of ACTH that is released).

Under extreme emotional arousal the integrated functioning of the amygdala and hippocampus falls apart. Acute panic can cause instant breakdown. Also, in chronic stress the stress hormone, cortisol, in the course of time overstimulates the amygdala and reduces the size of the hippocampus, impairing its operation. The hippocampus and related structures (the observing ego?) are then prevented from evaluating incoming information from the amygdala and its related structures (the experiencing ego?).

The result of new information not being categorized in time and space or integrated with existing mental schemata is that traumatic memories are dissociated: the emotional memories of the trauma remain ready to be triggered while the factual memories of the trauma are only spottily recalled, if at all. Hence, too, the familiar clinical finding that traumatic memories are timeless and ego-alien. Not being collated and transcribed into personal narratives, they come back as concrete emotional and sensory states with little verbal representation. This failure to process information symbolically and integrate it with other experience is at the very core of the pathology of post-traumatic stress disorder (van der Kolk *et al.*, 1996: 295–296).

It is striking that this is the converse of the effect of art. Precisely those functions that one finds damaged or failed due to trauma are those we have long postulated as being enhanced and even ideally realized in the dynamics of aesthetic structure and experience. Art succeeds, above all, in helping one process information symbolically and relating it in novel ways to the self and world at large. While art is not "traumatolytic," it aids in transforming private trauma into ego-syntonic and more universal experience.

Neither art nor psychotherapy can always undo all the devastating effects of trauma. What it can do, however, is to help restore the synchronous operations of the experiencing and observing ego – the destruction of which is the structural source of the effects of trauma.

In terms of neuroscience, psychosocial stress can impair hippo-campal plasticity, but rhythmic–melodic interactions with care-takers limit adverse interactions (Panksepp, 2001), neurons continue to proliferate in the adult hippocampus, and SSRI (selective sero-tonin reputake inhibitors) antidepressants may protect hippocampal neurons by increasing the concentration of serotonin. Finally, modern neuroscience offers some basis for the beneficial results of playful, joyous and *aesthetic* activities.

We do not yet know whether art or psychotherapy actually promotes hippocampal neuron regeneration. We do, however, have an overarching idea of some neuroanatomical sites of damaged integration resulting from trauma where antidepressants, psy-chotherapy and art can all help to facilitate psychological healing.

* * *

Loss is close to the heart of trauma. We have concentrated on the intrapsychic aspects of loss: the loss of the sense of wholeness of the self caused in part by the loss of integration between the observing and experiencing aspects of the ego; and their possible neurobiological correlates in the amygdala and hippocampus. Needless to say, other loci beyond our scope may well be involved; for example, the orbital frontal lobe, particularly that of the nondominant hemisphere (Schore, 1997a).

Collective external trauma, like private subjective loss, involves a loss of an important part of the self. Kai Erikson writes eloquently of what happens when a common disaster damages the sense of communality that binds people together in mutual support.

> People begin to emerge hesitantly from their protective shells into which they have withdrawn [and] learn that they are isolated and alone . . . . "I" continue to exist, though damaged and maybe even permanently changed. "You" continue to exist, though distant and hard to relate to. But "we" no longer exist as a connected pair or as linked cells in a larger communal body.
>
> (Erikson, 1976: 154)

The two traumas, he adds, are of course closely related, but distinct in the sense that either can take place in the absence of the other.

Returning to individual trauma, loss is an intrinsic consequence of "engaged" living – living with emotional attachments and, hopefully, the patterns of action to make them real. Loss entails mourning – more overt grief at first and more private mourning later. It is not necessary to differentiate it here from clinical depression. It should be pointed out, however, that a degree of trauma is frequently, perhaps invariably, involved with loss. Some hypervigilance and intolerance of stimulation reflect this. Reactive hyperactivity of one kind or another may also serve defensive purposes.

Uncomplicated mourning over loss presents a developmental conflict, perhaps even a crisis, at any age of occurrence. Mourning, like activity/passivity, bisexuality and autonomy/dependence, is a "divergent conflict" that requires alternating expression of the two sides rather than an either/or choice (Kris, 1992).

The painful process of alternation between wishing to hold onto the lost relationship and wishing to live on in the present and into the future cannot be resolved by choosing one or the other. Freud (1917) famously opined that reality requires that a mourner must eventually relinquish all libidinal attachments to the lost object and redistribute them.

Personal experience, however, caused him to modify this paltry view. In a letter to Ludwig Binswanger, April 12, 1929, he wrote:

> My daughter who died would have been thirty-six years old today . . . . Although we know that after such a loss the acute state of mourning will subside, we also know we shall remain inconsolable and will never find a substitute. No matter what may fill the gap, even if it be filled completely, it nevertheless remains something else. And actually this is how it should be. It is the only way of perpetuating that love which we do not want to relinquish.
>
> (quoted by E.L. Freud, 1960: letter #239, p. 386)

The insight that comes from mourning is different from that which comes from the lifting of repression. Loss needs to be acknowledged, to be sure, and this is the task of the observing ego. It may even require cognizance of the fact that a particular emptiness is not to be averaged out. It is irremediable: notes on the keyboard are missing; the melody broken.

So what is needed is not only an observing ego but one with the capacity for self-comforting such that painful affective states can be moderated and more positive ones reestablished. In other words, the quality of the pre-existing internalizations determines how the observing ego accomplishes its task: reestablishing its interplay with the experiencing ego, influencing the affective tone objectively but benevolently; as earlier, the holding environment of maternal attunement and one's responsive resonance converted potential trauma into the challenge of further emotional differentiation.

Again this returns us to music – and the possibility that it, like mourning, can facilitate internalization and thereby affect regulation.

* * *

Adam reached back for his mother's comforting song and soothed himself with it when he anticipated the fear of coming across big fish while snorkeling. When he found another little fish like himself he offered him his friendship through music.

The embattled woman in the Lodz ghetto who listened to her own voice singing "became" two people and, even though it was a sad song, no longer felt lonely.

Adam's grandfather lost his life-companion to a nursing home. Her mind slowly dying, he compared her paradoxical presence and absence to him with the pain of a phantom limb. He dreamed as follows.

He saw his wife approaching on an empty street. She was wearing a black lace dress reminiscent of one his mother wore on special occasions. They embraced and danced slowly, shyly, solemnly, as in their ritual first dance at their wedding fifty years ago – several steps together forward, then walking side by side holding hands, then several steps dancing backward, and again walking side by side. The melody was a light airy dance tune with German lyrics that he remembered from an old 78 r.p.m. record from childhood. He had never spoken the language and only barely understood it, but he remembered these words: *Schon ist das leben, wenn die musik spielt* (Life is beautiful, as long as the music plays).

He awoke moved but puzzled, because it was the tune on the other side of the record that he had really loved and now he could not recall it. Then, suddenly, he did. This melody was slower, nostalgic, with downward progressions and somber ending. The words were unsparing, fateful: *Es gibt nur einmal, es kommt nicht wieder. Das ist ein scherz, ein traumerei.* (It happens but once, it never returns. It's a plaything, a dream.) And, as he said, the dam spilled over.

Neither the lilting melody, nor the young lovers' embrace, nor the image of his mother, could shield him from the latent melody and words on the other side and what he knew only too well: it *was* over; but, also, their music together – intact – was becoming part of him, internalized, joining the music of other loving presences there from the beginning.

* * *

We turn now to internalization and affect regulation. According to current developmental studies, what the infant internalizes is the process of mutual affect attunement, fittedness, and regulation and not the object itself or part-objects. There is general agreement, for example, that the internalization of the soothing quality of good affective attunement in early infant–caregiver relationships is the source of affect regulation itself – the capacity to differentiate, tolerate and modulate painful affect states.

Neuroscience has much to contribute to this discussion, if with a different terminology. "Experience-dependent internal regulatory systems" (Schore, 1996, 1997b) or "internal representations of external human interpersonal relations" (Hofer, 1984, 1990) encapsulate the essence of the psychoanalytic concept of "internalization" as the transformation of external interactions into intrapsychic structure and dynamics.

Neuroscience holds that the primary caregiver acts as a "hidden" regulator of chemical agents that influence the maturation of centers in the temporal and orbital frontal cortices (Hofer, 1990). Affect-regulating experiences, as in mutual gaze and facial mirroring, become imprinted in the right orbital frontal cortex and trigger high levels of endogenous opiates in the child's growing brain. These are responsible for the pleasurable qualities of social interaction, affect and attachment and may have an enduring effect on the ability to modulate affect and tolerate negative affect states (Schore, 1996, 1997b).

Other studies in neuroscience further support the affect-regulating significance of the *internalized* caretaker. Moreover, the withdrawal of these sensorimotor interactions from the beginning and extending into one's contemporary life has a continuing demonstrable effect on one's mind and *internal biologic systems*.

It seems possible that the regulating action of important human relationships upon biologic systems may be transduced, not only by sensorimotor and temporal patterning of the actual interactions, but also by the *internal experiences of the relationship* . . . . [Conversely,] these internal representations may serve as active but symbolic surrogates that prevent the release of withdrawal responses after separation through their associative connections with biologic systems.

(Hofer, 1984: 193; italics added)

Now to the internalization of music and its affect-regulating significance. Like poetry, the affective power of music most likely has its origins in the infant's earliest vocal experience of the mother. Not that vocal experience can ever be simply vocal: the attributes of mother's voice are indistinguishable from her touch and movement; all become fixed in the rhythm of the baby's body and comprise a rich medley of sensorimotor and affectomotor components, linking mother and infant prior to the latter's differentiation.

The sensorimotor and affectomotor components of music are likewise indistinguishable. The affectomotor response to music comprises many physical concomitants of affects or preverbal affect precursors – tactile, kinesthetic, rhythmic, respiratory. It can be no coincidence that listening to music is often accompanied by sub-vocal singing along with the music, perhaps harking back to one's earliest musical interplay. (Recall the earlier example of singing to elicit the illusion of two-ness to relieve loneliness.)

Pablo Casals, Glenn Gould and other instrumentalists were famous for being hardly able to restrain their singing accompaniment to the music they were performing; they seemed merged with it. It is possible that for them, explicitly, as for others in the audience of music, less overt and more implicitly, the interaction with the music becomes itself internalized as a more or less silent and perhaps enduring affective presence.

If it is possible as I suggest that music (and art) may not only evoke but perhaps embody internal representations of significant relationships, how may we conceptualize the relationship between music and internalization?

This question is intimately connected to the more basic one as to how we distinguish inside from outside, subjective from objective. A review article on developments in neuroscience cites the prevailing consensus that current perception requires comparisons with the past:

> The separate features of the environment stimulate particular patterns of neuronal activity in the brain. The brain does not perceive the external environment, nor the separate stimulus features. Rather, the brain recognises the patterns of neuronal activation within the brain itself. For perception to occur, the brain searches for a match between the current pattern of neuronal activation and patterns stored in memory from prior experience . . . . The brain . . . makes a quick assessment of just enough details to find a "good enough match." When a "good enough" match is found, perception occurs.
>
> (Pally, 1997: 1025)

How well this "matches" Freud's repeated assertions (in the 1895 "Project" (pp. 327–330) and the "Dream Book" (1900–1901: 565–567)), foreshadowing the following:

> All presentations originate from perceptions and are repetitions of them . . . . The antithesis between subjective and objective . . . only comes into being from the fact that thinking possesses the capacity to bring before the mind once more something that has once been perceived, by reproducing it as a presentation without the external object having still to be there. The first and immediate aim, therefore, of reality-testing is, not to *find* an object in real perception which corresponds to the one presented, but to *refind* such an object . . . . The reproduction of a perception as a presentation is not always a faithful one; it may be modified by omissions, or changed by the merging of various elements . . . . A precondition for the setting up of reality-testing is that objects shall have been lost which once brought real satisfaction.
>
> (Freud, 1925a: 237–238)

As we have repeatedly discussed, the "good enough" match between the virtual tension and release dynamic of art (music) on the one hand and affect on the other, recalls early affective attunements and stimulates affective resonance; the underlying concordance between art and affect may be so close that it leads to a preconscious illusion that one's emotional responsiveness to art is mutual and reciprocated, that is, that music itself is a witnessing presence. This facilitates further affectomotor responsiveness (G.J. Rose, 1996).

At its least, music thus comes to act as a sensorimotor bridge between the illusion of an external witnessing presence and latent affecto-motor memory traces or lasting engrams of early self–object interactions, namely, internalizations. Because some of these early self–object interactions or internalizations were symbiotic in nature – that is, their boundaries having been relatively unformed and permeable – the affective, memorial experience they give rise to often has transitional characteristics. They merge self and other.

At its most, the interaction with music may itself become internalized. In either case, whether by facilitating internalization or the interplay with music itself becoming an internalization, it may well be through its relationship to internalization that music contributes to affect regulation.

In summary, we suggest that:

1   Music elicits preverbal internalizations that embody and encode affective memories that contribute to affect regulation.
2   The affective interplay with music may itself become internalized as a nonverbal affect-regulating presence.

* * *

At the outset we asked: "What dreams, memories or maps go into the body of Song to orient one in an uncertain reality?" Our journey has led from developmental psychology, through clinical neurology, trauma theory and psychobiological aesthetics, pointing finally to internalization as one possible key to affect regulation.

Summarizing, the emotional response to music lies in the self-recognition and self-soothing to be found there. It represents an externalized auxiliary body ego built in concordance with the tension and release patterns of neurobiological rhythms (cf. Chapter 5 on music as temporal prosthesis) as well as the structure of affects.

A person seeks music as a temporal/rhythmic holding environment within which one can feel both stimulated and protected as in neonatal life by the responsive presence of the mother. At that time, infant and primary caretaker together formed a nonverbal system that contained the tension and release of affect within tolerable limits.

Music is a *transformation* of this *inter*personal system of affect regulation to an *intra*psychic, abstract level; through rhythmic sensorimotor stimulation, it comes to embody and evoke early internalizations, in all their unconscious, symbiotic, memorial and affectomotor aspects. Affective interaction with the music may itself become internalized.

Ideally, all these internalizations retain the power to promote self-comforting. Through them, music supports an optimal working relation between the observing and experiencing aspects of the ego; this intrapsychic integration helps bring about more positively toned affect regulation. Likewise, dipping back and touching the symbiotic elements in internalization in order to repeat for the moment the separation–individuation process also helps restore and renew one's sense of wholeness.

From the point of view of neuroscience, the limbic and orbital frontal systems, especially in the nondominant hemisphere, may be some of the neuroanatomical sites of these operations.

Is it possible through aesthetic experience, either actively creating it or responding to it, to reach new levels of integration of the personality without the intermediation of language?

The lines of thought presented in this book suggest that the answer is "yes." Nonverbal art may play a fundamental if silent role in emotional development and accessing affects such as those blocked by trauma. Perhaps it bypasses verbalization by stimulating internalizations which, in turn, stimulate the reintegration of experience.

If, by whatever internal route, reintegration occurs through profound aesthetic or other nonverbal experiences, we know little or nothing about its quality or duration, let alone how it compares to that achieved by psychoanalysis. Nor do we know if or how this line of thought is related to learning within the "implicit system" where, neuroscience holds, learning does proceed without language.

Since internalizations are representations of the *quality* of personal interactions, abstracted and transformed into intrapsychic structure, they are not faithful mirrors of the external world; they are created images that correspond with rather than reproduce the outside. Thus, they are prime examples of the creativity of everyday life – each moment a reciprocal inscription that fuses "objective" with subjective.

As we move into the unknown we embolden ourselves by projecting comforting, familiar aspects of ourselves to temper fearful anticipations of the strange and foreign. Perhaps more eager to refind than to discover – whatever may be discoverable through a system which is necessarily less than fully open yet more than merely solipsistic.

If such a formulation also describes ongoing personal development, how fitting to our subject that a biological process essentially enacts a fundamental *musical* gesture and vice versa: recurrences, variations, and recapitulations, alluding to the past, selectively amalgamating old and new; advancing – perchance to grow – through the music of time.

Chapter 8

The power of implicit motion: "it goes straight through"

A standard musical practice is to recapitulate recurrent themes in order to develop and elaborate them further. We shall do the same, aiming always for an overview of art and the creative process in the light of contemporary psychoanalysis.

Two working assumptions:

1   Psychoanalysis and art each enhance self-recognition; the former, verbally and explicitly; the latter, nonverbally and implicitly.
2   The mid-ground between feeling and thought is a seed-bed of creative imagination.

Neuroscience data and the work of artists, Paul Klee and Alberto Giacometti, will illuminate the material.

Let us return to the temporary therapeutic miracles that music and art can sometimes accomplish with victims of neurological devastation. Recall that listening to music, performing it or just imagining it can sometimes restore motor ability, emotional range and psychological identity for a brief period of moments or even hours. This may be accompanied by a revival of normal EEG patterns.

Not that all music will work. Some individuals respond to romantic composers like Chopin or Schubert but not to Bach or Bartók. Music can be anti-epileptic for some and precipitate seizures in others; in movement disorders, if the music is overloud or forceful it can cause some patients to jump or jerk with the beat (Sacks, 1998).

We begin with a clinical vignette.

Anne was in a late stage of vascular dementia. At a much earlier point she would succumb nightly to escalating panic and agitation uncontrolled by drugs. Music, however, could often restore a degree of calm. As we discussed earlier in relation to the Sundown Syndrome of nocturnal psychosis, perhaps the external periodicity of music entrained and supported the faulty internal periodicity of neurobiological mechanisms. In addition, music may recruit early soothing internalizations that help one regain a core sense of identity that stabilizes affect regulation.

Now she was no longer subject to panic; she was mostly withdrawn and indifferent to music as well as the presence of intimates (whom she may or may not have still recognized). She rarely spoke. When she did utter a word or two, it was without affect or any obvious referential context.

What about art? She had been an avid painter and had twice run her own art gallery. Painters had been among her closest friends.

One day she was shown colored illustrations of Monet and abstract paintings of Jimmy Ernst, an old friend. She looked at them all intently for many minutes and with unswerving attention. Asked what she thought, she replied immediately and with the intensity that had once been so characteristic: "This is really beautiful!" Then, more astonishing still: "It goes straight through!"

What goes straight through? I suggest that implicit motion at the core of nonverbal aesthetic form evokes implicit motion at the heart of affective responsiveness. Let us elaborate. Implicit motion comprises both the tension and release of the virtual motion that has been built into the formal structure of visual art and music, and the actual muscular tension and release that makes up a significant part of one's total bodily responsiveness to affect.

How does it go straight through? We borrow a metaphor from physics.

A magnet moving inside a coil of wire will generate an electric current in the wire. Suppose that the formal structure of art and music acts like a magnet; that is, it shapes perceptual fields of virtual tension and release – like a magnet sets up actual magnetic fields of force. The flowing currents of bodily affect that one experiences in responding to the arts is like the electric current induced in the coil of wire. In other words, actual waves of affective bodily response will be generated (the currents in the wire) as one's perception actively engages the virtual implicit motion that is built into these nonverbal aesthetic forms.

As to the sudden return to normality brought about by music and art, a number of elements are involved: range of motion (if this has been disabled) and range of emotion. Also, one's sense of identity. All respond together.

Is there an underlying factor that bundles these therapeutic responses together? Motion. Music, art and affective responsiveness all involve motion in some form. The relation of identity to motion is problematic though, arguably, indirectly involved.

We will examine this contention about motion in some detail, but first a historical point is worth mentioning. Apparently, the significance of movement at one time connected art history and the early history of psychoanalysis. It was an established research theme for both psychoanalysts and art historians in Europe. At the same time that Freud was exploring the meaning of expressive movements, hysterical symptoms and dream imagery, art historians were studying the image of movement. Neither discipline referred to the other (L. Rose, 2001).

Movement and music. The basic ingredient of music is not sound but motion (Sessions, 1950). To be more precise, the basic ingredient of the experience of music is the sense of motion – virtual implicit motion. Moreover, it is the sense of virtual motion, built into the structure of music, that some believe conveys affect. This conclusion, it will be recalled, was derived from a musical analysis of examples from different composers (Epstein, 1993).

Further, musical – in contrast to musicological – listening leads to rhythmic engagement with the music. It is heard to "move" or "breathe." This reflects that each musical phrase must be performed in a single breath as a unique gesture moving toward completing a cadence. Of course music cannot actually move or breathe. We "ride" the phrases and cadences within the parameters of our breathing. It makes bodily sense, for that is the level where we recreate it.

The main engine that drives the sense of harmonic motion forward towards a goal is dissonance striving to resolve in consonance. Nietzsche (1870–1871: 143) put it that dissonance contributed a "forward propulsion" in the course of a "playful shattering and rebuilding." The most famous example of this – said to be the starting point of "modern music" – is the first chord of Wagner's *Tristan und Isolde.*

It contains within itself not one but two dissonances, thus creating within the listener a double desire . . . for resolution. And so the music proceeds: in every chord shift something is resolved but not everything . . . the musical ear is being partially satisfied yet at the same time frustrated . . . [until] the final chord of the work.

(Magee, 2000: 208–211)

According to Magee, this movement of music from expectation to expectation instantiates Wagner's philosophical understanding of the world as he understood it from Schopenhauer. Schopenhauer believed that music corresponded to our deepest human nature: perpetually besieged by an endless train of unsatisfiable longings, each following hard on the last. The movement of music, in short, mirrors the movements of *desire* – making up so much of our innermost life.

We return now to the hypothesis that the implicit motion of virtual tension and release in aesthetic form is what "goes straight through" to restore affective responsiveness and, perhaps, one's sense of identity. First, the relation of motion to affect their "dynamic congruency" (Sheets-Johnstone, 2003: 197).

Rhythm, the felt periodic recurrence of a pattern of stimulation, bears special mention as one form of the sense of motion. Freud (1924) speculated that the fluctuating strength of rhythmic motion underlies sensations of pleasure and unpleasure. It is unquestionably an essential ingredient of many powerful emotional experiences as well as constituting one of the basic elements of aesthetic form.

Looked at more closely in relation to affect, one may say that patterns of actual tension and release represent the motoric or kinesthetic aspects of an individual's affective response. Conversely, different contours of tension and release can be reliably identified with different affects (Tomkins, 1962–1963; Clynes and Nettheim, 1982). Further, one may speculate that these rippled motor discharge patterns of affect provide feedback that enhances affective intensity, i.e. they are generative as well as expressive.

A metaphorical way of expressing the relation of affect to motion is to say that just as a body needs a skeleton, feelings require an armature to bring them to self-awareness. Implicit motor patterns of muscular tension and release provide such a matrix. Thus, the remark (attributed to Nietzsche) that one listens to music with one's muscles highlights the *motoric* component of the affective response. This is now validated by finding that the motor areas of the brain are activated when listening (Benzon, 2001; cf. also,

Sheets-Johnstone, 1999: "affective feelings and tactile-kinaesthetic feelings are experimentally intertwined", p. 264; "movement-notation systems demonstrate empirically the dynamic congruency of movement and emotion in real life", p. 273).

Audition is also intimately involved with motion due to the abundant connections between the auditory pathways and the reticular system. The reticular system is concerned with a regulation of cortical electrical rhythms. It also has extensive connections with both the whole cerebral cortex and large subcortical areas. Perhaps the rhythmical component of the auditory input impacts on the whole brain by dint of the reticular system (Wertheim, 1997).

The reticular system might enable music to bypass cortical damage and stimulate subcortical areas on which rhythm probably depends (Henson, 1977). In addition, in the vicinity of the reticular activating system there are monamine modulators. These produce momentary facilitation in circuits that are actively involved in processing significant events (LeDoux, 2002: 313). Moreover, since the auditory nerve has an intimate and nearly immediate relation to the limbic system, considered to be the emotional center of the brain, music would provide access to emotional responsiveness.

Music and audition are widely represented in the brain in both cortical hemispheres. So even if one is deaf, imagined music will be processed by both hemispheres and gain immediate access to emotional centers. This helps provide access, too, for that quality of wholeness that constitutes each person's identity.

Finally, identity, the third element that along with motion and emotion sometimes responds with dramatic improvement to music. Like music and audition, identity is widely represented in the brain. This is reflected in the fact that it is perhaps the last psychic property to be lost.

> Identity has such a robust, widespread neural basis . . . as if personal style is so deeply ingrained in the nervous system, that it is never wholly lost, at least while there is still any mental life present at all . . . . This makes a continuing possibility of being affected by music, even in the most deeply damaged patients . . . . The same [widespread neural representation] is true for music too . . . and not only cortical but subcortical . . . . Where there is human consciousness, there can be a response to music; and it may be too . . . even when there is not.
>
> (Sacks, 1998: 10–11)

Self-recognition being an important aspect of one's sense of identity, let us recall the significance of movement as the basic way by which people recognize the constancy at the core of their identity. We earlier discussed the old (1931) experiment (reported by Allport, 1937) on how people recognize themselves. When all extraneous cues are blocked out, the experimental subjects frequently could not identify their own voices, styles of speech, pictures of their own hands or profiles. When they were filmed walking, however, they all recognized their own gait. Yet 70 per cent of the time they failed to identify the gaits of friends, despite the fact that one often sees the gait of friends but seldom one's own. We concluded earlier in discussing this that the most important element of self-recognition was not simply one's own motion *observed* but the inner, *kinesthetic* experience of rhythmic motion.

Another dimension by which we recognize ourselves, and are recognized by others, is that inner constancy throughout the apparent movement and variations in the course of time. It is what characterizes the unchanging nature of a person's identity. It lends itself by analogy to a musical theme and all its possible variations. It is worth a detour to consider two examples.

Bach's thirty Goldberg variations have been described by pianist Vladimir Feltsman as two two-sided mirrors. They start out facing each other, move toward each other, pass through each other to the other side to end at the same point in space and time where it began. Since there are a total of four sides, the result is the reflection of the whole piece inside and an eternity from outside.

Beethoven, who was brought up on Bach, crosses paths with him in his thirty Diabelli variations. They consist of melodic, harmonic, chromatic and dynamic variations which, as many writers have noted, are less transformations than, at moments, transfigurations to the sublime.

Both the Goldberg and the Diabelli variations show how wide a range of variations are possible on a single theme. Bach's Goldberg takes off on a single aria; Beethoven's Diabelli on an insipid waltz tune. Each builds a world.

As alluded to earlier, the idea of psychological identity describes an inner world of sameness and consistency despite and alongside the changes of time. This useful biological organizational principle does not imply that identity necessarily means inner homogeneity; there are many facets of an enduring identity. While this diversity within unity has been highlighted recently and referred to as requiring "normal dissociation" or "a necessary illusion of integration" of "self-states" (Bromberg, 1998), these terms carry an inevitable pathological coloration.

The older literature, on the other hand, enhanced the concept of identity with a felicitous musical image. The idea of theme and variations was intended to illustrate the coexistence of change with constancy. Applying a developmental perspective, Lichtenstein (1961) postulated that the early contact with the mother imprints an invariant primary identity theme on the infant. (I would say: "on the infant's constitutional givens.") He compared it to the unchanging inner form of a musical theme that remains constant despite subsequent transformations of that theme on other levels.

This "primal identity" at the beginning is based on narcissistic mirroring whereby self and other are seen as extensions of each other. In the course of time, later developmental variations of the primary identity theme include lessening degrees of symbiosis extending on to autonomy and true mutuality. It is significant that the earlier and later variations may continue to fluctuate among each other. (Freud (1925b) referred to a rhythm of transformation between ego libido and object libido; Lichtenstein preferred "rhythmic changes in the patterns of identity" (1964: 55).)

A contemporary take on identity might be that many identity patterns coexist as part of a rhythmically shifting polyphony of voices from the past. They consist of a spectrum of internalized object relations, ranging from symbiotic narcissism to separate mutuality and autonomy, each with its own contours of feeling. They might be termed "feeling forms of identity" to indicate both aspects – the range of internalized object relations and the feelings that inhere to them – together maintaining an equilibrium of constancy throughout the changes of Time.

Clinically, one measure of health is the ability to stay in touch with them and tolerate the ambiguity and complexity inherent in a broad spectrum of affective identity patterns – one that comprises both the capacity to let boundaries melt when appropriate as well as regain separateness. Another consideration is that some aspects contribute to a person's stability and others detract from it. In contemporary culture, especially, the sheer diversity and need for accommodation predispose to problems of identity diffusion. (We will discuss this later in relation to postmodernism.)

* * *

Let us suppose we are about to enter a new situation with few anticipatory clues as to what to expect. At our disposal are a number of different facets of one's self or identity to deploy and project like antennae or radar to probe the atmosphere. Intuiting the presence or absence of aspects of one's self in others goes a long way initially to allay or alert, confirm or discomfit.

This may be conceptualized in various ways: significant internalizations, "feeling-forms of identity," representations of one's body ego. It is an automatic and preliminary narcissistic test of how well one's bodily self-feelings are attuned to resonate with unfamiliar others.

When the new territory to be explored is some creative activity of one's own, such narcissistically-based testing – intrinsic to any initial approach to novelty – is probably central. Is it perhaps because the creative impulse puts so much at stake, springing from so intimate a need and attached to so bold an aspiration?

> A verse seeking a rhyme
> A note its overtones
> A Rhythm – Resonance.

On some level creative work is bound to be a self-portrait of one's own active mind in constantly shifting focus. Reaching into one's sense of self invites the projection of inner experience, to be objectified, re-subjectified and re-externalized. Filtering, replenishing, refining; losing, recovering, (re)discovering.

A clinical example will lead us into the therapeutic usefulness of creative work. A woman reacted to separation from her therapist with a feeling of being left without a skin.

> At the worst moment I thought about painting in order to feel better, and in fact I succeeded in painting three little pictures; and when I looked at them I felt a lot better. It was as if I could see myself, as if I could see that I existed. I recognized myself more than if I was looking at myself in the mirror.
>
> (Gaddini, 1982: 382–383)

Perhaps she recognized herself better than in a mirror because it was the functioning of her own mind projected onto the canvas, slowed down and magnified, that she recognized. Her own creative efforts of decomposing and recomposing on the canvas (Nietzsche's "shattering and rebuilding") allowed her to experiment and discover out there the healing process of loss and recovery.

The feeling-forms of her body-ego, projected, could be played with, refined and *perfected* in the course of making art. Working on the canvas offered a better external scaffold or prosthesis – a more proficient auxiliary ego – than her own workaday one. In its externalized version of decomposing in order to recompose more ideally, it could provide that improved narcissistic support its author required in order to function better when deprived of therapeutic support.

Artistic composition demands a peak level of integration; it presupposes a prior disassembly before attaining a new assemblage. To state it another way: art is mind playing repeatedly with decomposition and reintegration – idealized and realized.

This suggests a rationale as to why participating in art, either actively or passively, can temporarily "normalize" a mind, even one crippled with psychosis (e.g. Wolfli; see Rose, 1996). The artistic act is one of objectification of subjectivity; objectified, it offers the opportunity for vicarious reintegration. Needless to say, the same holds equally for an already well-functioning mind to optimize itself through artistic objectification and reintegration.

The therapeutic value of the arts lies in their offering an opportunity and a model of high-order reintegration. Either as an observer or as a participant one may feel consciously that which may have been unformed and latent – and thereby experience an enhanced sense of wholeness. Needless to say, this is independent of the work's creative status, if any.

Creative art, on the other hand, transforms subjective personal affects into more objective and relatively conflict-free nonverbal aesthetic forms. If an audience can avoid reflexively rejecting what is radically new and potentially traumatic (is there enough there that is reassuringly familiar?), the objective feeling-forms may resonate with emotional recognition of one's own mind, illuminated and transcended.

* * *

Just as the sense of *motion* plays a crucial a role in listening to music, this also holds for looking at art. The artists Paul Klee and

Alberto Giacometti both managed to bypass and/or transcend the content of personal problems by shifting their focus to the abstract forms of perception. Of special interest to us is the importance to both artists of the implicit virtual motion in visual perception. Their examples also illustrate how art can simultaneously serve privately defensive and publicly creative ends.

For Paul Klee color held many intensely personal meanings. As we will later describe, he learned to deal with these weighty *contents* through artistic *forms*.

The second entry of his diary (Klee, 1964) records how the colors red and gray became connected with infantile shame and conflict. At ages two to three years he had to wear his older sister's underwear that was too long for him. So, when the doorbell would ring he would hide to keep the visitor from seeing the gray flannel with the wavy red trimmings. White became related to gender envy at age three to four years when he wished he were a girl so he could wear lace-trimmed white panties. The color black was associated with his mother's morbid pessimism and always "seeing black" – she was wheelchair-bound for the last twenty-three years of her life.

Being intensely introspective and articulate, he was able to describe in later life not only his early color-related conflicts but his multifaceted identity. Self as a dramatic ensemble of prophetic ancestor, brutal hero, bon vivant, professor – all of whom amaze him!

Throughout his diary (Klee, 1964) we learn how, almost from the beginning, music permeated his life. His father taught music at a college in Berne. As a young man Paul regularly played violin or sometimes viola in both a quartet and a symphony orchestra. The diary is full of spirited references to concerts he attended or in which he participated.

Central to Klee's intuition about the nature of art is the idea of music as a metaphor to approach the dynamics of light and color movement. "I must some day be able to improvise freely on the chromatic keyboard of the rows of watercolor cups" (p. 244). "Colored bass notes . . . ward off flabbiness, not too dark" (p. 244).

During the course of fourteen years, Klee discovered that the essential thing in a work of art is how forms move. He described this in sexual terms:

> In the beginning . . . insertion of energy . . . form-determining sperm: the primitive male component . . . . [Then] shaping of

form: the primitive female component . . . . The final
consequence of both . . . is form. The energetic stimulus. Then
the fleshly growth of the egg. (pp. 310, 312)

For Klee, light and color are manifestations of the movement of
energy in the creation of forms.

I am now trying to render light simply as unfolding energy.
Light as color movement is somewhat newer. (p. 253)

Color possesses me. I don't have to pursue it. It will possess me
always, I know it. That is the meaning of this happy hour:
Color and I are one. I am a painter. (p. 297)

The real truth . . . remains invisible beneath the surface. The
colors that captivate us are not lighting, but light . . . diffused
clarity . . . . It is difficult to catch and represent this, because
the moment is so fleeting. It has to penetrate into our soul. The
formal has to fuse with the Weltenschauung . . . . Simple
motion [is] banal. The time element must be eliminated.
Yesterday and tomorrow as simultaneous. In music, polyphony helped . . . to satisfy this need . . . . Polyphonic painting
is superior to music in that, here, the time element becomes a
spatial element. (p. 374)

I understand this to mean that, in Klee's view, music provides the
illusion of having vanquished temporality by means of interweav-
ing many voices simultaneously and recurrently. "Polyphonic
painting," however, goes a step further. It converts the flow of *time*
into *spatial forms* that appear to move by dint of the implicit
virtual motion inherent in the perception of light and color.
  This construction allowed Klee to explore the movement and
qualities making up the nature of light and color perception. Safe
on an abstract plane far from the originating source of stressful
color, he succeeded in liberating color from infantile shame and
conflict. At the same time, however, let us not forget that his
theoretical formulation of how he determined and shaped aesthetic
forms retained its sexual construction unabashedly. As the saying
goes: he could have his cake and eat it, too. "What a fascinating
fate it is to master painting today (as it once was to master music)"
(Klee, 1964: 393).

A recent study (Danckwardt, 2002) independently supports the view of how aesthetic form can transcend personal conflict. It even details the formal means by which Klee bypassed the problematic content of color, directing attention instead to exploring the movement of light and color. It describes how, in *Untitled* 1914/94, multiple small squares encourage the eye to "enter only step by step." By circumscribing the scope and order of one's visual inspection, Klee is in effect dosing it out – to himself and us – in small amounts. The tonality of complementary colors guides the direction of one's visual inspection into a rhythm of motion. A yellow square at the bottom interacts with a pillar of color on either side: red-brown and gray-olive; their interaction with the yellow "creates an intense stretching of the light . . . the yellow has suddenly turned into energy"; overlaying it with varnish transforms it into green; this prevents its light from escaping forward; forced backwards, the light appears to diffuse and emerges as though from inside the whole watercolor.

This strategy encourages deep viewing "into the origins of the colors and the light" and on to an expanded way of seeing. Look! A color can be bent, boxed in, covered up, made to turn corners, diffuse and come up elsewhere. As Marion Milner (1957: 163) wrote: a color needs "listening to . . . allowing it to call for what colors it need[s] around it, colors that gr[o]w out of its own nature." Colors that "call" to each other and "grow" are colors that move and call out to each one's own perceptual motion to respond affectively.

The central importance of the *movement* of forms was Klee's transformative insight into his own work. The contrast with Giacometti's oeuvre is illuminating for, on the surface, the latter's creative vision appears to have been just the reverse. He endlessly explored the absolute *immobility* of figures as they are suspended in the void of space (and "silence") that surrounds them.

I argue, however, that their effect is essentially identical by opposite means: Giacometti's work forces the viewer into an aesthetic partnership. One has no choice but to project the movement of one's own perceptual processes into what is objectively total immobility. This subjective enactment is restorative and fortifying, for by just barely "reanimating" the artistic portrayal with one's own breath of life, one can imaginatively tolerate Giacometti's visions of the "silence" of Death.

It is apposite to interpose that this projection of one's own movement is well known to experimental psychology, where it was termed the "autokinetic phenomenon." It refers to the fact that a dot of light in a dark space without any referential frame will appear to move. The apparent direction of such perceived movement can be unconsciously conditioned experimentally. It is particularly pertinent to our discussion of *implicit* motion that the durability and speed of this perceptual learning is correlated with the amount of muscular effort *explicitly* exerted in recording the movement by pencil on paper (Haggard and Rose, 1944).

Returning now to Giacometti, we offer some background to his life and the importance of the element of trauma therein.

Giacometti suffered from a stultifying creative block for more than nine years until he saw a newsreel containing documentary footage from the Nazi death camps. His creative energy was suddenly released.

He described what happened in an ecstatic letter to his mother: "I see reality for the first time . . . . Every day I find something new. I almost never sleep . . . . I haven't read a paper for eight days or more" (quoted by Wilson, 2003).

Years later in an interview (Clay, 1963), he stated:

> I no longer knew just what it was that I saw on the screen. Instead of figures moving in three dimensional space I saw only black and white specks shifting on a flat surface. They had lost all meaning . . . . The unknown was the reality all around me, and no longer what was happening on the screen! . . . At the same time, there was a total revalorization of reality. It became passionate, unknown, marvelous . . . .
>
> By contrast . . . to the black and white specks [on the screen that] had lost all meaning . . . the Boulevard [Montparnasse] had the beauty of the *Arabian Nights* . . . . Everything was different, spaces and objects and colors and the silence, because the sense of space generates silence, bathes objects in silence . . . . I began to see heads in the void, in the space that surrounds them . . . fixed, immobilized definitively in time . . . not like any other object, but like something simultaneously living and dead . . . as if I had just crossed a threshold, as if I was entering a world never seen before. All the living were dead . . . . The waiter . . . become immobile, leaning toward me, with his mouth open, without any relation to the preceding moment, to the moment following, with his mouth open, his eyes fixed in an absolute immobility. And not only

people but objects at the same time underwent a transformation . . . .

(quoted by Lord, 1983: 258–259)

Note within the space of a page or so the repetition: "immobilized,"
"immobile," "immobility."

Giacometti is describing two phenomena: derealization of the
human images on the screen transforming them into black and
white specks; and a manic hyper-appreciation of brand new aspects
of the appearance of the world at large around him. In addition,
the transformation represents a drastic shift away from the *content*
and affective charge of the visual images of dead and dying humans
on the screen. In its place he discovers a novel way of viewing the
world at large. He reverses figure and ground. Instead of focusing
on *objects* in the visual field he forces us to become feelingfully
aware of the *spaces* in which his made-objects are suspended. In
which all objects – we too, potentially – become disconnected from
the steady din and its diverting illusion that we occupy a reserved
place in the flow of time.

Such a radical shift from objects to the surrounding space
defamiliarizes the world. It necessarily stimulates affect in each
viewer according to one's personal memories and associations. We
are immersed in a strange new perceptual landscape of Death in
Life and back again and again and yet again, with each of us both
victim and agent.

As, indeed, Giacometti must have experienced. His clinical elation was tantamount to a rebirth following a near-death encounter.
Nearly flooded by what he saw, though denying it, he transformed
the images into black and white specks. Then he dosed it out to
himself in small tolerable amounts, yes – but drawing from these
unliving and abstracted "specks" of living skeletons – managing
also to stretch us into a novel experience, at once profoundly
destabilizing and reassuring, of the unspeakably precarious world-
space we blithely inhabit.

Needless to say, viewing a documentary film of the Holocaust
cannot be equated with the actual and sustained physical traumatic
experience of the Holocaust. The film was thrice removed from
actual experience; at most, Giacometti had a mediated "traumatic"
experience. Secondly, the typical outcome of massive psychic
trauma is to precipitate or aggravate a creative block. Giacometti's
experience rather seems to have allowed him to overcome his

previous block and stimulated him to produce a flood of new work in a new style.

Massive and prolonged psychic trauma, on the other hand, leading to excess cortisol secretion, ultimately destroys the hippocampal memory system. This impairs the capacity to reflect, contextualize and experience and leaves only the now unregulated and over-stimulated amygdala to flood the organism with unassimilable memories. Thus, instead of finally working through memories to a successful conclusion, their repetition leads to the opposite – retraumatization (for a review, see Yovell, 2000).

Giacometti's coping with the Holocaust documentary mobilized his creative perceptual and contextual flexibility. He transformed private raw passions and conflicts into a new organizational structure of malleable, abstract perceptual data in new and relatively non-conflicted contexts. This made it possible to convoy intense and potentially traumatic stimulation safely through his own normal stimulus barriers and those of his audience.

In his charge as an artist, Giacometti provides a dynamic new *aesthetic* balance to allay the psychic imbalance of his disturbing vision of death in the midst of life. He provides us, the viewers, with tools to recompose new visual and psychic balances of our own. These had come out of his own phenomenological analysis of common visual experience. "Every time I look at the glass, it seems to remake itself" (Giacometti, 1990: 273). "The nearer you get the farther away the thing goes. It's an endless quest" (Giacometti, 1990: 275).

In other words, his own astutely observed optical experience invests his work with subjectivity and creates a new synthesis that forces the observer to experience the implicit motion in apparent immobility (Figures 8.1–8.4). In Figure 8.1, *Man Pointing* (1947), the observer's eye and bodily tension are forced in the same direction; likewise in *Man Walking II* (Figure 8.2, 1960), the downward drag of *Dog* (Figure 8.3, 1951); or, in *Man Falling* (Figure 8.4, 1950), in the direction of the fall. This last example is one of his most slender and fragile figures, perched on tiptoe and about to fall from its tiny pedestal while its head is hyper-extended backwards as if ecstatically. It creates an almost intolerable tension between "about to fall" and "not falling" (thus embodying what some consider the central dynamic of the art of dance).

As Giacometti wrote: "The heads, the figures, are nothing but continual movement . . . . They constantly remake themselves"

Figure 8.1   Representation of Giacometti's *Man Pointing* (1947).

(p. 218). A viewer must constantly refocus his/her gaze. In *Large Head of Diego* (1954), it shifts between the distances within the face and the security and weight of the narrow front-view torso. On the other hand, in other examples one is not forced to enact the implicit motion. It is implied in the tension between a tiny head and a heavy, sloping pedestal, as in *Woman of Venice, II, V, VIII* (1956). Or it is

Figure 8.2   Representation of Giacometti's *Man Walking II* (1960).

referred to symbolically, as in *The Chariot* (1950), where a filiform figure is mounted on a small platform between two immense wheels.

Distortions, ambiguities and asymmetries – widely distributed and illusory – turn each moment of concentration into flickering immediacy. They force one to see, sort and re-sort with quickened affects at the same time that they impose delay along the path of

Figure 8.3 Representation of Giacometti's *Dog* (1951).

habitual perception. The normally lazy search for familiarity is defeated and one must look and listen again. All this magnifies and recruits into awareness the normally subliminal pre-stages of perception – stimulating the interplay of primary and secondary process perception that underlies everyday perception (as so importantly disclosed by Charles Fisher's (1954, 1956) tachistoscopic studies).

This visual equilibrium of apparent mobility and stasis is to be found in the auditory sphere in the music of late Beethoven. The Diabelli variations, the slow movements of the string quartets, the Adagio movements of the Sonata in C Minor, opus 111, seem outside space and time. How is this brought about? According to recent musical analysis (Solomon, 2003), in opus 111, for example, a combination of accelerated motion, rhythmic diminution and minimal harmonic action leads to a blurring of any distinction between rapid movement and stasis. They condense into a time-stopping experience – a "shimmering sonic barrier" (pp. 207–209).

Thus, art and music both have their ways to reopen paths for the perception of implicit motion to "go straight through" to an increased tolerance for the coexistence of logical opposites – leading, in turn, to a more rapid interplay of feeling and thought. To what end? To rediscover how much more lies out there and inside beyond the unattended moment.

Current knowledge at the interface of visual art and neurology suggests that artists, especially those of the late 19th and 20th centuries, have tapped into brain specialization the details of which

Figure 8.4   Representation of Giacometti's *Man Falling* (1950).

are only now becoming clear. Recent research discloses that the brain harbors a whole mosaic of interconnected visual receptive areas. Some cells are responsive to color, others to movement, and still others to the direction a line makes along a visual field.

The art of Cezanne, the Cubists, of Mondrian and Malevich reflects the thesis (Zeki, 2001) that there is a strong relation between painting and how the brain works. Abstract and representational modes of painting enlist different cerebral systems. Many artists have distilled the same essential features of the visual world as physiologists have revealed based on anatomical properties of the central nervous system. In other words, modern art and neuroscience have both been exploring the outer dimensions of perception.

In a late letter to Stefan Zweig (July 27, 1938) in relation to art, Freud (1960: 444) mentioned "the quantitative proportion of unconscious material and preconscious treatment." Where was he pointing?

What is the relationship between the system Unconscious (Ucs) and the preconscious pre-stages of perception? I would surmise that the more equal distribution of (primary process) imagination in the former and (secondary process) realistic perception in the latter, as in dream imagery, provides the essential quality of ambiguity. This can be "ridden" into either neurotic regression, or – given the necessary gift – creative progression, or both.

In the course of their work, both Klee and Giacometti seemed also to have been engaged in self-healing and identity clarification. As Klee said of himself, from a cramped self he gradually experienced the reemergence of a self without blinkers. Both apparently succeeded in parallel evolutions of personal and artistic development – transforming inner problems into externalized aesthetic forms for which they could discover a new balance through creative play.

Much of how this comes about remains an enigma. How does a musical performer transfer the expression of affects via muscles to musical instrument? Or a painter via the brush?

How can distinct finger pressure patterns corresponding to various emotions be correctly recognized – though not necessarily transmitted – as the emotions they represent (Clynes and Nettheim, 1982)?

As for the separate acts of making and responding to art, let us try to describe the path of (bodily) affect.

Whether a painter working with pigment, or a musician with sound, an artist treats the aesthetic medium as plastic material. Through imaginative play, he/she transmutes an inner world of thought and feeling into an external art-product.

In the making of art, affect may often be experienced in waves of actual bodily tension and release of implicit motion accompanied by excitation and/or discomfiture. However they become mysteriously embodied in the art-work, their objective realization there ultimately forms the dynamic balance of *virtual* implicit motion of tension and release that characterizes aesthetic structure. This, in turn, is conducive to stimulating an other's responsive affect in the form of the implicit motion embodied in *actual* tension and release patterns. Not, be it again noted, necessarily by dint of *communication*, whether conscious or unconscious, of the art-maker's own affects; rather, by the *concordance* between the implicit motion – virtual and actual tension and release – that constitutes the dynamic inner structures of both art and affect.

As to words, in *Speak, Memory*, Nabokov (1947: 217) writes that poetry is a sign "of passing or having passed, or hoping to pass, through certain intense human emotions." In the course of this passage, the verbal transmission of "certain intense human emotions" into an expressive medium remains as much a mystery as the bodily transmission of affect in nonverbal art.

In summary, the implicit motion of *mind, itself*, generates states of being and activates affectomotor pathways that somehow transmute the mind's own motion into the virtual motion of nonverbal art. This, in turn, reflects, magnifies and thus makes the implicit motion of mind *perceptually* manifest to oneself.

The implicit motion of nonverbal art, then, indeed "goes straight through": it enlivens affective consciousness, and recharges – even reawakens – bodily sources of identity and the sense of self.

Chapter 9

A psychoanalyst listens to a musician listening to himself composing

How does music mean? Does "meaning" include evoking emotions? Whose? Composer's? Performer's? Listener's?

Evoking emotions through music is not the same as musical "communication," itself a controversial matter. Most musical scholars adhere to the concept that a composer sends out messages with objectively ascertainable content. Listeners receive it. This orthodox view is only now being challenged by a minority of scholars – "new musicologists."

For a composer the questions around music and emotion are especially complicated. A composer is not only a musical technician but a person who may have a deep expressive involvement with the occasion for which he/she is composing. How do these theoretical commitments and personal emotions interact? Do they affect a listener?

My take is that music is not produced by spontaneous generation in cyber space. Composers and performers have personal feelings and professional know-how. Together with their audience, all are listeners, too, each with a history of voice-prints: songs, sounds, rhythms. These must impart some unique emotional coloration to any musical experience.

Jonathan D. Kramer, composer, found himself thinking deeply about what the music meant to him as an individual with expressive needs uniquely his own. "I simply wrote the music I needed to write, feeling what it meant (to me) but not pondering too much about *how* it meant" (unpublished: 4). He remained "dubious of music's ability to communicate specific thoughts, ideas, or images" (p. 5). But he found that "listening to music can be a powerful experience, evoking real and raw emotions . . . . *How* this is possible [is] the major unexplained mystery of the musical art" (p. 5).

When Kramer was writing *Requiem for the Innocent*, a Vietnam protest piece for orchestra – three minutes of untexted music – it took only eighteen hours to write what he felt flat out, including orchestration and copying parts. Deeply involved in a cause, he felt good, then bad about feeling good because people were dying in Vietnam while he was writing far away in safety. In this experience, technical task and personal feelings were inextricably interwoven.

It took almost nine months to write *No Beginning, No End* for orchestra and chorus. This commemorated fifteen Soviet Jewish poets, intellectuals and leaders whom Stalin had had executed. "It was obligated to mean something beyond itself," namely, "a symbol of the indestructibility of truth." Note "it" – not "I."

It also had a private meaning: *as a Jew*, a solidarity with the murdered poets. One of the harrowing experiences of Kramer's youth was hearing at age ten his grandfather tell of how he narrowly escaped death in escaping from Lithuania because of being a Jew – "not because of his beliefs, but because of his being. And that being is mine."

The third time, thirteen years later, was a Holocaust remembrance event. *Remembrance of a People*, for piano, string orchestra or string quintet, and optional narrator is more personal and less political. It took eleven months to write. During that time he kept a diary because he felt a conflict between his identity as a detached musical theorist and as an emotionally involved composer: in the former aspect he remained committed to the belief that music is incapable of communicating specific ideas, but in the latter he wished to invoke specific emotional reactions in others.

There was a yet more intimate necessity beyond the technical matter of crafting the music, and the personal one of wishing to transmit his feelings. "I needed to use *my* musical art to help *me* come to terms with memories of the Holocaust" (p. 24): composing as working through.

A painter said, "I paint in order to see what I couldn't see unless I painted it." Attempting to objectify thoughts and feelings in whatever form discloses them more fully to oneself. We talk, write, perform, in part, to uncover what we think and feel as well as to experience the sense of mastery that comes from expressive self-actualization. If others can be made to feel deeply within themselves what one has projected out there like a message in a bottle, it may help one recognize oneself the better; reflected back from out there, and by repeated projections and reflections, one may continue to learn and grow.

The wish to communicate embodies a full spectrum of objective and subjective elements. The more subjective end ranges from the conscious wish to experience a sense of personal attunement and responsive resonance to a more unconscious impulse for momentary oneness with an other. The latter probably harks back to the earliest preverbal affective interplay between infant and caretaker.

The act of communicating with oneself by writing a diary in the course of one's own creative process is an act of objectification in the service of recruiting more self-involvement. In Kramer's case it led to his happily achieving a closer collaboration between both aspects of himself.

In technical jargon, this refers to the subjectively expressive aspects of one's self working in close harmony with the more objectively reflective ones – subjectivity and objectivity alternating and informing each other. Asking which is the more important in eliciting affective resonance in an audience is probably analogous to the question of what ultimately is successful in psychoanalysis: the intellectual insight and perspective one gains, or the emotional ambience of the therapeutic relationship that one internalizes. A pragmatic "answer" may lie less in understanding how this works – we do not know exactly – than in facilitating and trusting the power of the Unconscious to integrate both aspects.

Turning to Kramer's diary, the first entry has to do with the "surprising" course the music is taking when the work proceeds "intuitively." Without conscious intention, Kramer finds the music moving around transforming themes – something he would have ordinarily found "utterly uninteresting." Not surprisingly, the interval of a minor third assumes importance.

The next month, "the movement seems to be done" as it ends with "the music break[ing] off unexpectedly." Does this refer, he wonders, to "lives cut short"? Much of the piano part also "cuts off." It is rarely integrated with the rest of the ensemble. "It either plays against the others, accompanies discreetly, is a soloist, or is silent." Are all these musical metaphors for alienation? Along with this and also unexpectedly, two fragments intrude; one is from Tchaikovsky's *Pathétique* symphony and the other an altered fragment of the *Dies Irae* tune. "Neither quotation [is] intentional."

Another discovery: towards the end of the second movement, he realizes that the whole movement has been more tonally integrated in F-minor than he had realized. He asks himself what tonality or atonality has to do with grief. Theoretically he would have assumed that atonality would have been more fitting to express Holocaust grief than tonality. However, since tonality sets up firmer expectations [of continuity] than does atonality, maybe deliberately frustrating them is more wrenching and thus actually more suitable.

Valid or not, this is an interesting attempt to correlate musical tonality/atonality with the actual psychological experience of continuity/discontinuity; this linkage is the connection to the matter of loss and grief.

Eight months into the piece, and now in the fourth movement, Kramer realizes he is fulfilling a long-standing wish.

> I had always planned to write a piece that sits on the fence between tonality and atonality . . . without a huge contradiction of language. I have just figured out that the Holocaust piece *is* this music . . . . It scares me . . . . I must be careful . . . . [It could] come perilously close to an atonality-as-ugliness aesthetic. I must not let that happen . . . .
>
> I find myself wanting to write a long (too long?) series of sighs, or cries, of anguish in the middle of the movement . . . [they] trail off into (brief) silence. This seems to happen again and again, phrase after phrase . . . . The sighing phrases are now beginning to resolve toward consonance.

These diary entries sound like a struggle with the power of emotions and an attempt to use atonality as a defense against expressiveness: specifically, his own feelings about the Holocaust. Composing has helped him deal with them. "The Holocaust . . . is no intellectual exercise. *It happened* . . . . The final movement deals not with specific images and feelings but with inescapable reality." The nature of this reality: ultimately inexpressible – awesome.

As the diary proceeds we find Kramer thinking less and less about technical matters and just writing. Musical relationships work and become more believable when they arise out of intense involvement with the materials rather than conscious intention. "The process is not calculated but felt." Conceptual logic does not always lead to musical logic. At one point there was a problem about whole-tones. It went away when he became "less rigid about . . . procedures – allowing in a few foreign notes when they knocked at the door. The problem was not with the idea but with its realization."

Clearly, the very process of composition had taught its composer to experience first-hand the expressive power of music. Perhaps closer to the mark, he learned something about the depth and intensity of his own power to feel – while holding it at arm's length behind a cognitive shield.

The last dated entry in the diary has to do with a big break-through in trying to write a "poignant melody" in his imagination. This had "yielded up awful possibilities." The melody had centered on a previously missing E-flat. He found it not in his imagination but in another movement. He then was able to proceed quickly with the task of editing. Finally, he felt released.

One wonders if this detail represents an important micro-enactment of a private response to the Holocaust: through com-posing the music, he put himself through an actual experience of loss and recovery – of an E-flat.

* * *

How, then, does music mean? While it remains mysterious, a possible outline may be ventured.

An early overall view offered by Kramer was that meaning results from a complex interaction of composer, score, editor, performer, performance, recording engineer, playback system, and – above all – listener. A striking example of why "above all, with the listener" is how two professionally trained musicians heard a particular passage from one of Kramer's compositions (*Serbelloni Serenade*, 1995): one heard Russian contrapuntal music like that found in some Shostakovich fugues, and the other heard Mexican bullfight music.

My formulation begins with a sense of wholeness as a criterion of aesthetic form. Such wholeness used to be compared to that of a whole organism growing out of nature as a living being (Coleridge, 1817). Hence, it was termed an organic unity that succeeds in making the art "work" or "live" (Hospers, 1967). Every essential element is present; every non-essential element has been eliminated.

It should be noted, however, that contemporary postmodernism in music may seek a unity that is not organic; or an organicism that does not necessarily lead to unity. In short, in postmodern thought, organicism and unity are not equated.

Kramer (1995) has offered a number of clarifications. For example: the alleged unity of a composition is textual unity; the performer's perceptual unity imparts the textual unity of performance; music as constituted by the experiencing person who listens to it is perceptual unity. These are not the same.

Continuing, Kramer argues that the postmodern aesthetic of disunity is to force our minds to make sense of disorienting and disunited experiences inherent in modern life. Those who have found the concept of order to be oppressive may welcome disunity, even chaos, and court them as liberating.

While postmodernism and modernism are difficult to distinguish, the latter incorporates and reinterprets the past; the former takes a fundamentally ironic attitude to the past and places the burden of making sense of the pastiche or collage of past and present upon the individual listener. Fundamentally, the postmodern challenge arises from a cacophony of contemporary values and processes that defy any external notion of unity and leaves any ordering principle up to the individual.

It is claimed (Kramer, 2001) that postmodern music not only exploits an interpenetration of past and present but reflects multicultural, social, political, and technological contexts. It embraces a pluralism of contradictions, fragmentations, discontinuities, meanings and temporalities. It shares with contemporary art in general a common feature: it leaves it up to the audience to ascribe meaning and apply structure, rather than leaving it primarily with the musical scores, performances or composers.

The criticism of postmodernism in general is that the seeming freedom of its cultural relativism and perspectivism presents a danger: it can be exploited to replace emotion and reason as the traditional values whereby order replaces cacophony. In other words, instead of limitations being seen as spurs to creativity, their abolition in the name of freedom may be declared, *ipso facto*, creative. The "saturated self" of a postmodern consciousness, instead of being enriched by immersion in other perspectives, then risks losing a reliable sense of identity and drowning (Gergen, 1991).

This direct linkage to "identity" suggests a clinical comparison. Creative ferment and growth for an individual require a favorable dynamic balance between the two components of identity, constancy and change. Equal dangers are stagnancy on the one hand and overstimulation to the point of flooding on the other.

The flooding of overstimulation is the inner essence of psychic trauma. Under the threat or actuality of trauma, flooding signals existential anxiety: danger of catastrophic loss of structure and sense of self.

In clinical situations, one defense against the fear of loss of self is to create an array of "as-ifs" or "false selves" – often unconscious. In postmodern art, so-called "appropriations," for example, are (defiantly) conscious. Whether conscious or unconscious, false selves offer an illusion of safety and distance behind which one's true but vulnerable self can hide. The price: loss of authenticity.

"Inauthentic" is, in fact, a criticism leveled against postmodern art (Kuspit, 2000). Some postmodern artists, however, do not take this label as a put-down but choose to relish it as celebrating a virtue. In any case, we may ask: "Is postmodern art a post-traumatic regression and/or a social and political commentary more than a movement of aesthetic significance?"

Attempting to extrapolate these considerations to individual human psychology, one may thus adopt different points of view: pejoratively diagnose conditions like counterphobia, identity diffusion, a dissociation of thought and feeling; or declare that anomie – lack of adherence to usual individual or group norms – has become the new norm. On this latter view, postmodernism would appear as an attempt to come to terms with pervasive unpredictability and potential trauma. In short, a (short-term?) adaptation in the name of creativity.

Leaving the significance of postmodernism to history to decide, how does music mean? I postulate the following guidelines.

Central to a traditional psychological sense of wholeness is a harmonious coming together of thought and feeling: feelingful thought, thoughtful feeling. Early in life, in the preverbal period, they were interwoven; with maturation and conventional education they become more and more separated; when they are reunited in love, varieties of religious experience and historical notions of art, something of this original sense of wholeness is temporarily and ineffably restored.

The dynamic core of feelingful thought or thoughtful feeling is an implicit motion of balanced tension and release; tension is related to thought, and release to feeling.

The same dynamic lies at the center of aesthetic form, except that now it is a matter of virtual implicit motion of balanced tension and release.

The recognition of this implicit motion and structural concordance between the external wholeness of aesthetic form and one's own internal wholeness of thought and feeling leads to an automatic responsive resonance, perhaps even a brief sense of union on the part of an audience. Its own sense of wholeness has been vicariously validated and reinforced.

However, the specific thoughts and feelings making up any individual listener's responsive resonance will still depend in large measure on that person's history, associations and present circumstances.

An attempt to locate these formulations in a wider context would go something like this. Nonverbal art, like music:

1 stimulates and gratifies the expectancies of a motivational system that
2 seeks corroborating reflections of the flow of one's own mental life by
3 offering augmented and slowed-down external images of virtual tension and release in the form of aesthetic equivalents of the flow of mental life. They
4 invite an external–internal interplay of implicit motion that
5 recruits affect and latent memory,
6 approximating the early developmental experience of wordless attunement and resonance between caretaker and infant. It thereby
7 enhances a sense of wholeness of self within an expanded awareness of the world.
8 Not unlike Love.

As for creative gift and neurotic deficit, they may flourish in their separate spheres or interact. One need neither demonize nor romanticize any relationship between them as might appear, so long as they are not conflated.

One is rare and the other run-of-the-mill. Another distinction is that with art, as with fine wit, less is more. Reality is permanently enriched as the world, ever-newly experienced, continues to grow. Whereas, in the compromise formations, condensations and fusions of neurotic conflict, reality becomes stereotyped, automatized, constricted. Less is, indeed, less.

Much modern art has to do with highlighting the ambiguity and irreconcilability inherent in reality; it forces one to acknowledge and live with the contrasts and the coexistence of logical opposites and existential conflicts. Like grief, these are incapable of emotional "arbitrage."

The power of memory, for example, to repossess lost love is not to be "averaged out" with the craving to continue to live at the full. Each is a rich note of a complex chord combining consonance and dissonance – together propelling the "musical" action forward in endless elaborations of lived Time.

As one moves into the unknown we embolden ourselves by projecting comforting, familiar aspects of ourselves to temper fearful anticipations of the strange and foreign. Our central nervous system is necessarily both less than fully open and more than merely solipsistic. Perhaps we are all more eager to refind than to discover – whatever may be discoverable through such a system. Art experiments with various combinations of self and other, internal and external, and offers them for objects of contemplation.

This much seems clear. The "truth" of art does not lie simply in the repressed Unconscious as the surrealists naïvely believed. Not, that is to say, in the veridicity of unconscious fantasy. Or in the psychopathological "return of the repressed." Postmodernism, for its part, grapples in its own way with its own truth.

Is it too much to say that, in making certain things conceivable and feel-able – if not reasonable and understandable – (primary process) imagination and (secondary process) realistic cognition achieve a dynamic new equilibrium? Or, more simply, that the area between feeling and thought is the seed-bed of creative imagination? Where this leads is unforseeable. Limitless. Therefore, ungraspable. This, our "truth"?

* * *

One might like to hope that verbalization and psychoanalytic insight into oneself could also expand one's perceptual awareness of the world. Likewise, one might hope that a fine-tuned aesthetic sensibility could bring knowledge and personal insight. Alas, for both areas. However much harmonious overlap we may attain between words and music, thought and feeling, mind and body, conscious and unconscious, a gap and a mystery will remain.

The urge to overcome the earliest sense that a gap exists between Self and Other lends itself to later epiphanous experiences packaged in various forms, including mystical, sexual, aesthetic, chemical, philosophical and religious varieties. It is opposed by the biological necessity to preserve the integrity of the self. The tension between the twin impulses for fusion and separateness can spark moments of instant spontaneous engagement from within. As with music.

Why is music instantaneously apprehensible in contrast to speech about music that reflects a secondary interpretive approach? In answer to this, an ethnologically based theory (Keil and Feld, 1994) holds that a listener is enticed into a feelingful engagement with music – "*getting into*" and "*getting off on*" it – by minor discrepancies or subtle irregularities in performance. For example, timing being a split second apart, pitch being just a shade off, overtones, harmonics, and textures being maximized. In jazz this may be referred to as "inflection," "pulse" or "timbre."

This view holds that these micro-discrepancies reflect that "the universe is open, imperfect, and subject to redefinition by every emergent self . . . [who] has a different time feel . . . a different signature and . . . dances differently" (Keil and Feld, 1994: 171). Hence the instantaneous joyful participation in the delights of music.

A psychoanalyst might intuit that the attraction of the "slight out of syncness" and "out of tuneness" might itself reflect that the original developmental union we hypothesize between infant and caretaker was less perfect than the one we are inclined to idealize in safe retrospect.

For psychoanalysis, reason is a weak reed to lean on but it is the best we have to try to answer unconscious conflict now made conscious; and it probably does nothing to cure artistic insensitivity. As for the arts, except for the greatest literature, they may as well lay down their arms before the problem of *understanding* neurosis.

If aesthetic feeling-forms succeed in expanding perception and with it the apprehension of our representations of reality – knowing they are but representations as well as irreducibly circular – and thereby gain a greater degree of wholeness of self, they serve their author and a grateful audience well.

Why "grateful?"

But for the grace of Art – and its double mirror – we might have continued in the semi-torpor of habitual daily-ness. Music above all bypasses language and concepts to give explicit shape to the implicit motion of mind.

Identity is the internal face of feeling and thought; creative form, its outer one. With fresh affect and clarified perception we glimpse the richness within and without, and learn not answers, but awe.

Bibliography

Abel, D. (1969), "Frozen Movement in *Light in August*", in D.L. Minter (ed.) *Twentieth Century Interpretations of Light in August*, Englewood Cliffs, NJ: Prentice Hall.

Aiken, C. (1960), "William Faulkner: The Novel as Form", in F.J. Hoffman and O.W. Vickery (eds) *William Faulkner: Two Decades of Criticism*, East Lansing, MI: Michigan State College Press.

Akhtar, S. (2000), "Mental Pain and the Cultural Ointment of Poetry", *International Journal of Psychoanalysis* **81**:229–243.

Allport, G.W. (1937), *Personality*, New York: Henry Holt.

Amati-Mehler, J., Argentieri, S. and Canestri, J. (1993), *The Babel of the Unconscious*, trans. J. Whitelaw Cucco, Madison, CT: International Universities Press.

Arlow, J.A. (1986), "Psychoanalysis and Time", *Journal of the American Psychoanalytic Association* **34**:507–528.

Balter, L. (1999), "On The Aesthetic Illusion", *Journal of The American Psychoanalytic Association* **47**:1293–1333.

Beck, W. (1951), "William Faulkner's Style", in F.J. Hoffman and O.W. Vickery (eds) *William Faulkner: Two Decades of Criticism*, East Lansing, MI: Michigan State College Press.

Becker, J. (1979), "Time and Tune in Java", in A.L. Becker and A.A. Yengoyan (eds) *The Imagination of Reality*, Norwood, NJ: Ablex Publishing Corporation.

Beckett, S. (1955), *Molloy*, in *Three Novels by Samuel Beckett*, New York: Grove Press.

Benzon, W.L. (2001), *Beethoven's Anvil*, New York: Basic Books.

Berenson, B. (1950), *Aesthetics and History*, London: Constable.

Bergson, H. (1944), *Creative Evolution*, New York: Modern Library.

Bernstein, L. (1976), *The Unanswered Question: Six Talks at Harvard*, Cambridge, MA: Harvard University Press.

Bonaparte, M. (1940), "Time and the Unconscious", *International Journal of Psychoanalysis* **21**:427–468.

Brody, M.W. (1952), "The Symbolic Significance of Twins in Dreams", *Psychoanalytic Quarterly* **21**:172–180.

Bromberg, P.M. (1998), *Standing in the Spaces. Essays on Clinical Process, Trauma, and Dissociation*, Hillsdale, NJ: The Analytic Press.

Brooks, C. (1969), "The Community and the Pariah", in D.L. Minster (ed.) *Twentieth Century Interpretations of Light in August*, Englewood Cliffs, NJ: Prentice Hall.

Buber, M. (1963), "Man and His Image-Work", trans. M. Friedman, *Portfolio* **7**:88–99.

Bucci, W. (1985), "Dual Coding: A Cognitive Model for Psychoanalytic Research", *Journal of the American Psychoanalytic Association* **33**:571–607.

—— (1997), *Psychoanalysis and Cognitive Science: A Multiple Code Theory*, New York: Guilford.

Cassirer, E. (1923), *The Philosophy of Symbolic Forms*, Vol. 1. New Haven, CT: Yale University Press.

Clay, J. (1963), "Alberto Giacometti: Le Long Dialogue avec le Mort d'un Tres Grand Sculpteur de Notre Temps", *Realités*, **215**:135–145.

Clynes, M. and Nettheim, N. (1982), "The Living Quality of Music", in *Music, Mind, and Brain. The Neuropsychology of Music*, New York and London: Plenum.

Coleridge, S.T. (1817), *Biographia Literaria*, New York: Everyman's Library, 1906.

Cummins, P.F. (1992), *Dachau Song*, New York: Peter Lang.

Damasio, A. (1994), *Descartes' Error*, New York: Grosset/Putnam.

—— (1999), *The Feeling Of What Happens*, New York: Harcourt Brace.

—— (2003), *Looking for Spinoza*, Orlando, FL: Harcourt.

Danckwardt, J.F. (2002), "Comments on a Possible Relation between Fine Arts and Psychoanalysis. Panel on Colour and Music: Voices of the Unconscious", (reporter) A. Sabbadini, *International Journal of Psychoanalysis*, **83**:263–266.

Dewey, J. (1934), *Art as Experience*, New York: Minton, Balch.

Dufrenne, M. (1953), *The Phenomenology of Aesthetic Experience*, trans. E.S. Casey *et al.* (1973), Evanston, IL: Northwestern University Press.

Elkisch, P. (1957), "The Psychological Significance of the Mirror", *Journal of the American Psychoanalytic Association*, **5**:235–244.

Emde, R.N. (1983), "The Prerepresentational Self and its Affective Core", in *The Psychoanalytic Study of the Child*, **38**:165–192, New Haven, CT: Yale University Press.

Epstein, D. (1988), "Tempo Relations in Music. A Universal?", in E. Rentschler, B. Herzberger and D. Epstein (eds) *Beauty and the Brain. Biological Aspects of Aesthetics*, Basle: Birkhauser Verlag.

—— (1993), "On Affect and Musical Motion", in S. Feder, R.L. Karmel and G.H. Pollock (eds) *Psychoanalytic Explorations in Music. Second Series*, Madison, CT: International Universities Press.

—— (1995), *Shaping Time. Music, the Brain, and Performance*, New York: Schirmer.

Erikson, E. (1958), *Young Man Luther: A Study on Psychoanalysis and History*, New York: Norton.

Erikson, K.T. (1976), *Everything in Its Path*, New York: Simon and Schuster.

Evans, L.K. (1987), "Sundown Syndrome in Institutionalized Elderly", *Journal of the American Geriatrics Society* **35**:101–108.

Faber, M.D. (1988), "The Pleasures of Rhyme: A Psychoanalytic Note", *International Review of Psycho-Analysis* **15**:375–380.

Faulkner, W. (1932), *Light in August*, New York: Random House (Modern Library).

Feld, S. (1974), "Linguistic Models in Ethnomusicology", *Ethnomusicology* **18**:197–218.

Ferenczi, S. (1913), "Stages in the Development of the Sense of Reality", in *Sex in Psychoanalysis*, 1950, New York: Brunner.

Finn, D. (1992), *The Story of Ernest*, Redding Ridge, CT: Black Swan Books.

Fisher, C. (1954), "Dreams and Perception", *Journal of The American Psychoanalytic Association* **2**:389–445.

—— (1956), "Dreams, Images, and Perception", *Journal of The American Psychoanalytic Association* **4**:5–48.

Flam, G. (1992), *Singing for Survival. Songs of the Lodz Ghetto, 1940–1945*, Urbana, IL and Chicago: University of Illinois.

Freeman, W. (2000), "A Neurobiological Role of Music in Social Bonding", in N.L. Wallin, B. Merker and S. Brown (eds) *The Origins of Music*, Cambridge, MA: MIT Press.

Freud, E.L. (ed.) (1960), *Letters of Sigmund Freud*, (trans.) T. and J. Stern, New York: Basic Books.

Freud, S. (1891), *On Aphasia*, 1953, New York: International Universities Press.

—— (1895), "Project for a Scientific Psychology", in *The Origins of Psychoanalysis*, 1964, New York: Basic Books.

—— (1900), *The Interpretation of Dreams*, Standard Edition **4 & 5**, 1955, London: Hogarth.

—— (1913), *On Psychoanalysis*, Standard Edition **12**:207–211, 1958, London: Hogarth.

—— (1917), *Mourning and Melancholia*, Standard Edition **14**:243–258, 1957, London: Hogarth.

—— (1920), *Beyond the Pleasure Principle*, Standard Edition **18**:1–64, 1955, London: Hogarth.

Freud, S. (1924), *The Economic Problem of Masochism*, Standard Edition **19**:157–170, 1961, London: Hogarth.

—— (1925a), *Negation*, Standard Edition **19**:233–239, 1961, London: Hogarth.

—— (1925b), *An Autobiographical Study*, Standard Edition **20**:7–74, 1959, London: Hogarth.

—— (1940), *An Outline of Psychoanalysis*, Standard Edition **23**:139–207, 1964, London: Hogarth.

Fromm, E. (1965), "Hypnoanalysis: Theory and Two Case Excerpts", *Psychotherapy: Theory, Research, and Practice* **2**:127–133.

Fuller, P. (1980), *Art and Psychoanalysis*, London: Writers and Readers Publishing Cooperative.

Gaddini, E. (1982), "Early Defensive Fantasies and the Psychoanalytic Process", *International Journal of Psychoanalysis* **63**:379–388.

Gergen, K.J. (1991), *The Saturated Self: Dilemmas of Identity in Contemporary Life*, New York: Basic Books.

Giacometti, A. (1990), M. Leiris and J. Dupin (eds) *Ecrits/Alberto Giacometti*, Paris: Hermann.

Gilot, F. and Lake, C. (1965) *Life with Picasso*, New York: New American Library.

Gombrich, E.H. (1972), "The Visual Image", *Scientific American* **227**:82–96.

Gorelick, K. (1989), "Perspective: Rapprochement Between the Arts and Psychotherapies: Metaphor the Mediator", *The Arts in Psychotherapy* **16**:149–155.

Gray, D.D. (1993), *I Want to Remember*, Wellesley, MA: Roundtable.

Greenacre, P. (1957), "The Childhood of the Artist", *The Psychoanalytic Study Of the Child* **12**:47–72.

Greene, D.B. (1982), *Temporal Processes in Beethoven's Music*, New York: Gordon and Breach.

Haggard, E.A. and Rose, G.J. (1944), "Some Effects of Mental Set and Active Participation in the Conditioning of the Autokinetic Phenomenon", *Journal of Experimental Psychology* **34**:45–59.

Harrer, G. and Harrer, H. (1977), "Music, Emotion and Autonomic Function", in M. Critchley and R.A. Henson (eds) *Music and the Brain*, London: Heinemann Medical Books.

Hartocollis, P. (1976), "Time as a Dimension of Affects", *Journal of the American Psychoanalytic Association* **20**:92–108.

Hasty, C. (1997), *Meter as Rhythm*, New York: Oxford University Press.

Heisenberg, W. (1958), *Physics and Philosophy*, New York: Harper & Row.

Henson, R.A. (1977), "Neurological Aspects of Musical Experience", in M. Critchley and R.A. Henson (eds) *Music and the Brain*, Springfield, IL: C.C. Thomas.

Hindemith, P. (1945), *Craft of Musical Composition*, revised edn, New York: Associated Music Publishers.

—— (1961), *A Composer's World*, Garden City, NY: Doubleday Anchor Books.

Hofer, M.A. (1984), "Relationships as Regulators – A Psychobiological 'Perspective on Bereavement'", *Psychosomatic Medicine* **46**:183–197.

—— (1990), "Early Symbiotic Processes: Hard Evidence From a Soft Place", in R.A. Glick and S. Bone (eds) *Pleasure Beyond the Pleasure Principle*, New Haven, CT: Yale University Press.

Hoffman, F.J. (1951), "Introduction", in F.J. Hoffman and O.W. Vickery (eds) *William Faulkner: Two Decades of Criticism*, East Lansing, MI: Michigan State College Press.

Holland, N. (1975), *Five Readers Reading*, New Haven, CT: Yale University Press.

Hospers, J. (1967), "Problems of Aesthetics", in P. Edwards (ed.) *The Encyclopedia of Philosophy*, **1**, New York: Macmillan.

Humphrey, N. (2000), "Now You See It, Now You Don't", *Neuro-Psychoanalysis* **2**:14–17.

Isaacs, S. (1943), "The Nature and Function of Fantasy", in M. Klein, P. Heimann, S. Isaacs and J. Riviere (eds) *Developments in Psychoanalysis*, 1952, London: Hogarth.

Jackendoff, R. (2000), "Unconscious, Yes. Homunculus, ???", *Neuro-Psychoanalysis* **2**:17–20.

Jaffe, J. and Feldstein, S. (1970), *Rhythms of Dialogue*, New York: Academic Press.

James, W. (1892), *Psychology*, New York: Henry Holt.

Jaques, E. (1982), *The Form of Time*, New York: Crane, Russak.

Keil, C. and Feld, S. (1994), *Music Grooves*, Chicago: University of Chicago Press.

Klee, P. (1964), *The Diaries of Paul Klee 1898–1918*, ed. F. Klee, Berkeley and Los Angeles: University of California Press.

Klein, M. (1957), "Envy and Gratitude", in R. Money-Kyrle (ed.) *The Writings of Melanie Klein*, Vol. 3, London: Hogarth Press.

Knoblauch, S.H. (2000), *The Musical Edge of Therapeutic Dialogue*, Hillsdale, NJ: The Analytic Press.

Kohut, H. (1957), "Observations on the Psychological Functions of Music", *Journal of the American Psychoanalytic Association* **5**:389–407.

—— (1971), *The Analysis of the Self*, New York: International Universities Press.

Kohut, H. and Levarie, S. (1950), "On the Enjoyment of Listening to Music", *Psychoanalytic Quarterly* **19**:64–87.

Kramer, J.D. (1981), "New Temporalities in Music", *Critical Inquiry*, Chicago: University of Chicago Press, Spring, 539–556.

—— (1988), *The Time of Music*, New York and London: Schirmer.

Kramer, J.D. (1995), "Beyond Unity: Toward an Understanding of Musical Postmodernism", in E.W. Marvin and R. Hermann (eds) *Concert Music, Rock, and Jazz Since 1945: Essays and Analytical Studies*, Rochester, NY: University of Rochester Press.

—— (2001), "The Nature and Origins of Musical Postmodernism", in J. Lochhead and J. Auner (eds) *Postmodern Music/Postmodern Thought*, London: Routledge.

—— (unpublished) *Coming to Terms with Music as Protest and Remembrance: One Composer's Story*.

Kris, A. (1992), "Interpretation and the Method of Free Association", *Psychoanalytic Inquiry* **12**:208–224.

Kubler, G. (1962), *The Shape of Time: Remarks on the History of Things*, New Haven, CT: Yale University Press.

Kuspit, D. (2000), *Redeeming Art: Critical Reveries*, New York: Allsworth Press.

Langer, S.K. (1942), *Philosophy in a New Key*, Cambridge, MA: Harvard University Press.

—— (1953), *Feeling and Form*, New York: Scribner's.

—— (1957), *Problems of Art*, New York: Scribner's.

Laub, D. and Auerhahn, N.C. (1993), "Knowing and Not Knowing Massive Psychic Trauma: Forms of Traumatic Memory", *International Journal of Psychoanalysis* **74**:287–302.

Laub, D. and Podell, D. (1995), "The Art of Trauma", *International Journal of Psychoanalysis* **76**:991–1005.

LeDoux, J. (1996), *The Emotional Brain*, New York: Simon and Schuster.

—— (2002), *Synaptic Self*, New York: Simon and Schuster.

Lewin, B. (1950), *The Psychoanalysis of Elation*, New York: Norton.

Lichtenstein, H. (1961), "Identity and Sexuality", *Journal of the American Psychoanalytic Association* **9**:179–260.

—— (1964), "The Role of Narcissism in the Emergence and Maintenance of a Primary Identity", *International Journal of Psychoanalysis* **45**:49–56.

—— (1971), "The Malignant No: A Hypothesis Concerning the Interdependence of the Sense of Self and the Instinctual Drives", in *The Unconscious Today*, New York: International Universities Press.

Lord, J. (1983), *Giacometti: A Biography*, New York: Farrar, Straus, Giroux.

Lourie, R.S. (1949), "The role of rhythmic patterns in childhood", *American Journal of Psychiatry* **105**:653–660.

Magee, B. (2000), *The Tristan Chord – Wagner and Philosophy*, New York: Henry Holt.

Mahler, M. (1966), "Notes on the Development of Basic Moods: The Depressive Affect", in *Psychoanalysis – A General Psychology*, New York: International Universities Press.

Mahoney, P.J. (1987), *Freud as a Writer*, New Haven, CT: Yale University Press.

Margolis, N.M. (1954), "A Theory on the Psychology of Jazz", *American Imago* **11**:263–291.

Matthis, I. (2000), "Sketch for a Metapsychology of Affect", *International Journal of Psychoanalysis* **81**:215–227.

Melges, F.T. (1982), *Time and the Inner Future. A Temporal Approach to Psychiatric Disorders*, New York: John Wiley.

Merleau-Ponty, M. (1961), "Eye and Mind", in *The Primacy of Perception*, Chicago: University of Chicago Press.

Meyer, L.B. (1956), *Emotion and Meaning in Music*, Chicago: University of Chicago Press.

—— (1967), *Music, the Arts and Idea*, Chicago: University of Chicago Press.

Millgate, M. (1969), "Faulkner's *Light in August*", in D.L. Minster (ed.) *Twentieth Century Interpretations of Light in August*, Englewood Cliffs, NJ: Prentice Hall.

Milner, M. (1957; 2nd edn 1979), *On Not Being Able To Paint*, Oxford: Heinemann.

—— (1952), "Aspect of Symbolism in Comprehension of the Not-Self", *International Journal of Psychoanalysis* **33**:181–195.

Mursell, J. (1937), *The Psychology of Music*, New York: Norton.

Nabokov, V. (1947; First Vintage International Edition, 1989), *Speak, Memory*, New York: Random House.

Nietzsche, F. (1870–1871), *The Birth of Tragedy in the Spirit of Music*, 1956, New York: Doubleday.

Noy, P. (1968), "The Development of Musical Ability", *The Psychoanalytic Study of the Child* **23**:332–347.

—— (1993), "How Music Conveys Emotion", in *Psychoanalytic Explorations in Music. Second Series*, Madison, CT: International Universities Press.

Olds, C. (1984), *Fetal Response to Music*, Wickford, Essex: Runwell Hospital.

—— (1985), *A Sound Start in Life*, Wickford, Essex: Runwell Hospital.

Orgel, S. (1965), "On Time and Timelessness", *Journal of the American Psychoanalytic Association* **13**:102–121.

Ostwald, P. (1988), "Music and Child Development. The Biology of Music Making", in F.R. Wilson and F.L. Roehmann (eds) *Proceedings of the 1984 Denver Conference*, St Louis, MO: MMB Music.

Pally, R. (1997), "II. How the Brain Actively Constructs Perceptions", *International Journal of Psychoanalysis* **78**:1021–1030.

Panel (1980), "New Knowledge about the Infant from Current Research: Implications for Psychoanalysis", (reporter) L. Sander, *Journal of the American Psychoanalytic Association* **28**:181–198.

Panksepp. J. (1999), "Emotions as Viewed by Psychoanalysis and Neuroscience: An Exercise in Consilience", *Neuro-Psychoanalysis* **1**:15–38.

—— (2000), "The Cradle of Consciousness", *Neuro-Psychoanalysis* **2**:24–32.

—— (2001), "The Long-Term Psychological Consequences of Infant Emotions: Prescriptions for the Twenty-First Century", *Neuro-psychoanalysis* **3**:149–178.

Penfield, W. and Perot, P. (1963), "The Brain Record of Visual and Auditory Experience: A Final Summary and Discussion", *Brain* **86**:595–696.

Pratt, C.C. (1952), *Music and the Language of Emotion*, Washington, DC: US Library of Congress.

Read, H. (1951), "Psychoanalysis and the Problem of Aesthetic Value", *International Journal of Psychoanalysis* **32**:73–82.

Riviere, J. (1936), "On the Genesis of Psychical Conflict in Earliest Infancy", *International Journal of Psychoanalysis* **17**:395–422.

Rizzuto, A. (2000), "Panel Report. Spontaneity versus Constraint: Dilemmas in the Analyst's Decision Making", *Journal of The American Psychoanalytic Association* **48**:549–560.

Rose, G.J. (1961), "Pregenital Aspects of Pregnancy Fantasies", *International Journal of Psychoanalysis* **42**:544–549.

—— (1963), "Body Ego and Creative Imagination", *Journal of The American Psychoanalytic Association* **11**:775–789.

—— (1964), "Creative Imagination in Terms of Ego 'Core' and Boundaries Sessions", *International Journal of Psychoanalysis* **45**:75–84.

—— (1966), "Body Ego and Reality", *International Journal of Psychoanalysis* **47**:502–509.

—— (1969), "*King Lear* and the Use of Humor in Treatment", *Journal of The American Psychoanalytic Association* **17**:927–940.

—— (1971), "Narcissistic Fusion States and Creativity", in *The Unconscious Today*, New York: International Universities Press.

—— (1972), "*The French Lieutenant's Woman*: The Unconscious Meaning of Any Novel to Its Author", *American Imago* **29**:165–176.

—— (1978), "The Creativity of Everyday Life", in S. Grolnick and L. Barkin (eds) *Between Reality and Fantasy. Transitional Objects and Phenomena*, New York: Jason Aronson.

—— (1980; 2nd edn 1992), *The Power of Form. A Psychoanalytic Approach to Aesthetic Form*, Madison, CT: International Universities Press.

—— (1987), *Trauma and Mastery in Life and Art*, New Haven, CT: Yale University Press. 2nd edn 1996, Madison, CT: International Universities Press.

—— (1996), *Necessary Illusion: Art as Witness*, Madison, CT: International Universities Press.

Rose, L. (2001), *The Survival of Images. Art Historians, Psychoanalysts, and the Ancients*, Detroit: Wayne State University Press.

Rose, R.D. (1980), *An Ethnomusicological Look at Bebop Jazz*, unpublished.

Rosen, C. (1980), *Sonata Forms*, New York: Norton.

Sacks, O. (1973), *Awakenings*, London: Duckworth.

—— (1985), *The Man Who Mistook His Wife For A Hat*, New York: Summit Books.

—— (1995), *An Anthropologist On Mars*, New York: A.A. Knopf.

—— (1998), "Music and the Brain", in *Clinical Applications of Music in Neurologic Rehabilitation*, St Louis, MO: MMB Music.

Salk, L. (1965), Study abstracted in *SKF Psychiatric Reporter*, May–June, No. 20.

Sartre, J.-P. (1951), "Time in Faulkner: The Sound and the Fury", in F.J. Hoffman and O.W. Vickery (eds) *William Faulkner: Two Decades of Criticism*, East Lansing, MI: Michigan State College Press.

Schenker, H.K. (1935), *Introduction to Free Composition*, trans. and ed. E. Oster, 1979. Reprinted in J. Hermand and M. Gilbert (eds) *German Essays on Music*, 1994, New York: Continuum.

Schilder, P. (1936), "Psychopathology of Time", *Journal of Nervous and Mental Disease*, **83**:530–546.

Schore, A.N. (1996), "The Experience-Dependent Maturation of a Regulatory System in the Orbital Prefrontal Cortex and the Origin of Developmental Psychopathology", *Development and Psychopathology* **8**:59–87.

—— (1997a), "A Century after Freud's Project: Is a Rapprochement between Psychoanalysis and Neurobiology at Hand?", *Journal of The American Psychoanalytic Association* **45**:807–939.

—— (1997b), "Early Organization of the Nonlinear Right Brain and the Development of a Predisposition to Psychiatric Disorders", *Development and Psychopathology* **9**:595–630.

Seeger, A. (1987), *Why Suya Sing*, Cambridge: Cambridge University Press.

Sessions, R. (1950), *The Musical Experience of Composer, Performer, Listener*, Princeton, NJ: Princeton University Press.

Sharpe, E.F. (1940), "Psychophysical Problems Revealed in Language: An Examination of Metaphor", in *Collected Papers on Psychoanalysis*, 1950, London: Hogarth Press.

Sheets-Johnstone, M. (1999), "Emotion and Movement", *Journal of Consciousness Studies* **6**:259–277.

—— (2003), "Ongoing Discussion: David D. Olds's 'Affects as a Sign System'", *Neuro-Psychoanalysis* **5**:195–199.

Shetler, D.J. (1988), "The Inquiry into Prenatal Musical Experiences: A Report of the Eastman Project", in F.R. Wilson and F.L. Roehmann (eds) *Music and Child Development, the Biology of Music Making: Proceedings of the 1984 Conference*, St Louis, MO: MMB Music.

Silverman, S.E. and Silverman, M.K. (2002), "From Sound to Silence: A Preliminary Investigation of the Use of Vocal Parameters in the Prediction of Near-Term Suicidal Risk", work in progress.

Siomopoulos, G. (1977), "Poetry as Affective Communication", *Psychoanalytic Quarterly* **46**:499–513.

Slap, J.W. and Brown, J.H. (2001), "Ongoing Discussion of Yoram Yovell (Vol. 2, No. 2): Commentary", *Neuro-Psychoanalysis* **3**:111–120.

Slatoff, W.J. (1963), "The Edge of Order: The Pattern of Faulkner's Rhetoric", in F.J. Hoffman and O.W. Vickery (eds) *William Faulkner: Three Decades of Criticism*, New York and Burlingame, KS: Harcourt, Brace and World.

Solms, M. (1997), "What is Consciousness?", *Journal of the American Psychoanalytic Association* **45**:681–703.

Solms, M. and Nersessian, E. (1999), "Freud's Theory of Affect: Questions for Neuroscience", *Neuro-Psychoanalysis* **1**:5–14.

Solomon, M. (2003), *Late Beethoven. Music, Thought, Imagination*, Los Angeles: University of California Press.

Spence, D. (1982), *Narrative Truth and Historical Truth*, New York and London: Norton.

Spitz, R.A. (1957), *No and Yes. On the Genesis of Human Communication*, New York: International Universities Press.

Stein, J. (1963), "William Faulkner: An Interview", in F.J. Hoffman and O.W. Vickery (eds) *William Faulkner: Three Decades of Criticism*, New York and Burlingame, KS: Harcourt, Brace and World.

Stern, D. (1985), *The Interpersonal World of the Infant: A View from Psychoanalysis and Developmental Psychology*, New York: Basic Books.

Terr, L.C. (1984), "Time and Trauma", *Psychoanalytic Study of the Child* **39**:633–665.

Toch, E. (1948), *The Shaping Forces in Music*, New York: Criterion Music.

Tomkins, S. (1962–1963), *Affect, Imagery, Consciousness*. 2 vols. New York: Springer.

Turner, T. and Poppel, E. (1983), "The Neural Lyre: Poetic Meter, the Brain, and Time", *Poetry* **2**:277–309.

—— (1988), "Metered Poetry, the Brain, and Time', in I. Rentschler, B. Herzberger and D. Epstein (eds) *Beauty and the Brain. Biological Aspects of Aesthetics*, Basle: Birkhauser Verlag.

Van der Kolk, B., McFarlane, A. and Weisaeth, L. (eds) (1996), *Traumatic Stress. The Effects of Overwhelming Experience on Mind, Body, and Society*, New York and London: Guilford.

Von Bertalanffy, L. (1968), *General Systems Theory*, New York: Braziller.

Wertheim, N. (1997), "Is There an Anatomical Localisation For Musical

Faculties?", in M. Critchley and R.A. Henson (eds) *Music and the Brain*, Springfield, IL: Charles C. Thomas.

Whitehead, A.N. (1920), *The Concept of Nature*, Cambridge: Cambridge University Press.

Wilson, L. (2003), *Alberto Giacometti: Myth, Magic and the Man*, New Haven, CT: Yale University Press.

Winner, E. (1982), *The Psychology of the Arts*, Cambridge, MA: Harvard University Press.

Winnicott, D.W. (1953), "Transitional Objects and Transitional Phenomena", *International Journal of Psycho-Analysis* **34**:89–97.

Yovell, Y. (2000), "From Hysteria to Posttraumatic Stress Disorder: Psychoanalysis and the Neurobiology of Traumatic Memories", *Neuro-Psychoanalysis* **2**:171–181.

Zeki, S. (2001), *Inner Vision*, New York: Oxford University Press.

Zuckerkandl, V. (1956), *Sound and Symbol. Music and the External World*, Princeton, NJ: Princeton University Press.

—— (1973), *Man the Musician: Sound and Symbol*. Vol. 2. Princeton, NJ: Princeton University Press.

Index